Myth

and Modern American Drama

by THOMAS E. PORTER

University of Detroit

Wayne State University Press, Detroit

1969

Copyright ©, 1969
by Wayne State University Press,
Detroit, Michigan 48202.
Published simultaneously in Canada by
The Copp Clark Publishing Company
517 Wellington Street, West
Toronto 2B, West.
All rights are reserved.
No part of this book may be reproduced without formal permission.
Library of Congress Catalog Card Number 68-21543
International Standard Book Number 0-8143-1512-7
First paperback reprint, September, 1973
Waynebook number 36

Acknowledgments

To the Viking Press for permission to quote from *Death of a Salesman, The Crucible,* and *Collected Plays* by Arthur Miller.

To Harcourt, Brace & World, Inc. for permission to quote from *The Cocktail Party* by T. S. Eliot.

To New Directions for permission to quote from *A Streetcar Named Desire* by Tennessee Williams.

To Random House, Inc. for permission to quote from *Mourning Becomes Electra* by Eugene O'Neill, *Actfive and Other Poems* by Archibald MacLeish, and *Detective Story* by Sidney Kingsley.

To Houghton Mifflin Co. for permission to quote from *J.B.* and *Streets in the Moon* by Archibald MacLeish.

Quotations from *Who's Afraid of Virginia Woolf?* by Edward Albee are taken from the Atheneum edition.

To my uncle, John Connell,
with grateful affection

Preface

Although there are numerous studies devoted to modern American drama, few attempt to deal with the difficult basic questions of structure and meaning. The criticism of poetry and fiction has kept pace with the development of these genres, and the interested student has a large body of theory and analysis to work with. The student of drama, on the other hand, is faced with a heterogenous collection of aphorisms and traditional tags ("the tragic hero," "tragic flaw," "conflict the essence of drama") that can be applied in various ways to particular works at the whim of the critic. While some of the issues dealt with in the following pages have been touched on by such writers as Gassner, Bentley and Fergusson, on the whole the critics have been satisfied to shift ground whenever their reaction to a particular drama required it. We are all indebted to their insights, especially to the theoretical investigations of Fergusson, but, if a more fundamental approach to dramatic criticism is to be developed, a fresh starting point is imperative.

The suggestions of the Cambridge Anthropologists about the mythic and ritualistic nature of Greek drama, it seems to me, offer such a point of departure. Not that we can begin hunting down a unified world-view in American drama, this would be Procrustean. A significant contribution of the works of Harrison, Cornford and Gilbert Murray is their vision of the relationship between the drama and the cultural milieu in which it is produced. Whether or not their historical arguments hold water, they do show an intimate connection between what happened in the theatre of Dionysus and the beliefs, attitudes and institutions of the Athenian citizen. On the grounds that the connection between drama and culture is significant today, the following essays examine American drama in the light of its cultural milieu.

I would also like to acknowledge the influence of Mircea Eliade, whose studies in the philosophy of anthropology continually enlarged my cultural perspective. That there are "mythic" qualities in any world view, even the most scientific, is amply illustrated in his works. Under his influence, "culture" escapes its narrow confines and is seen as the process by which a community interprets its own experience: its origins, its institutions, its history and its values.

The methodology in this volume is intended to be inductive. Many of the ideas set forth in the Introduction are proposed as theses to be explored rather than as assumptions which the reader is asked to take on faith. Each essay will, hopefully, demonstrate how the cultural milieu contributes functional attitudes and patterns to the action of the play. The reader can, then, judge for himself.

This book was begun as a doctoral dissertation at the University of North Carolina under the direction of Professor O. B. Hardison, Jr. His superior critical acumen was matched by his thoughtful consideration in suggesting new directions. Without his help this study might have perished among the microfilms. I am also grateful to Professors E. W. Talbert, C. Hugh Holman of the same University and George Harper of the University of Florida, to Professor J. V. Holleran of the University of Missouri, for valuable suggestions, to the Reverend John A. McGrail, S.J., for encouragement and support, and to Mrs. Sandra Shapiro for reading the manuscript. I owe a debt long outstanding to Mrs. Mabel Strong LeFevre for introducing me to the drama which I should like to acknowledge here.

T.E. PORTER, S.J.

Detroit, Michigan
September, 1968

Contents

Introduction:

The Dramatic Milieu and American Drama

In the Introduction to his *Collected Plays* Arthur Miller records a
remark overheard in the lobby after a performance of his *Death of a
Salesman:* "I always said that New England territory was no
damned good." On the face of it, this comment represents a naive,
grass-roots reaction worthy of Willy Loman himself. For the anonymous theatre-goer who made this remark, the source of Willy's
troubles was not his false ideals and lack of self knowledge, but the
sales-resistant New England territory. A more sophisticated observer
would, perhaps, emphasize the pathos of the anecdote only to miss
the kernel of truth it contains. Here "territory" refers to something
more than geography; it refers also—and primarily—to a cultural
climate and a state of mind. Willy fails because he does not "know
the territory"; he neither recognizes nor understands the cultural
forces that have shaped his ideals and his destiny. Willy's problem
is the problem of the Salesman, the man who lives out there in the
blue, on a smile and a shoeshine. And this is the problem of every
American who has followed the dream of success to the end of the
rainbow. As Willy failed to sell the hard-nosed New England mer-
chandizers, he also failed to cope with his own milieu. So the kernel
of truth contained in Miller's pathetic anecdote is that the play is as
much about the milieu as it is about the character, as much about
"the territory" as about the tormented psyche of the salesman.

As a reflector of the American scene, *Death of a Salesman* is not a
unique case. A close look at American drama after Eugene O'Neill
reveals that the plots and the dramatis personae of representative
plays show a similar relationship to the milieu. As Miller deals with
the "little man" in American society, so Tennessee Williams explores the mind of the Southerner caught between an idyllic past

and an undesirable present. Thornton Wilder dramatizes the ideals of small-town America and Edward Albee satirizes the middle-class suburbanite in the affluent sixties. Both plot-situations and character-types are recognizable counterparts of problems and people on the American scene. There is a tendency in dramatic criticism to consider these cultural features of the drama as so much window-dressing, a technique for soothing the audience with familiarity while the real business of character portrayal goes on. This approach takes the territory for granted and focuses on an analysis of the hero as psychological specimen.[1] It ignores the fact that drama deals with character-in-a-situation and that this situation is not static, but a developing action. The personae exist only in the situation and as agents of the action. Because the situation reflects the cultural milieu and the personae types in it, the play speaks from the culture to the culture. Thus the way in which the drama represents the milieu is essential to an understanding of the drama as a whole.

The purpose of this book is to examine a number of representative American plays in the light of their cultural milieu. We will consider plot-structure, character-types and setting to discover how these elements of drama relate to the milieu. The various paths that this kind of study can follow are not uncharted; this relationship has been explored, with enlightening results, in the drama of other eras—for example, in Greek and Elizabethan drama. We understand the plays of the Athenians better for the studies of Greek ritual by Gilbert Murray and F. M. Cornford; we have a firmer grasp on Shakespeare's world-view because of the scholarship of E. M. W. Tillyard and Theodore Spencer. These scholars and others like them have painstakingly reconstructed the milieu of these periods from archeological and literary remains. Our task is relatively simpler. We have first-hand experience of our culture; its attitudes and ideals and strategies work deep in our own consciousness. For evidence we need not appeal to potsherds or black-letter pamphlets; we need only scan our book-shelves. It is true enough, as Francis Fergusson has pointed out, that the contemporary cultural picture is complex and fragmented, without a neat cosmic focus, but even at this juncture it continues to supply attitudes and ideals that are grist for the dramatist's mill.[2]

This is not to say that the dramatic milieu includes only the immediate cultural situation, that it contains no traditional elements. It includes, along with the American milieu, the dramatic traditions that the playwright inherits from his predecessors, and the heritage of Western culture, especially as reflected in literature. These matrices are available to the dramatist not merely as conscious techniques of presentation or patterning like impressionism or surrealism, for example; rather they permeate the atmosphere in which he works in the same way attitudes and values permeate a culture—as a milieu, a largely unarticulated set of attitudes that structures societal institutions, creates behavioral patterns and, in general, presents the members of a given society with goals and with strategies for achieving those goals. The dramatic milieu is the atmosphere in which the playwright works. It comprises the immediate cultural situation, dramatic conventions and traditions, and the heritage of Western culture—in effect, all those attitudes, ideals and traditions that determine or affect values, supply strategies and pattern human activities.

Though we are speaking here as though the dramatic milieu functions primarily as a matrix for the playwright, it should be clear that the milieu of the playwright is also the milieu of the audience. It provides that common ground between stage and audience, the common stock of experience which makes communication possible. The play speaks from culture to culture precisely because the play and the audience occupy the same territory—at least for the duration of the play. What the playwright creates, what the play expresses and what the audience experiences relate, at least ideally, to the same milieu.

The creative process of the playwright and the experience of the audience are both focused in the play, the medium which incorporates the milieu according to its own laws. The milieu appears, not as a sociological or psychological treatise or as a series of rhetorical flourishes, but dramatized in plot and personae. It contributes attitudes like the success ideology, strategies like personality development à la Dale Carnegie and dramatic patterns like the tragic triad of guilt-suffering-purgation. But these elements are woven into the action so that their meaning is experienced as well as stated. No matter what the playwright's intent, the drama creates its own effect and makes its own statement, through plot-structure and character delineation, about the culture to which it speaks. It is the critic's job to illuminate the experience and the statement as the drama effects them.

There are, as we indicated above, three working areas into which the dramatic milieu can be divided for purposes of analysis: 1) the immediate cultural situation, 2) traditional dramatic forms, 3) the heritage of the past, especially as it is reflected in literature. Each of these areas deserves attention, though they overlap in some instances. The contribution made by traditional forms is, in theory, most obvious because these forms include ready-made patterns with conventional meanings. "Tragedy" and "comedy" as traditional forms establish certain expectations in the mind of the audience, and, at a deeper level, they employ structures that make conventional statements. The non-dramatic heritage of Western culture provides traditional motifs and symbols for their conveyance. The struggle between good and evil, the significance of light and darkness can be dramatized in a good many ways, while the basic images continue to hold a cosmic meaning for the audience. The treatment of the immediate cultural milieu deserves a whole section, and we will deal with it in due time.

Tragedy and comedy are traditional forms that include patterns of action with conventional meanings. Obviously, the meaning of these forms can be seen only in an historical perspective. When we look at tragedy from a distance, the pattern emerges; stripped to its essential framework, *the tragic action is a movement from guilt through suffering to purgation and insight.* The way in which this pattern is filled out differs considerably from age to age and culture to culture and even playwright to playwright, but its outlines persist in Western drama. Whether the play is Aeschylus's *Oresteia* or *Oedipus* or *Hamlet* or *Death of a Salesman,* the structure is a progress from guilt to purgation. In the Eumenides, the climactic third play of the *Oresteia* trilogy, Orestes is acquitted of the charge of blood-guilt; this acquittal is accomplished by a providential intervention that recapitulates a cultural transition from rule by tribal code to rule by democratic procedure. Oedipus determines to search out the criminal who is polluting the city; he suffers through to a discovery of his own guilt and so learns that he is a fallible member of an error-prone race. Hamlet is forced to cope with a totally corrupt court and country, a world that has gone to seed. His problem is cosmic: how, in such a universe of disorder, one man can begin to set it right. It is the world that needs cleansing, and this is accomplished only at the cost of the Prince's life. In *Salesman* Willy Loman searches for the key to the success that has eluded him; he suffers very deeply because of his "guilt." If the search is unsuccessful and Willy goes to his death without the vision of the Theban king, it is because he is the Salesman caught in his milieu who cannot relinquish his ideals without destroying his identity. Each dramatization of the conventional tragic pattern finally makes a statement through the specific experience of the individual play about the relationship of the guilty individual to his society.[3] The pattern reflects a basic human desire to be free from guilt—as the specific culture may define it—and to join or rejoin a purified society. This is the conventional meaning of the traditional tragic structure; it is a progress by which the guilty individual is reconciled to society and in which society itself is renewed.

Comedy as a traditional term covers a wider spectrum of dramatic usage; from its Greek origins it reveals a two-fold potential for the satiric and for the sentimental. Aristophanes and Menander represent two different thrusts within the same pattern, and these directions persist through Western drama so that Shakespeare can unite the satiric and the sentimental in individual plays and mock romantic love while he is ratifying it. Rosalind can poke fun at Orlando's idealism while she falls deeper in love with him. Edward Albee hurls his suburbanite couple at one another's throats for two-and-two-thirds acts and leaves them holding hands at the final curtain.[4] Whether the satirical or the sentimental treatment is foremost in a given play, the final image projected by the last movement in a comedy is that of the harmonization of individuals in society with their own cosmos. The basic movement of the comic action often involves a progress to a "wedding," the unification of a society on its own terms. This "wedding" can represent a new social order rising from the ashes of the old, or the expulsion of undesirable elements—personae or character-traits—from society, or a celebration of harmony with the forces of nature, or any combination of these motifs. The happy reunion of separated lovers is the most conventional comic pattern, a mode that can be traced from the latest boy-meets-girl Broadway comedy through Shakespeare's forest comedies to the plays of Menander and the "satyr-tragedy" of Euripides.

The "boy-meets-girl" pattern of comic action has its own struc-

ture and its own meaning. The structure focuses on the reconciliation of lovers: a temporary liaison is followed by separation or
alienation, then the lovers are united in a permanent union, at least
for purposes of the play. Other images that surround the wedding
serve to emphasize its meaning; a new society is born in harmony
with the cosmos. So when Rosalind marries Orlando in *As You Like
It,* not only are two congenial spirits happily paired, but the usurper
Ferdinand is foiled, Orlando is restored both to his brother and to
his rightful place in the body politic. At the wedding of Hippolyta
and Theseus in *Midsummer Night's Dream,* the fertile forces of nature in fairy-form bless the marriage-bed. The moon-drenched,
flower-strewn bower that is the setting for romance surrounds the
progress to the wedding with images of fertility. Even when this
conventional pattern is adapted in a way that radically alters its
meaning, as in Albee's *Virginia Woolf,* it makes a statement about
man's aspirations to exist in an harmonious union both with his fellows and with a fruitful cosmic order.

These traditional patterns with their conventional meanings never
function in isolation; they are always assimilated to the whole. As
the cultural situation changes, the significance of the pattern is modified. The tragic pattern in Aeschylus and the tragic pattern in
O'Neill relate very differently to the total meaning of the play. The
salient point is that the conventional significance provides a point of
departure for the modern playwright. Because the form does make
its own statement, the playwright may modify it to suit his own
purposes.

The other traditional aspect of the dramatic milieu, the heritage of
Western culture, offers both conventional imagery and motifs to the
drama. The Judaeo-Christian tradition is the most durable contrib-
utor in this area. Archibald MacLeish begins *J. B.,* his drama about
the problem of evil, by invoking the Book of Job; T. S. Eliot uses a
meld of Greek ritual and Christian philosophy in *The Cocktail
Party.* O'Neill, Miller, Williams and Wilder deal with values that
look back to the Puritan theology of election and the signs of election. Perennial imagery, with its attached values, becomes transmuted in the crucible of assimilation into the drama and thus makes
a contribution to the meaning of the play.

Whether the dramatist adapts traditional patterns and motifs or
forges new structures from material at hand, he cannot avoid reference to his immediate cultural situation. He views the traditional in

the light of his immediate environment; the conventional signficance of the traditional elements in his milieu serves the present rather than embalms the past. For the American dramatist, specifically American ideals and attitudes contain material that the playwright can shape into plot and press for character-types. Ultimately the immediate cultural situation, woven into the texture of the drama, modifies the past and provides a key to the meaning of the action.

Dealing with such concepts as "cultural milieu," "cultural situation" and "cultural attitude" is like trying to hold quicksilver in the hand. Squeeze such concepts for precise definition and they vanish. Fortunately, illustration and example provide an alloy that makes slippery notions manageable. From the outset we have been dealing with the notion of "milieu"; it is the territory in which the dramatist works and whose qualities are absorbed in the play. As the territory is more a matter of attitude than of geographical location, so the immediate cultural situation is a milieu—the ideals, attitudes and institutions that distinguish the American group-mind.

Like other cultures, the American culture is a product of adaptation and experience. Some of our attitudes are traditional, native adaptations of the cultures from which we sprang; others are unique, products of our attempts to cope with new situations. It is possible, for instance, to trace the unique American attitude toward "success" to roots in our Puritan past, to see this ideology as a secularization of the Protestant ethic. It is likewise true that our fanatical faith in self-reliance was confirmed by the experience of the frontier. No scientific method can measure the relative influence of these two components on the American psyche, but it is clear that both have contributed to the shaping of a uniquely American attitude. It is likewise clear that success and self-reliance provide an underpinning for our social, economic and political systems, though the meaning of these terms might be differently understood by different groups in American society. That minority groups have variant definitions explains, to some extent, why they are in the minority. We can identify (and if we are dramatists, project) such concepts because they exist not only as concepts and images but also as programs for action. "Success" implies the acquisition of wealth by industry and/or invention; inheritance of a fortune does not count. "Rags-to-riches" is a variant (and extreme) statement of a group-attitude toward success that implies a program of action.

Images and programs for action that go to make up a cultural situation depend ultimately on what we may call, for want of a more precise term, "cultural attitude." Attitudes are the internal constituents of situation and milieu, psychological orientations from which images and patterns of action proceed. The most widely accepted cultural attitudes are expressed in social ideograms like "democracy," "law-and-order," "frontier," "success." The use of these ideograms implies the existence of a complex of inter-related images and emotions working in the psyche in a way that defies scientific analysis. "Democracy" strikes the ear of an American with a good deal more force than the dictionary definition can explain. To a long tradition of Anglo-Saxon parliamentary history, a revolutionary background and two-hundred years of republican experience add the images of "the land of the free," "equal opportunity," "freedom of choice," "free enterprise," "rights of the individual," and so forth. No other nation or race can quite appreciate the complex of feelings and meanings signified for the American by "democracy." Here we have a folk-idea which cannot be formulated or defined precisely, yet which has a normative influence on the culture.

It goes without saying that the force such cultural attitudes exert on society is directly proportionate to the credence which its members give them. Belief in the "democratic way" will override confusions and even contradictions in theory and practice. So the cultural attitude represented by the ideogram provides the necessary consensus that supports social, economic and political institutions. Such a "belief" does not, of course, represent itself as such; rather the believer simply accepts the attitude as the best, the most logical, often the only acceptable way of viewing reality.

Fortunately the literary critic does not have to handle cultural patterns and attitudes in the abstract or even, as the sociologist does, in relation to polls, graphs and census forms. They are expressed—and perhaps most clearly—in a variety of literary and subliterary forms, many of which have, themselves, had a powerful effect in shaping or reinforcing or giving new direction to the attitudes they express. The success ideology, for instance, bears the imprint of Benjamin Franklin's aphoristic formulations of it: "Early to bed and early to rise makes a man healthy, wealthy and wise"; "Keep your shop and your shop will keep you." Horatio Alger, in the late nineteenth century, evolved a stock-pattern of "rags-to-riches" that reaffirmed faith in the American drive for success and gave it a definite shape. Dale Carnegie enshrined, in persuasive essays, the cult of personality as a major factor for advancement in the business world. The popularity of these works testifies to the firmness with which the public embraced the ideology they express. Literary expression, then, has often been the alloy that has defined an attitude and encouraged popular belief in it.

Three major categories of literary and sub-literary expression reflect and shape cultural attitudes: 1) the literary tradition of Western civilization; 2) folk myth: tales and legends, capsulated in popular sub-literary forms; 3) "authoritative" analyses of institutions and behavior patterns popularized from a scientific background. Literary tradition, as we have seen, is a carrier of those attitudes which the group shared at its origin and which still persist, at least in vestigial form. It includes, for example, the great formulation of attitudes found in the Old Testament, as well as the literary heritage of Greek and Roman culture. Folk myth and its surrogates are products of those specific experiences that make a culture unique. "Authoritative" analyses interpret societal structures and behavior patterns, thus making the group-mind more conscious of its own cultural assumptions. While no hard-and-fast lines separate these three categories, each has its own distinctive features.

The artist has at hand, in the first instance, the corpus of Western literature and can draw on presumed knowledge of it by his audience. When the playwright uses literary models or allusions from the Bible, he creates a dramatic context which allows him to raise ultimate questions. Where this tradition contains elements alien to the modern mind, the meaning of the play is mediated through the dramatic interplay of the traditional (as the culture understands it) and the contemporary attitudes. He may also model his work on Greek or Elizabethan forms; if he does so, then the meaning of these forms is modified by the type of motivation he supplies or the adaptations he makes in the structure itself. The traditional form— as received by the culture—supplies the dramatist with a framework; he must then shape it to convey his own meaning to the audience.

Folk-tale and legend are specific interpretations of ethnic experience that express primarily the ideals and aspirations of the group. They treat typical situations and events, major historical moments and national heroes. Events and personages are metamorphosed to fit the predispositions of the community. Thus the image of the pioneer carries with it an aura of isolation, self-reliance, independence and resolution. The westward movement is fitted with a stereotyped pattern—the wagon train crossing the wide prairie; its representative cast of characters overcoming heat, cold, hunger, and thirst; fighting Indians; climbing the mountain barrier and finally settling down in a green valley in Oregon or California. Daniel Boone, Davy Crockett, Buffalo Bill lose their historical identity to become models of frontier manhood. In the Western movie or novel both the pattern of action and the hero are reduced to a formula: the lone cowboy who depends on endurance and dexterity with a gun brings law and order to a lawless land. After a physical struggle with the forces of evil—always well-defined—justice triumphs. Other such sub-literary genres employ similar cultural attitudes in formulaic fashion: the detective story, the rags-to-riches success story, the boy-meets-girl slick romance. Because these "entertainments" are simple, they embody folk-myth in clear outline. Because they are popular, they provide both artist and critic with a pattern which reflects certain ideals and aspirations in the community.

"Authoritative" analyses attempt to define cultural attitudes by a sociological or psychological exploration of institutions, mores or behavior patterns. This kind of analysis makes the public conscious of its own cultural predispositions by drawing attitudes to the surface and fixing them in an image. The "organization man" is exposed in all his conformity; the member of "the lonely crowd" is made aware of his lack of inner direction. Once such a study becomes popular and the coined image passes into the public domain, the attitude thus analyzed is substantially modified. Once the "organization man" recognizes his own image, he can never be exactly the same kind of organization man again. Such analyses may do as much to form the consciousness of the public as to reveal its subconscious attitudes. On a less scientific level, the "how-to" literature also helps to identify and establish group goals and values. The "self-help" literature of the first quarter of this century reveals a preoccupation with success and a determination to justify the pursuit of the dollar to God and man. The Freudian vogue of the twenties chopped away at the foundations of "puritanism" and established a psychological orientation in the popular mind that is still prevalent. Whatever the scientific value of such work, like the literary tradition of the past and the folk-myth, they supply the dramatist with images and patterns that embody cultural attitudes.

When we say that these formulations are available to the dramatist, we do not necessarily imply that he is conscious of incorporating them in his work. Insofar as they appear explicitly in the drama, they form a backdrop against which the action develops and, of course, they can often be identified as the "problem" that engages the attention of the dramatis personae. By and large, however, significant contemporary plays are not social drama or "thesis" plays in the technical sense. Rather, cultural attitudes and patterns operate in these plays in exactly the same way that they operate in the literary and sub-literary forms mentioned above—as structures that, by giving expression to the attitude or pattern and to the problem it generates, give shape and meaning to the action.

To see the cultural milieu as providing *structural principles of the action* is to supply a link that is often missing in dramatic criticism. We can speak of the "social force" of certain plays and thus consider their potential for "reforming" society, but in so doing we are not considering the cultural element—formulation of underlying attitudes—in its full aesthetic import. These elements are not merely extraneous background to the psychology of the personae or local color to hold audience interest while the real business of the play goes on; cultural attitude is the spine of the drama because it directs and regulates the action.

It will not help our analysis to enter upon a discussion of the tangled question about the meaning of dramatic action; we can stop short by treating its most basic expression—the plot. Plot, as Aristotle defines it, is the arrangement of the incidents. This arrangement delimits the action by giving it a beginning, a middle and an end. Plot is, then, a structural principle: boy-meets-girl, boy-loses-girl, boy-gets-girl. The stereotyped sub-literary form, a product of naive dependence on cultural attitudes, can serve serious artists by establishing a plot-pattern. The detective story, for instance, stripped down and capsulated, involves the commission of a crime, the detection of the criminal, his capture and the restoration of order in society. The Civil War romance, à la Thomas Nelson Page and Margaret Mitchell, sets up categories that can be filled out with variations: provocation, invasion, struggle and defeat-victory. Such patterns can become plot-structures; they can "arrange the incidents," define the limits of the action, and so provide a form which the dramatist can use to project his meaning.

Because these plot-patterns are related to a complex of cultural attitudes, they also control, to some extent, the type of dramatis personae and their motivations. Sub-literary genres make extensive use of stereotypes; the cast of characters is frequently as determined by the cultural milieu as the plot is. The cowboy-hero of the Western, the hard-boiled detective of the Dashiell Hammett-Raymond Chandler-Mickey Spillane school have certain physical attributes and ethical traits in common. They provide a fantasy image with which the American male can identify. Each has his place in the genre and fulfills certain expectations which the reader brings to the work. The physically tough, shrewd, more-or-less upright individualist who is not shackled by family responsibilities or social code is an agent of justice in his own society. Whatever variations are introduced into his personality or motivation, the genre outlines in considerable detail both the appearance and the ethos of the hero. On a more serious level, Willy Loman's personality and his basic motivation are determined by the context of the success ideology in which he appears; he is the Salesman and his "personal" problem cannot be separated from the cultural issue dramatized in the plot-pattern. The "stock" character, then, is more than a vehicle of convenience for the uninventive hack; rather, it is a determination that issues from the cultural context. The dramatist can avoid stereotype by giving his personae ambivalent motives and by drawing round characters whose seemingly contradictory qualities are reconciled in a cohesive psychology, but he does so within the limits of the cultural pattern and its related images. The dramatis personae, as they approximate or diverge from the stereotype, reflect the same cultural attitudes that structure the plot-pattern.

Since the plot-pattern and the character types, considered in their cultural context, may not be altogether a product of the dramatist's conscious artistry, they do not often appear in simple combinations. Significant drama deals with the complexities of the cultural situation rather than the fantasy-ideal. The structure may be latent, carefully concealed by a wealth of realistic detail; occasionally it makes an ironic comment on the theme, or conflict, of the play; in every case, it has a meaningful function to perform. Appreciating this function involves digging out the pattern, identifying the type-characters and exposing to view the underlying cultural attitudes. It may seem that this process demands the kind of reflection that cannot be achieved at a dramatic performance—and that is true enough. But in so reflecting we are merely drawing to the surface what is submerged in the subconscious of the audience at the play. The complexity of the experience and, therefore, of the analysis is no argument against its significance.

The plays treated in the following chapters have been chosen because they are at once representative and superior examples of American dramaturgy. They fall into two distinct groups. *Mourning Becomes Electra, The Cocktail Party* and *J. B.* make conscious use of literary models which come from the three major traditions influencing Western drama—Greek tragic, Greek comic and Judeo-Christian. They illustrate the varied ways in which these traditions can be used (and, occasionally, abused) by the playwright. In *Mourning Becomes Electra* O'Neill follows the sequence of events of his model almost point-for-point, but changes the motivations of the personae to make the action plausible for the audience. Because the Greek attitude toward blood-revenge and the Olympian theological machinery are unacceptable to our way of thinking, he replaces these alien cultural patterns with contemporary psychology, opposing a popular Freudianism to the Puritan ethic as understood by emancipated thinkers of the 1920s. Eliot uses the *Alcestis* of Euripides as a model, but he reproduces the conventional structure that underlies the action rather than the actual sequence of events in the original. He fills out this conventional comic structure with details culled from the anthropological studies of F. M. Cornford and with his own theory about the nature of a Christian society. The inclusion of Eliot's work in a study of American drama is justified not only by his origin and education but also by the fact that his viewpoint reflects New England as much as Canterbury, if not more. He is a unique figure in modern drama, a pedant who is able to incorporate esoteric scholarship in dramatic form. Archibald McLeish modifies both the structure and the events of his Biblical model, the Book of Job, by doubling the plot and introducing the dilemma of modern man as he faces atomic annihilation. Each playwright modifies his model by altering the milieu and the motivations and so renders his drama coherent in terms of the cultural attitudes of his audience.

The second group of essays deals with dramas that use folk-myths, legends and images expressed in popular sub-literary forms. None of these dramas adapts an already existing story or play as does O'Neill's *Mourning Becomes Electra,* nor do they consciously employ traditional literary models. Each uses the cultural pattern itself as a basis for its plot, characters and motivations. Sidney Kingsley's *Detective Story,* as the title indicates, draws on the hard-boiled hero of the Dashiell Hammett-Raymond Chandler school. This variety of detective story makes a statement about the American hero confronting an evil world—his ideals and the dilemma he faces because he is both member and opponent of a corrupt society. *Death of a Salesman* treats the Horatio Alger success story in reverse—the fall of a man who accepts the success ideology and fails to achieve its goal. *A Streetcar Named Desire,* typical of the work of Tennessee Williams, deals with Southern society, the plantation legend and its fate in the "New South." Williams is working with the closest approximation to a unified cultural milieu that exists in America, even though he depicts it in its death-throes. Miller's *The Crucible* examines, in an historical context, the American attitude toward the Law and uses the most ritualistic of American institutions, the trial, to project his meaning. He draws on the currency of the "witch-hunt" and on the Salem trial of 1692, thus treating a present problem against the perspective of the past. *Our Town* presents, in a mythical mode, the ideal American community. By mythicizing the small town, Thornton Wilder manages to create effective theatre with stereotypes for dramatis personae and soap-opera motivations. Edward Albee, in *Who's Afraid of Virginia Woolf?,* employs a conventional structure to attack convention. The patterns on which these playwrights draw express attitudes that characterize the American group-mind.

The story of modern American drama is the story of a courageous struggle against odds. Unlike the novel and the poem, the play creates a private world at the risk of being unintelligible and irrelevant. The very existence of a theatre depends on common ground, on the congruence of the universe of playwright and audience. The playwright can only present what the members of the audience will credit. If his values and his problems and his attitudes differ from theirs, then his play does not move them. When a play purports to speak to them, to depict their culture and describe their values, they will not willingly suspend their disbelief if it fails to do so.

Thus, if the culture fails to provide the dramatist with an adequate world-view, but only provides detached patterns that move in a vicious circle or spiral down into contradiction, a personal solution, arbitrarily supplied from outside the culture, cannot redeem the play. This is *deus ex machina*—and that the machine in our time has a gasoline engine or an atomic generator does not alter the case. The frustration sometimes felt at the conclusion of an honestly written, complex drama cannot be laid immediately at the door of the dramatist. If Miller cannot solve Willy Loman's problem, is it because the culture itself is helpless in the face of failure? The mirror that our drama holds up to nature reflects a familiar face; we need to take a long, hard critical look before judging the dramatist harshly. The face in the glass is our own; to understand it is to understand ourselves and our world.

Puritan Ego and Freudian Unconscious:

Mourning Becomes Electra

Modern American drama, by common critical consent, begins with Eugene O'Neill. His work so firmly limits our dramatic horizons that anyone but the expert has difficulty recalling the best-known plays, or even the names, of his immediate predecessors. When Jig Cook's amateur company performed *Bound East for Cardiff* in a converted fish-house on Cape Cod, the mainstream of American dramatic tradition was a melodramatic romanticism. Even the "big names" of the period before O'Neill—Augustus Thomas, William Vaughan Moody, William Gillette, Percy MacKaye, Clyde Fitch—were bound to a formula which now seems as remote as gaslight. This melodramatic formula was eminently simple; as George M. Cohan put it: in the first act you get your man up a tree, in the second act you throw stones at him, in the third act you get him down again. It enshrined an equally simple and orthodox set of American attitudes: virtue was always properly rewarded and vice punished; when the hero got down from his perch, he got the girl and a pot of gold for his trouble. A pure heart and dogged industry always triumphed over adversity, an even-handed Deity helped those who helped themselves, evildoers inevitably came to no good. These were the rules, and they reflected a semi-official attitude toward life and human nature. Bronson Howard said in a Harvard lecture:

In England and America, the death of a pure woman on the stage is not "satisfactory," except when the play rises to the dignity of tragedy. The death, in an ordinary play, of a woman who is not pure . . . is perfectly satisfactory, for the reason that it is inevitable. Human nature always bows gracefully to the inevitable.[1]

The wages of sin is death, as everyone knew, and therefore Frou-Frou the cabaret girl did not survive Act III. These attitudes and the dramatic formula that expressed them served the popular playwright for a century-and-a-half, from *The Contrast* through *Secret Service* and *The Heart of Maryland*.

Even after the public had begun to suspect that these rules did not apply to practical, everyday life, the playwright kept to the traditional formulae. What had been the representation of a firmly held faith became a vehicle for fantasy and escape. The melodrama still offered its audiences sentiment, excitement, moral aphorisms and personalities; most of all, it offered a glimpse of a simpler world the audience had lost—a world of naive virtue and immediate rewards which they piously believed their forefathers had inhabited. As belief in the rules declined, the playwrights dressed the formula in the finery of earlier ages—the Civil War and Revolutionary eras, period plays and costume drama—where these attitudes seemed less incredible. Lavish stage settings, richly costumed leading actors, the perspective of historical drama conspired to keep the audience from noticing how little drama had to do with life.

O'Neill spent his boyhood and early youth with one of the most successful versions of this formula. *The Count of Monte Cristo* had all the clichés: the historical setting, spectacular and thrilling episodes, the hero's rise through adversity to fame and fortune, poetic justice at the denouement, and, in production, a leading "classical" actor. For the young O'Neill, the contrast between the *Monte Cristo* world and the real world was sharp and well-defined. From his vantage point in the wings the rolling surf was only canvas and the crag, nothing but painted burlap. Each time Edmund Dantes emerged dripping from the canvas sea to proclaim the world his, O'Neill saw his hail-fellow, pinch-penny "Irish peasant" father. His later insistence, when he turned his hand to playwrighting, that "life" was the only thing worth writing about may have stemmed in part from his prolonged contact with *Monte Cristo*.[2] This resolve initiated a revolution in American drama.

In order to destroy one tradition, the playwright must create another. When O'Neill rejected the conventional formula, he had to forge his own form. So his dramatic career is a series of experimental efforts to find a satisfactory vehicle for "life." The autographical bias of his plays, which has been extensively documented by biographers and critics,[3] is not so much an instance of narcissistic preoccupation as it is evidence of dissatisfaction with a dramatic tradition. O'Neill wanted to write about contemporary life. The life he knew best was his own. His experimental method consisted in casting about for ways to embody his experience, in trying various approaches that range from stern "realism" in *Desire Under the Elms* and *Beyond the Horizon,* to expressionism in *The Hairy Ape* and *Emperor Jones,* to adaptations of Greek and Renaissance stage conventions like the mask and chorus or the aside. He was never satisfied; he would not settle for forms that did not encompass the whole of life. Drama, he said, had to deal with life: "fate, God, our biological past creating our present, Mystery, certainly"; this was the only subject worth writing about.[4]

One of his most interesting and, for our purposes, most informative experiments is his adaptation of the *Oresteia* of Aeschylus to an American situation. In the light of his search for form, it is understandable that O'Neill should be attracted to Greek tragedy. After a century of puritanism, sentimentality and scientific attack, the Christian tradition that had served Renaissance drama so well was —at least for the time—defunct. Greek tragedy dealt with "the Mystery" within a conventional structure; it came out of a relatively homogeneous culture and was well supplied with legendary themes. In short, the Greek playwrights had a form at hand; they needed only to shape their material to it. O'Neill set out to borrow both form and content from Aeschylus. In 1926 he noted in his work diary his intention to create a modern psychological drama based on Greek legend.[5] This entry began a five-year progress toward the Broadway production of *Mourning Becomes Electra.*

Because O'Neill followed the plot of the *Oresteia* so closely, his modifications of Aeschylus' plot stand out very clearly. He used the sequence of events point for point; he adopted character-types and relationships that the plot required. In borrowing these components from the Greek play, he perforce accepted the conventional ritual structure of conflict (agon), suffering (pathos) and revelation (epiphany) that influenced the Greek tragedian in the construction of his plot.[6] What O'Neill could not adapt from the Greek play were the culturally determined attitudes that the *Oresteia* expressed, the view of history as a providential development from a code of private vengeance to a system of trial by jury. By changing the situation of the drama from Athens to New England, O'Neill changed the cultural milieu and so had to find a comparable set of American cultural attitudes with which to motivate his personae. By looking at the Greek model and studying O'Neill's version, we can determine the contributions made by the Greek plot and structure as contrasted with the contributions of American situation and motivation to the over-all meaning of *Mourning Becomes Electra.*

In his treatment of the legend of the House of Atreus, Aeschylus is drawing on the resources the culture offers him. The legend that provides the base for the trilogy is a traditional story that expresses the experience of the people on three levels: the individual, the societal, the transcendental.[7] These levels are presented by the playwright as interpenetrating so that the history of the House becomes the history of the tribe and ultimately part of the history of the human race and its relationship with the gods. The action dramatizes 1) the family curse that follows the Atreides like Fate, 2) the effect of the code of blood-revenge on the city of Argos, and finally 3) "the gradual evolution, according to the master plan of Zeus, of the institution of civilized justice." [8] The legendary sources, the plot incidents and the structural elements all conspire toward the reconciliation of the individual with a reconstituted society under the guidance of divine providence.

Aeschylus establishes the legendary backdrop of his drama by weaving the relevant details into the texture of the play. These details include a record of the crimes of the House of Atreus beginning with the struggle of the sons of Pelops, Atreus and Thyestes, over their father's throne and the seduction of Atreus' wife by Thyestes. Atreus drove his brother out of the county and brought him back only to feed him the flesh of his children at the infamous banquet. In this context, the conflict is not merely a personal feud—accompanied by deeds however blood-curdling—between two brothers; its repercussions extend to the whole society and into the dimension of the gods. The family vendetta is an affair of state, a dynastic struggle. Moreover, the Thyestian banquet recalls an earlier τεκνοφαγια, child-eating, by the divine ancestors of the sons of Pelops. In order to protect his throne, Chronos swallowed up his children as soon as they were born. Though there is no description of child-eating by Chronos' son Zeus, the father of the gods, the "Dithyrambos" is reborn from Zeus's "male womb." [9] The traditional significance of the cannibalistic banquet relates to all three levels of the action in the *Oresteia:* the legendary motive of personal revenge is linked to the dynastic fear of being superseded as King; both these motifs recall the ritualistic entry of the young god Dionysus into Zeus's "male womb" in order to be reborn. This series of associations situates the action in a broad perspective relevant to the audience, reaching back into their tribal legends and up into the dimension of the Olympian gods.

The main incidents of the plot dramatize these same motifs of blood-guilt, dynastic struggle and the persistent working of the curse through the generations of the House of Atreus. Clytemnestra's motive for murdering her husband, King Agamemnon, is twofold: to avenge the ritual murder of their child, slain by Agamemnon to obtain favorable winds for the Argive war-fleet, and to retain the regency of Argos for herself and her lover. Sexual intrigue and kinsman-murder are the continuing fruits of the Thyestian curse on the House of Atreus. Orestes, the third-generation Atreides whose hands are yet unstained, faces the dilemma central to the action: he too must avenge a kinsman, his father, according to the tribal code. He can accomplish this only by violating the tabu against matricide and so perpetuating the curse. The cosmic powers of Earth and Sky are engaged in the action when Apollo, Zeus's messenger, orders Clytemnestra's death and, after Orestes carries out his command, the Furies—dark, maternal Earth-spirits—pursue him. Aeschylus solves the dilemma and reconciles the polarities inherent in the tribal code by abrogating it in favor of the juridical and social system of the *polis*. Orestes is brought to trial for his "crime" before the goddess Athena and a jury of Athenian elders. When the jury of citizens split their votes, Athena casts the deciding ballot for acquittal. The Furies are pacified by Athena's arguments and transformed into guardians of the city. This conclusion draws explicitly on Athenian history, and celebrates the institution of democratic processes—symbolized by the Areopagus, the ancient court for the adjudication of murder cases. The common law of the community is no longer the tribal code that sets kinsman against kinsman, but trial by a jury of citizen peers. The cosmic antagonism between the patriarchial Olympians and the defenders of matriarchy is reconciled by the transformation of the Furies into the gentle Semnae who bless the city from their caves on the Areopagus and lend their name to the oaths in the law courts.[10] It is clear that Aeschylus is drawing here on materials that are part of his audience's cultural heritage.

The structural pattern, too, which undergirds the action fulfills audience expectation, though perhaps a less precise and conscious one. The legendary plot fills out ritual categories with which the audience would be familiar: agon, pathos and epiphany. In the *Oresteia* the agon can be reduced to the struggle between polarities in the tribal code: filial piety and blood-revenge. From this springs the pathos, the suffering of generations of Atreides, culminating the dilemma which faces Orestes. The epiphany reveals the divine teleology that dissolves the old social system and creates a new, more enlightened one.[11] On the level of the ritualistic pattern, the hero's experience culminates in rebirth. He passes from guilt through suffering to purgation and emerges a "new man." This pattern is an analogue of the rebirth of the god. The legend as dramatized, then, includes both the historical resolution of a cultural dilemma and the ritual pattern that gives this resolution a cosmic dimension.

Even in this summary treatment of the trilogy its unity of concept and execution is evident. We see how this unity flows from the dramatist's ability to shape the cultural components with which he works. Aeschylus inherited the ritual structure, the legend of the House of Atreus, the tradition of Athenian democracy. That he was able to forge these elements into a dramatic unity is testimony to his artistry; that the elements were available to him is testimony to the homogeneity of Greek culture. These components point to an organic complex of attitudes in the fifth-century Athenian mind which could view the development of civilization as a providential progress and the individual as a member of the community governed by divinely sanctioned laws. Thus Orestes, caught in the web of circumstance, can be redeemed by the same forces that produced his guilt. In the concluding movement of the drama, the hero is purged of all guilt and "reborn," a new society is initiated and the cosmos is ordered on all levels.

Mourning Becomes Electra follows the general outlines of the Aeschylean trilogy very closely. The playwright borrows the three-play division, the sequence of events and the climatic order. In *Homecoming,* the first play, Ezra Mannon (Agamemnon) returns from war and is poisoned by his wife Christine (Clytemnestra) who is carrying on an affair with Adam Brant (Aegisthus). In the second play *The Hunted*, Orin (Orestes) and Lavinia (Electra) avenge their father's death by murdering Brant and driving Christine to suicide. *The Haunted* culminates with a judgment on Orin and Lavinia for their part in the destruction of their mother.[12] This point-for-point parallelism in the plots makes the divergence in the conclusions more striking. O'Neill and Aeschylus both include a "judgment" in the last play. But O'Neill's does not open out into a social revolution and a theophany. He concludes with a self-judgment by the two remaining members of the House of Mannon. Lavinia immures herself in the sepulchral family mansion; she punishes herself with a living death. Orin is not vindicated and absolved of his mother's "murder"; he commits suicide. The difference between Aeschylus' ending and O'Neill's is all the more important because the American playwright borrows his structure from the Greek. The epiphany of the *Oresteia* vindicates, on three levels, those teleological processes by which suffering leads to a new life for the individual and the community. The epiphany of *Mourning* depicts an isolation imposed by self-judgment that leads to death. Mourning becomes Electra; death becomes the Mannons. This epiphany, however, is not a simple, disconnected cry of despair; it proceeds from the cultural determinants with which O'Neill situates and motivates his action: the Puritan heritage and Freudian psychology. The cultural attitudes that are formulated under these headings are as definite and describable as the dictates of tribal custom in the *Oresteia*. Each supplies a set of motivations for the personae, and together they constitute an agon like the filial-piety and blood-revenge components in Aeschylus. They function in *Mourning* to determine the direction of the action and the over-all meaning of the play.

The Puritan heritage of the personae in *Mourning* is established in a general way by the setting. O'Neill situates the action in New England. This locale—in literary convention at least—is rugged, cold, sea-bound. The thin-soiled, rock-strewn countryside with small, barren mountain-ranges and rivers running down to the gray Atlantic creates an atmosphere of severity, inflexibility, firmness. The people are like the landscape—tight, thrifty, joyless, merchant-class puritans, descendants of Anglo-Saxon non-conformists. The Mannons live in this setting; their attitudes are defined by the locale.

Within this general situation O'Neill specifies his Puritanism. It is not a careful historical approximation of New England attitudes vintage 1865; it is Puritanism as O'Neill understood it through the eyes of his own generation. And, in the early twentieth century, among the avant-garde of the literary world, it was the sum total of everything that was wrong with American society. The leaders of the 1912 "Renaissance," *duce* H. L. Mencken, took on what they called "Puritanism" in a paper war. Mencken and his colleagues—George Jean Nathan and Ludwig Lewisohn among others—made the term a pejorative tag. The attitudes it stood for were, according to Mencken, universal: "What could be more erroneous than the common assumption that Puritanism is exclusively a Northern, a New England, madness? The truth is that it is as thoroughly national as the kindred belief in the devil." [13] He set out to delineate and excoriate this feature of the American character wherever he found it.[14] The Puritan, according to Mencken, was first and foremost a pharisee, a hypocrite, for whom public morals, especially in the areas of sexual behavior and consumption of alcohol, were the main concern. In these two sensitive areas, Mencken proclaimed, practice did not agree with preaching. Actually, the Puritan was "rather more prone to fornicate than other men, when he drinks, he is apt to make a hog of himself," but he would never consider relaxing the prevailing tabus.[15] No matter what the private views of individuals, the official American posture was a hypocritical, righteously irreligious (or a-religious) Puritanism.[16]

O'Neill moved in an atmosphere of rebellion against this type of Puritanism. He knew and admired Mencken and his magazine, *The Smart Set*. Three of the early plays were published in this journal, and the co-editor, George Jean Nathan, became a life-long friend.[17] Moreover, the whole Provincetown group were allied in spirit with this rebellion against the genteel tradition. They were, in Lewisohn's words, "the rebellious children of the Puritans, nobly aware of the tradition of libertarianism which is the true tradition of America." [18] Whether or not his view really fitted the facts, Mencken created an image of American society that gained wide credence among the emancipated. The Puritan background of *Mourning* comprises, along with broader classical elements, that complex of attitudes described and decried by Mencken and his associates. O'Neill weaves these attitudes into the background of his action.

As the locale calls Puritanism to mind, O'Neill visualizes the tradition in his stage setting. The Mannon house characterizes the family. The façade of the mansion is fronted by a white Grecian-temple portico with six tall columns and a "gray stone wall behind." This portico, says a stage direction, is like an incongruous white mask fixed on the house to hide its sombre gray ugliness.[19] If the audience fails to mark the significance of the setting, early in the first act it is called to their attention:

Christine. Every time I come back after being away it [the house] appears more like a sepulchre! The "whited" one of the Bible—pagan temple front stuck like a mask on Puritan gray ugliness! It was just like old Abe Mannon to build such a monstrosity—as a temple for his hatred. (MBE, p. 31.)

It is highly unlikely that a New Englander of 1865 would see the family home in this light; the voice is the voice of Mencken. The action is played against this pharisaical façade as the house of the Mannons visualizes for the audience the traditional attitudes of the "House of Mannon."

This interpretation of the Puritan heritage rests on a broad cultural base; the Mannon background also includes those features characteristic of the nineteenth-century New Englander. Grandfather Abe, whose Biblical name has dynastic implications, established a shipping business that made the family fortune. (The name Mannon, with resonances of Aga*memnon*, also has an appropriate resemblance to "Mammon.") As a result of their dedication to business, the Mannons are the most prosperous family in the community. Ezra did not rest on his inheritance; like a good Puritan he went on to serve the community. After learning law, he became judge and mayor of the town. Devotion to business is part of the traditional Protestant mystique. Diligence and industry lead to financial success—and this success carries with it a debt to society.

God requires social achievement of the Christian because he wills that social life shall be organized according to his commandments, in accordance with that purpose. The social activity of the Christian in the world is solely activity *in majorem gloriam Dei*. This character is hence shared by labour in a calling expressed in the first place in the fulfillment of the daily tasks given by the *lex naturae;* and in the process this fulfillment assumes a particularly objective and impersonal character, that of service in the interest of the rational organization of our social environment.[20]

To all outward appearances, the Mannons are "the elect." Their prominence in the community and the lavishness of the mansion testify to their probity, according to the orthodox standard. Christine, whose adulterous union would hardly be explicable in a rigid Puritan, is set apart from the real Mannons; her ancestry is not New England or even Anglo-Saxon. She is "furrin lookin' and queer, French and Dutch descended." Her family has not been financially successful; "she didn't bring no money when Ezra married her." "She ain't the Mannon kind" sums up the xenophobic reaction of the townspeople. (MBE, p. 21.) This background is contrasted with the family's—Anglo-Saxon stock, old settlers, successful merchants, in short, Puritan "elect."

Though the family has all the visible earmarks of the predestined, these are simply outward show. Like the mansion, their Puritanism is full of dead men's bones, and their theology has no relish of salvation in it. "The Mannon way" is a preoccupation with death, the cold remnant of Calvinistic dogma.

> *Mannon.* Life had only made me think of death. . . . That's always been the Mannon way of thinking. They went to the white meeting-house on Sabbaths and meditated on death. Life was a dying. Being born was starting to die. Death was being born. . . . That white meeting-house. It stuck in my mind—clean-scrubbed and white-washed—a temple of death! (MBE, p. 82.)

According to the cultural analyses of historians like Weber, the virtues of the Puritan—industry, thrift, social responsibility, regular habits, careful avoidance of sensuality, all stemmed from a search for certainty about election. Somewhat oversimplifying Calvin's theology, they depended on cautious organization and a clock-like regularity as protection against an irretrievable lapse—a fall whose implications extended out of time into the *illud tempus* of predestined election, that "moment" which melds the beginning with the end of time, the archē with the eschaton. No redemption is possible for the sinner within this system; once fallen, he is forever reprobate. The Mannon concern with death, however, does not relate it to grace, election and the after-life. There is no theological foundation to the

Puritan code in *Mourning*. Like the Puritanism that Mencken describes, it is an appearance without a substance, an ethic without a dogma. These attitudes provide a basis for the motivation of the personae, but, unlike the tribal code of the *Oresteia*, they do not include an Olympian dimension.[21]

Along with this preoccupation with death, another prominent feature of the Mannons' Puritanism is their attitude toward sex. For O'Neill's generation, Puritanism was associated, first and foremost, with a repressive attitude toward sexual impulses. This appetite posed the greatest problem for the Calvinist; it exercised the strongest pull and thus had to be most zealously guarded against. The "fall from grace" gradually assimilated sexual overtones; the fallen woman fell only in one direction. The objection to liquor and tobacco was rooted in the feeling that such license might lead to sexual indulgence. The libertarian school insisted that this revulsion was the obverse of a strong fascination. Lewisohn notes that he found in a not-illiterate house in an American village, along with the Bible and Shakespeare, "a luridly illustrated exposure of the sexual wickedness of the Mormons." [22] Mencken objected both to the police tactics of the guardians of public morality and to the sex-hygiene publicity of the "emancipated woman." Both approaches divested sex of its beauty and mystery, and reduced it to a "disgusting transaction in physiology." [23] The Puritan attitude is summed up most succinctly in the dictum: sex is "dirty."

O'Neill's characters are caught between this revulsion and fascination. The origin of the family curse is, in the first instance, Abe Mannon's hatred toward his brother David because of David's seduction of, and subsequent marriage to, Marie Brantôme. He went so far as to destroy the house in which the seduction took place. This hatred has implicit approval in the Puritan way—no association of the elect with the reprobate. By sustaining the orthodox position on sexual errancy, Grandfather Mannon—who, it turns out, was in love with Marie himself—bequeathed his righteous hatred to the family. In the play this strain in the Mannon ethos finds full expression in the reactions of Lavinia and Orin. In her first conversation with Captain Brant, Lavinia declares that she "hates love" and equates it with "naked women and sin." "Love" means the physical act of love; the Captain, like all men, dreams "dirty dreams—of love." (MBE, pp. 39, 40.) Christine, whose descent explains her liberal attitude—the French are traditionally a passionate people—derides her daughter for prudishness: "Puritan maidens should not peer too inquisitively into spring! Isn't beauty an abomination and love a vile thing?" (MBE, p. 72.) Love is sometimes vile also for Christine; her own marriage soon turned "romance into disgust." She made her husband feel the burden of her distaste, and he expresses his reaction in good Puritan style:

> *Mannon.* What are bodies to me? . . . Ashes to ashes, dirt to dirt! Is that your notion of love? Do you think I married a body? . . . You made me appear a lustful beast in my own eyes—as you've done since our first marriage night. (MBE, p. 92.)

For the Mannons, dirt and animality and abomination spell out the implications of sex.

The obverse of the coin is depicted also; their revulsion is attended by a fascination. Though bodies are only bodies, when Ezra sets out to effect a reconciliation with his wife, he becomes passionate. Christine allays his suspicions about her affair with Brant by kissing him and allowing him to press her "fiercely in his arms." Lavinia's repugnance for her mother's sensuality is flavored with jealousy, especially about her father's affections. Of all the Mannons, Orin most reveals this fascination-revulsion syndrome. His passionate attachment to his mother, rife with sexual overtones, has kept him from marrying Hazel, but he is drawn by the girl's purity, and he sees her passionless love for him as cleansing. On their return from the Islands, he finds Lavinia's blossoming attractiveness repulsive—because he sees her now as desirable. The climax of the brother-sister relationship is Orin's proposal that they have incestuous relations; this would both satisfy his desire and cement their mutual guilt.[24] From the Puritan point of view, the physical act of love between brother and sister is the fullest expression of their mutual damnation. The "curse" which began with David's seduction of Marie Brantôme spirals down to an incestuous proposal. No seventeenth-century divine could conceive a more suitable symbol for the ultimate reprobation of the Mannons; no libertarian could devise a clearer picture of the fascination-revulsion combination that Mencken and his school saw in Puritanism.

The attitudes of the townspeople-chorus underscore the conventionality of the play's Puritanism. The middle-class conspiracy which aspires to Babylonian practices while proclaiming Christian values weds hypocrisy with a practical view of sex. The women gossip in orthodox fashion; coming away from Ezra's wake, one of them blurts out:

Mrs. Hills. You remember, Everett, you've always said about the Mannons that pride goeth before a fall and that some day God would humble them in their sinful pride. (MBE, p. 106.)

This version embarrasses the company; afterwards the men draw aside for a less pious assessment. They make sniggering references to the General's love-making as the probable cause of his angina. The lower classes are even blunter about their sexual preoccupations. Before the climax of the second play, the murder of Adam by Orin, the drunken sailor who serves as chorus complains about the "yaller-haired pig who put her arm around me so lovin' " and then cleaned his pockets. (MBE, p. 155.) Similarly, in the knocking-on-the-gate episode which opens *The Haunted,* the cronies who gather round the gardener allow that Christine was a "looker." One offers to let her ghost sit on his lap if "ghosts look like the living." (MBE, p. 191.) The middle-class and the proletariat fill out the picture; they reflect Mencken's contention that the Puritan sexual code does not really represent the aspirations of society. And, while practice and appearances may differ among the classes, their attitudes with regard to sex have a common root; sex is animal and degrading, not to be associated with "pure" love.

The main line of the plot which O'Neill borrowed from Aeschylus is thus given a local habitation and a name: New England and Puritanism. Death and sexual rivalry, the principal occurrences, are put in perspective by this situation and that complex of attitudes. The family tradition—conventional behavior based on Puritan standards —insures the perpetuation of the curse. The Puritan code provides no resources for purging guilt; in fact, this guilt cannot be publicly admitted, for the Mannons are the "elect" (to all appearances). Their fall from grace cannot be mended because it cannot be confessed.

Christine. [To Lavinia] So hadn't you better leave Orin out of it: You can't get him to go to the police for you. Even if you convinced him I

poisoned your father, you couldn't! He doesn't want—any more than you
do, or your father, or any of the Mannon dead—such a public disgrace
as a murder trial would be! For it would all come out! Everything! Who
Adam is and my adultery and your knowledge of it—and your love for
Adam! (MBE, p. 135.)

Dis-grace, the fall from grace, seals the guilt up within the family.
The Mannons are caught in their private hell, and the family circle
draws tighter around their mutual guilt.

This pattern of isolation and introversion which their guilt imposes on them is reflected in the tightening circle of relationships
among the members of the family. Each episode repeats the preceding episode; the murder of Adam duplicates the murder of Ezra
even to the identification of the victims. After the murder of Brant,
Orin exclaims: "By God, he does look like Father!" (MBE, p. 169.)
Adam and Christine have plotted to remove Ezra; Orin and Lavinia
conspire to murder Adam. The network of blood relationship grows
tighter: Adam and Christine are not relatives; Ezra is Adam's
cousin. Then brother and sister murder their cousin Adam. The
blood-tie is closer between these conspirators than between Adam
and Christine. The motivation is also more introverted. Orin mur-
ders to avenge his father and to reclaim his mother's affections;
Lavinia cooperates as accomplice in order to revenge her father, to
pay Adam back for spurning her and to punish her mother for stealing both her loves—Ezra and Adam. Juxtaposed to these complications, Christine's motive was comparatively simple—to get Ezra out
of the way. This pattern dramatizes the isolation of the reprobate
Puritan. Once he has sinned, no outside power can help him—
neither society nor God. The family is helpless in the face of guilt
and death; there is no prospect of salvation anywhere.

O'Neill's understanding of Puritanism provides conscious motivation for the personae. The Mannons think in Puritan categories;
they see their plight in these terms. But the playwright and the
audience see their actions in a wider context that conflicts with, but
also in some sense explains, the Puritan mentality. Puritanism does
not clarify the darker matters that make the action inevitable, that
link crime to crime in a necessary progress. In Aeschylus' drama the
blood-code supplies this inevitability because it is more than a social
convention; it is an expression of the will of the gods. Zeus, by his

messenger Apollo, orders Orestes to avenge his father. The structure of the *Oresteia* leads to an epiphany in which the hero is purged of his guilt, regenerated. It is clear that within the Puritan system, especially as the libertarians see it, there is no possibility of regeneration.

O'Neill is striving to revitalize the legend, to render its values in modern terms. He must, therefore, find a complex of cultural attitudes, which the audience will recognize and (hopefully) accept, to provide the dimension which an Olympian Providence supplies in the *Oresteia*. O'Neill tried to find this complex of attitudes in a theory of behavior that was "in the air" when he wrote the play—the psychology of Sigmund Freud.

Freudian theories of character are a version of reality that "explains" the crimes of the Mannons as their Puritan heritage "explains" their feelings of guilt. When intellectuals of the twenties characterized Puritanism as "repressive," they were using a word that has explicit Freudian sanction.[25]

When O'Neill chose Freudian psychology to motivate the action, he extended the dimensions of his play-world into areas as broad (if not as transcendent) as the Olympus of Aeschylus. The Freudian view of behavior invokes a region as mysterious as the dwelling-place of the gods and sees human motivation as guided by impulses as imperative as divine commands. As the social dimension of O'Neill's action extends into the Puritan past, so the broader dimension extends into the unconscious where drives are determined by infantile experience.

Like the Puritanism, the Freudianism of the play is popular and unscientific. *Mourning* is not a carefully documented case study nor was it intended to be. The fact that the doctrines of Freud were widely misunderstood and vastly oversimplified by the public and the popularizers, did not prevent the playwright or the novelist—who often did not understand them either—from using the attitudes toward human behavior that the theories suggested.[26] However imprecisely, the public knew that Freud insisted on the relevance of the sex drive to life-adjustment, on the dangers of repression, on the importance of dreams as a key to self-knowledge in these areas. The "Unconscious" or subconscious was a deep, dark, cellar-like place from which proceeded equally dark impulses like the urge to marry your mother; "repression" was a dangerous damming-up of such urges and led to abnormal inversions.[27] The biological determinism of nineteenth-century Naturalism also had prepared the ground for the psychological determinism of these theories. Whether or not the public approved, Freudianism, as it was understood or misunderstood, represented in the 1920s a definite complex of attitudes about the importance of the psychic as a key to human behavior.

O'Neill himself insisted that his knowledge of the psychoanalysts was unscientific and fragmentary, and that he was guided more by intuition than by any theory.

There is no conscious use of psychoanalytic material in any of my plays. All of them could easily be written by any dramatist who had never heard of the Freudian theory and was simply guided by an intuitive psychological insight into human beings and their life-impulsions that is as old as Greek drama. It is true that I am enough a student of modern psychology to be fairly familiar with the Freudian implications inherent in the actions of some of my characters while I was portraying them; but this was always an afterthought and never consciously was I for a moment influenced to shape my material along the lines of any psychological theory. It was my dramatic instinct and my personal experience with human life that alone guided me.[28]

There are pieces of autobiography to which O'Neill could have pointed to justify his stand, for instance, Jamie O'Neill's devotion to his mother and the fact that Eugene always thought that this devotion kept his brother unmarried. Eugene's own attachment to his mother was deep and firm, even under the strain of Ellen O'Neill's dope addiction. In his own experience, too, there was the idealistic Irish-Catholic identification of Mother with the Virgin—a Jansenistic preoccupation with "purity" that was tied tightly to the mother-image.[29] In the broader cultural perspective, there is the American reverence for "Ma" that assumes almost mythical proportions in folk tradition. The woman keeps the flame, "not only of the hearth, but of beauty and purity and faith and hope" in a rude masculine world.[30] Nonetheless, in spite of O'Neill's contention, there is a psychological theory built into the plot and characters of *Mourning Becomes Electra*. If O'Neill is working from his own experience, he interprets it according to the categories that popular Freudianism offered him. That hypothesis attaches a darker significance to the traditional attachment to Mother, and to Mother's attachment to "her boy."[31] The "folk-tale" attitude toward Mother, the American experience and O'Neill's own heritage establish a background for the Freudian position and indicate how the playwright is likely to interpret the "complexes."

The specific details of O'Neill's Freudianism in *Mourning* are elaborated from the over-simplified proposition that every male is attracted to the woman who resembles his mother in physical appearance and every female desires a man who resembles her father. The prototype of the female in the play is Marie Brantôme. Christine and Lavinia both resemble her, especially in their "peculiar shade of copper-gold hair."

Brant. [To Lavinia] You're so like your mother in some ways. Your face is the dead image of hers. And look at your hair. You won't meet hair like yours and hers again in a month of Sundays. I only know one other woman who had it. You'll think it strange when I tell you. It was my mother. (MBE, p. 37.)

The Mannon women are identified with one another through this symbol. The Mannon men, too, look alike—Adam, Ezra and Orin. These similarities visualize the tangled, interlocked relationships among the members of the family at the same time as they "explain" them. Given this pattern, according to the Freudian hypothesis, the involvements are predictable. Adam loves Christine; Lavinia loves her father, Brant and Orin; Ezra loves his wife and daughter; Orin loves his mother and his sister. Reciprocally, Lavinia hates Christine; Adam hates Ezra and Orin; Orin hates the rivals for his mother's love, Adam and Ezra. Christine's revulsion for her husband is explained by another Freudian postulate, her unfortunate experience on her wedding night, presumably Ezra's ineffective love-making. Orin's complex and Lavinia's are treated specifically in the course of the dialogue; Lavinia has a fixation on her father and her brother, and Orin is still his mother's "boy."

Christine. I know you, Vinnie! I've watched you ever since you were little trying to do exactly what you're doing now! You've tried to become the wife of your father and the mother of Orin! You've always schemed to steal my place! (MBE, p. 53.)

Orin's mother-complex is developed at some length. He has had his mother's love, he is her baby. And his love for her, while rife with sexual overtones, is reverential. His greeting on their first encounter in the play contains a curious juxtaposition: "Mother! God, it's good to see you!" (MBE, p. 114.) Christine deals with him in seductive terms, emphasizing the physical in their relationship.

Christine. You're a big man now, aren't you? I can't believe it. It seems only yesterday when I used to find you in your nightshirt hiding in the hall upstairs on the chance that I'd come up and you'd get one more goodnight kiss. (MBE, pp. 132–33.)

According to the play, the "Oedipus complex" arises because the mother loves the father too little and the son too much.[32] This Freudian hypothesis explains the attractions and attachments that motivate the events—each Mannon is drawn by an unconscious impulse to that person who resembles the parent of the opposite sex. In Orin and Lavinia, the third generation, this impulse has grown into a fixation, a "love-hate" directed primarily at Mother.

The most illuminating instance of the operation of this Freudianism is the hero's mother-fixation. His fate turns on his complex; in him the pattern of psychological forces works out to a conclusion. He is mother's boy, with all that implies, and his attachment, moreover, includes an explicit connection of Mother with peace, innocence and the security of infancy. While away at war, Orin dreamed of his mother as an island of peace:

Orin. Those Islands came to mean everything that wasn't war, everything that was peace and warmth and security. I used to dream I was there. . . . There was no one there but you and me. And yet I never saw you, that's the funny part. I only felt you around me. The breaking of the waves was your voice. The sky was the same color as your eyes. The warm sand was like your skin. The whole island was you. (MBE, p. 133.)

The playwright leaves little to the imagination. The island surrounds Orin; it is warm, secure amid the wash of waters. It does not take a particularly acute dream-diagnostician to recognise the desire to return to the womb. Supplementary to this dream was the illusion that each man he killed at the front resembled his father. The wish to possess Mother and the acting-out of the father-murder give Orin the classic Oedipal symptoms. This complex moves him to murder Brant, and the brunt of his hatred falls on the father-figure, not on the mother. Christine's presence always has a softening effect. When he witnesses Christine's disintegration because of Brant's death, he pleads with her:

> *Orin.* Mother! Don't moan like that! How could you grieve for that servant's bastard? I knew he was the one who planned Father's murder! You couldn't have done that! He got you under his influence to revenge himself! . . . But you'll forget him! I'll make you forget him! I'll make you happy. (MBE, p. 178.)

In the midst of his jealousy, he is suffering from fractured idealism, a desire to preserve his mother immaculate.

This image of Mother remains inviolate throughout the play. As Mother, Christine symbolizes "pre-natal, non-competitive freedom from fear." [33] Even Christine's rejection of Lavinia does not make her an "unnatural mother"; it is the result of not being able to consider Lavinia *her* child. And Lavinia's hatred screens a longing for mother-love. "Oh, Mother! Why have you done this to me? What harm have I done you?" (MBE, p. 86.) After Christine's suicide Lavinia becomes Mother—she has assumed Christine's function along with her personality. She takes care of Orin, watches over him. More than ever Orin is caught by his complex:

> *Orin.* You don't know how like Mother you've become, Vinnie. I don't mean only how pretty you've gotten—. . . . I mean the change in your soul, too. . . . Little by little it grew like Mother's soul—as if you were stealing hers—as if her death had set you free to become her. (MBE, p. 204.)
>
> . . . .
> Can't you see I'm now in Father's place and you're Mother? (MBE, p. 225.)

The transformation into "Father and Mother" is complete, and Orin's complex made completely explicit, when he makes his proposal to his sister:

> *Orin.* I love you now with all the guilt in me—the guilt we share! Perhaps I love you too much, Vinnie. . . . There are times now when you

44

don't seem to be my sister, nor Mother, but some stranger with the same beautiful hair—(He touches her hair caressingly. She pulls violently away. He laughs wildly.) Perhaps you're Marie Brantôme, eh? And you say there are no ghosts in this house.

Lavinia. (staring at him with fascinated horror) For God's sake—! No! You're insane! You can't mean——!

Orin. How else can I be sure you won't leave me? You would never dare leave me then. You would feel as guilty as I do! You would be as damned as I am! (MBE, p. 239.)

By taking Lavinia, Orin would fulfill his desire to possess Mother completely; he would also be able to share the burden of his guilt. The pivotal point of the action here is Lavinia's horror at Orin's proposal; there is simply no question in her mind of actual incest. Lavinia in the Islands and with "clean, honest Peter" was sufficiently emancipated; "any love is beautiful." But emancipation draws the line at incest. The mother is ultimately attainable only by another, even darker, door.

Stripped of its "Island" imagery, the way back to the womb, to peace and security, is a return to the oblivion of prenatal unconsciousness. Orin cannot confess his guilt publicly; he cannot face life with its burden. When Lavinia cries out that he should commit suicide, he hears his mother's voice.

Orin. Yes, that would be justice—now you are Mother! She is speaking now through you! . . . It's the way to peace—to find her again—my lost island—Death is an Island of Peace, too—Mother will be waiting for me there. (MBE, p. 240.)

Orin's suicide is presented as a return to Mother; this is the judgment rendered by his complex. Death is the way to peace, rest, freedom from fear. It is also a passage into oblivion.

As Orin's suicide is the judgment leveled by his complex, Lavinia's self-immurement is the judgment of her Puritan heritage and her complex. She tries to break out of the circle, to escape with Peter and live, but her resolution breaks down when, in a Freudian slip, she calls Peter "Adam." The dead keep thrusting themselves between—her love for Adam, Orin's jealousy sealed in an incriminating letter. She accepts this fate with Puritan spirit and locks herself in the Mannon house to live with the ghosts of the past in expiation for all their crimes.

Lavinia. [to Seth] Don't be afraid. I'm not going the way Mother and Orin went. That's escaping punishment. And there's no one left to punish me. I'm the last Mannon. I've got to punish myself! Living alone here with the dead is a worse act of justice than death or prison! I'll never go out or see anyone! I'll have the shutters nailed closed so no sunlight can ever get in. I'll live alone with the dead, and keep their secrets, and let them hound me, until the curse is paid out and the last Mannon is let die! . . . I know they will see to it I live for a long time! It takes the Mannons to punish themselves for being born. (MBE, p. 256.)

The "Mannon way" catches Lavinia in the end; being born is starting to die. The house is a sepulchre, and her life henceforth a living death. So her determination—so much admired by the humanist critic—really amounts to the same decision Orin makes. She shuts herself off from the world to await the inevitable end. In Lavinia and Orin the Freudian and the Puritan, so opposed in particulars, meld into a unity.

Before we can evaluate the over-all meaning of the action, we must consider one other feature of the play which focuses the desires of the characters and constitutes a dimension of its own. The thematic image of the "Islands" runs through the entire drama and represents a uniquely American belief that a spatial remove is a panacea for all problems. The Mannons continually consider the possibility of escape. Adam Brant, the sea-captain, has been to the Islands; he describes them in idyllic terms to Lavinia:

Brant. Unless I'm much mistaken, you were interested when I told you of the Islands in the South Seas where I was shipwrecked my first voyage at sea. . . . Unless you've seen it, you can't picture the green beauty of their land set in the blue of the sea! The clouds like down on the mountain tops, the sun drowsing in your blood, and always the surf on the barrier reef singing a croon in your ears like a lullaby! The Blessed Isles, I'd call them! You can forget there all men's dirty dreams of greed and power. (MBE, pp. 39–40.)

Ezra considers the possibility of an escape when his difficulties with Christine become apparent.

Mannon. I've the notion if we'd leave the children and go off on a voyage together—to the other side of the world—find some island where we could be alone a while. (MBE, p. 84.)

On his return from the war, Orin tells his mother of the Islands which he, as noted above, identifies with the Mother image:

Orin. Have you ever read a book called "Typee"—about the South Sea Islands? . . . Someone loaned me the book. I read it and reread it until finally those Islands came to mean everything that wasn't war, everything that was peace and warmth and security. . . . The whole island was you. (MBE, pp. 132–33.)

For Adam, the Islands are a Garden of Eden, a *hortus conclusus* where sin is unknown and life simple and sweet. For Ezra, who does not pursue the idea, they represent isolation, freedom from the "children," a chance to begin again. For Orin, they represent peace in the embrace of Mother. But the Islands are not only a symbol in the play; they are also very real. Christine and Adam, now free of Ezra, are going to sail to the South Seas where they will be happy "once we are safe on your Blessed Isles." Orin's rage at Brant and his mother includes an outburst about "their" island:

Orin. I heard her asking him to kiss her! I heard her warn him about me! And my island I told her about—which was she and I—she wants to go there—with him! (MBE, p. 167.)

The geographical reality of the Islands, insisted on in Adam's description and Orin's reference to Melville's *Typee*, becomes inescapable when, in *The Haunted*, Orin and Lavinia describe their trip there. The freedom and naturalness of the environment and the primitive innocence of the natives transform Lavinia:

Peter. [To Lavinia] Gosh, you look so darned pretty—and healthy. Your trip certainly did you good! You stopped at the Islands?
Orin. Yes, we took advantage of our being on a Mannon ship to make the Captain touch there on the way back. We stopped a month. But they turned out to be Vinnie's islands, not mine. (MBE, pp. 208–209.)

47

The feminine features of the environment bring out the feminine in Lavinia; she blossoms out into a replica of Christine. For the nonce, she loses her Puritan cast of mind, her New England inhibitions, because of the experience. As symbol, the Islands represent release from Puritan guilt, the hope of an escape to love and freedom. But as reality, they project a spatial dimension and an escape "to another country." The Islands are also a real refuge that would put the house of Mannon half a world away.³⁴

In *Mourning Becomes Electra* O'Neill uses the Islands as the surrogate to the hope of a new life. They represent a paradise in which the climate and an abundance of material goods cancel the necessity for competition—"war" of all kinds. The Mannons need not protect their fortune, or assume responsibility in the community. No class distinctions keep people apart. Lavinia walked in the moonlight with a native and everything was "simple and natural."

> *Lavinia.* I loved those Islands. They finished setting me free. There was something there mysterious and beautiful—a good spirit—of love—coming out of the land and sea. It made me forget death. There was no hereafter. There was only this world—the warm earth in the moonlight—the trade wind in the coco palms—the surf on the reef—the fires at night and the drum throbbing in my heart—the natives dancing naked and innocent—without knowledge of sin! (MBE, p. 212.)

The Puritan ethic can be forgotten, is not necessary, because this remove is also a return. Evil does not exist on the Islands, there are no laws, there can be no consciousness of guilt. Emotions—impulses from the unconscious—have free play without the danger of remorse; there is no conflict between desire and control, between the good of the individual and the good of society. The fertile, vernal, tranquil qualities of the place at once create and reflect the psyche of the inhabitants.

> *Lavinia.* [to Peter] I've thought of you so much. Things were always reminding me of you—the ship and the sea—everything that was honest and clean! And the natives on the Islands reminded me of you too. They were so simple and fine. (MBE, p. 211.)

In the first play, Adam praises the life on the "Blessed Isles," and Ezra longs to go there. Adam and Lavinia plan their flight; Orin and Lavinia actually stop there on their voyage, and the experience transforms Lavinia. O'Neill, in using this image, is drawing on a yearning to escape, to return to paradise, that links the Puritan with the Freudian elements of the play. If the Islands are a refuge and a Paradise, they are also, as noted above, Mother.[35] The descriptions of Brant and Orin, the transformation of Lavinia, confer on the Islands a feminine image of warmth, softness, sea-bathed fecundity. Thus, in both the spatial and psychological dimensions, they represent escape, haven and a new life.

In the action the Islands are unattainable. The vision and the dream cannot be realized; for the Mannons, there is no escape from complex or heritage. Christine and Adam never make the journey; Lavinia and Orin return to find their dilemma unsolved, their guilt unpurged. Paradise cannot be regained by out-voyaging. Geographical islands will not serve—Orin's jealousy blights them for him and for Lavina also. They remain the symbol of a forlorn hope that is not transformed into a regenerating experience.

O'Neill does not arbitrarily assert the futility of this hope at the conclusion of the play; he foreshadows it throughout. One major device for this purpose is a choric-song, the sea-chanty "Shenandoah." *Homecoming* opens with Seth, the gardener-chorypheus, singing in the "wraith of what must once have been a good baritone" a chorus of that melancholy song. The desire to put to sea—the sailor is bound away "across the wide Missouri"—results in frustration and separation; the spatial dimension is not seen as an escape or a refuge, but as an unnavigable gulf: "Oh, Shenandoah, I can't get near you." The song recurs at Christine's suicide: "She's far away across the stormy water." (MBE, p. 181.) The separation is final. The image of the Islands and the hope of escape are countered from the outset by a song of hopeless longing. The stormy waters that separate man from his desire cannot be crossed except by death.

The plot of *Mourning Becomes Electra* is remarkably faithful to the *Oresteia*. Its characterization, symbolism and tone, however, are determined by O'Neill's interpretation of the Puritan heritage, by Freudian psychology, and by the corollary motif of salvation by spatial remove. The effect of these non-Hellenic elements is a shift of focus so radical as to produce a complete inversion of the play's meaning. The *Oresteia* proclaims a constant relationship between the individual and society. Orestes' crime does not isolate him from the community—he flees to Delphi, the communal shrine, he is judged by a jury of citizens, his personal fate changes the structure of society from clan-centered to city-centered. Conversely, the Mannons become progressively more isolated from the community. The townsfolk attend the funeral in the second act, but in the third they shrink from entering the "haunted house." The familial society contracts until only Orin and Lavinia are left; finally Lavinia shuts out *all* society. Secondly in the *Oresteia* the Greek code of blood vengeance provides the motivation for Orestes' crime and defines the nature of, and sets limits to, his guilt. He *must* murder his mother to avenge his father. The dilemma is perfect. In O'Neill's play, on the other hand, the "crimes" are rooted in the characters' subconscious, and the feeling of guilt is unlimited because it proceeds from the Puritan sense of damnation. Finally, the solution to Orestes' dilemma in the *Oresteia* is rooted in the popular history of the Athenian nation. The establishment of the jury-trial system makes the conclusion inevitable because it actually happened. Because the historical event is presented as the result of a providential process, Orestes' purgation is complete; it is sanctioned by the gods. O'Neill's solution to the Mannon curse is not purgation, but death. Orin "returns to Mother" by committing suicide; Lavinia's self-immolation is merely a surrogate for suicide. No Providence, benign or malicious, is invoked, and even the sense of inevitability is contingent on acceptance of O'Neill's Freudian coordinates.

These contrasts suggest that the "meaning" of *Mourning Becomes Electra* is derived not from the plot, but from the opposition between the psychological imperatives and the Puritan ethos. The polar tendencies of each set of attitudes are rendered absolute; the autonomous unconscious is seen to be locked in conflict with the Puritan ego. In her recent study of O'Neill, Doris Falk draws a message from this struggle:

All his life man is forced to wrestle with the unconscious in an attempt to reconcile its demands with those of his conscious ego. The Sin of Pride means to O'Neill what it does to Jung: Man is in fatal error when he assumes that his conscious ego can fulfill all his needs without acknowledgement of the power of the unconscious, the equivalent of the gods.[36]

On these grounds the theme of the play is the inability of man to walk humbly the *via media* between paralysis and destruction, the way of self-acceptance. The pride of the Mannons will not allow them to accept their "real" selves, to realize that active, creative men are doomed to suffer and that to avoid grief is to reject happiness because these conditions are opposite sides of the same coin.

This analysis is neat and perceptive, but it acknowledges only one of the two polar opposites. Precisely because the Mannons are defined by their Freudian impulses *and* their Puritan heritage, they can have no access to this hypothetical "real self." The implication that all the Mannons needed was a good psychiatrist begs the question and turns *Mourning* into a "thesis" play. Perhaps O'Neill intended that the audience take some such idea away from his play, but the development of his plot, and its conclusion, makes its own statement.

Beyond the stereotyped message that "adjustment is all," and in ironic contrast to it, there is in *Mourning Becomes Electra* an overwhelming, unrelenting sense of the imminence of Death. The events of the plot—murder, murder-suicide, suicide, immurement—objectify this sense as does the sepulchral façade of the Mannon house. Death is the goal of O'Neill's Puritan; he meditates on it, he walks in its shadow, he lives for it. Since this Puritanism does not include a theological dimension, Death is an end in itself, not a passage to another world.

Thus Death is not merely a thematic image in the play or simply a way of dispatching the personae and cleaning up the stage. It is the epiphany that concludes the action, the vision to which the plot progresses. If Greek tragedy included the death of the hero, it also provided a means of encompassing the idea of death in a framework of death-and-rebirth. O'Neill's modifications, however, result in a hopeless reiteration that death is final, absolutely conclusive, the end. In addition to the agon and the pathos, the conflict and the suffering, the *Oresteia* includes a "rebirth" or epiphany, in which the hero is purified by both society and the gods. In *Mourning,* however, the epiphany is a vision of Death, of existential nothingness, the individual confronted by the void. "Rebirth" and purgation become simple release from suffering through suicide or self-immurement.

The action of *Mourning* turns in an ever-tightening circle; its universe is bounded on every side by a void. There is no escape from experience, from guilt, from time. The undertone of *Angst*— the suffering of the characters in the face of this vision—gives the play the affective power it has. It reflects a major preoccupation of "mythless" modern man.

It is in trying to estimate this anguish in the face of Death—that is, in trying to place it and evaluate it in a perspective other than our own— that the comparative approach [to culture] begins to be instructive. Anguish before Nothingness and Death seems to be a specifically modern phenomenon. In all other, non-European cultures, that is, in the other religions, Death is never felt as an absolute end or as Nothingness: it is regarded rather as a rite of passage to another mode of being: and for that reason is always referred to in relation to the symbolisms and rituals of initiation, rebirth or resurrection.[37]

This *Angst* is nowhere explicit in the drama; it exists as the tension between the suffering of the personae and the epiphany. The Mannons push against the barriers of their space- and time-bounded existence; the desire for egress and the impossibility of finding it generate the tension, the psychic action of the drama. As Lavinia finally turns back into the sepulchral house of the Mannons, she moves not toward a rebirth, but toward an encounter with the void that makes a travesty of so long life.

The Old Woman, the Doctor and the Cook:

The Cocktail Party

The verse dramas of T. S. Eliot are the contributions of a poet, a critic, an amateur cultural historian, to modern theatre. Long before the production of his first dramatic effort in 1935, Eliot had published a significant corpus of poetry, and had laid the foundations for a new school of literary criticism by insisting that great literature is dependent on tradition—especially royalism and Anglo-Catholicism. When he set out to write poetic drama, he approached the task self-consciously, with certain definite ideas about the nature and function of this genre. His principles, in broad outline, can be gleaned from his critical essays on the possibility of poetic drama, on the Elizabethan and Jacobean dramatists, on the use of poetry, and *passim* in his other works. Eliot is as much an innovator as Eugene O'Neill, but, in spite of a superficial similarity like the use of Greek sources and devices, he takes a different approach to the use of literary models in drama. O'Neill advertised his literary source and followed it faithfully, adopting contemporary theories of motivation. Eliot eschews the personal, the "private mind," and the specifically modern. The surface of *The Cocktail Party* is modern, but it has roots in the traditional literary heritage of Western civilization. It is an attempt to tap this tradition, not merely to reshape it according to modern attitudes but to create a new embodiment of those traditional attitudes which he considers crucial to the maintenance and development of Western culture.

Eliot's approach to the drama rests on his conviction that literary tradition is the life's blood of art. The poet cannot rely on his personal experience; rather, he "must be quite aware of the mind of Europe—the mind of his own country—a mind which he learns in time to be much more important than his own private mind." [1] This mind is the vehicle of value and culture—it generates whatever art a generation produces. To neglect it is to fall into barbarism.[2] Thus the dramatist is presented with this heritage, and his task is to shape it into a new literary creation. "No man can invent a form, create a taste for it and shape it too. . . . To have, given into one's hands, a crude form, capable of indefinite refinement, and to be the person to see the possibilities" of a new and contemporary expression is the mark of the artist.[3] Refinement of this crude form, Eliot indicates in another essay, extends beyond the development of a more polished technique into an area of deeper significance, to a "kind of doubleness of action, an underpattern in which the reality of the action is felt to be in conformity with the laws of some other world we cannot perceive."[4] This statement suggests that the structure itself, as well as the mode of filling it out, can be consciously chosen by the artist. The indications of Eliot's approach—which could be amplified from other essays—do not make the plays plain as a pipe-stem any more than his poetic theories make his poetry completely accessible. They do point to a *modus procedendi* which involves conscious selection of cultural patterns and an artistic use of the literary tradition of the West.

In *Poetry and Drama* (London, 1950), Eliot has described briefly the results of his attempts to practice what he preaches. His first effort, *Murder in the Cathedral,* written for a special occasion and for a special audience, allowed him to concentrate on developing a suitable poetic diction which he describes as "neutral," i.e., neither authentic Anglo-Norman nor pseudo-Shakespearean, for a subject and theme that included an historical perspective. The world which the play evokes is twelfth-century England; the interpretation of such events as happen there do not put much of a strain on audience credibility. In *The Family Reunion,* Eliot tried a modernization of Greek drama, like O'Neill's *Mourning,* moving his action into the present and putting his verse into the mouths of people "dressed like ourselves, living in houses and apartments like ours, and using telephones and motorcars and radio sets."[5] His own appraisal of this version was largely negative—the play fell between two stools, being neither sufficiently Aeschylean nor adequately modern. His next attempt to cope with the problem of modernizing was *The Cocktail Party.* Eliot considered this play more successful, a good balance between literary tradition, basic Western cultural attitudes and a modern situation. He adroitly concealed the source of his inspiration —the *Alcestis* of Euripides—from reviewer and critic, thus eliminating distracting comparisons; he employed a comic format that allowed for a more realistic surface than in *Family Reunion;* he produced a three-stress verse line which approximated conversational prose. Nonetheless, the play impressed critics and reviewers as "mysterious." They scented a "kind of doubleness, an under-pattern" that belied the "comedy of manners" façade. The refinement of this contemporary "crude form" produced a number of levels or dimensions—the nature of these dimensions and their interaction constitute the critical problem of the play. The remainder of this chapter will be devoted to a discussion of this problem.

The structural components of *The Cocktail Party* are various and interlocked. They include the drawing-room comedy plot à la Noel Coward; the satyr-drama of Euripides as realized in the *Alcestis;* and finally, the conventional comic form which can be related to the Dionysian ritual and which includes strong archetypal overtones. Dramatic tradition reveals the links between each of these structures. The modern comedy is related, by a traceable genealogy, to Greek New Comedy: "The plot structure of Greek New Comedy, as transmitted by Plautus and Terence, in itself less a form than a formula, has become the basis for most comedy, especially in its more highly conventionalized dramatic form, down to our own day." [6] New Comedy is itself a descendant of Euripidean tragedy or satyr-drama, hence the connection with the *Alcestis.*[7] These connections, on which we will elaborate later, are part of a conscious design that Eliot creates to express his meaning.

That the playwright is consciously using these structures as a bridge to his audience is borne out by remarks scattered through his writings. In "The Possibility of a Poetic Drama," he speaks of adapting a "true structure, Athenian or Elizabethan, to contemporary feeling"; the *Alcestis* provides him with this kind of structure.[8] The mythical and ritual implications of this type of satyr-drama are spelled out in F. M. Cornford's *Origins of Attic Comedy* in scholarly detail; Eliot is acquainted with Cornford's work: "Few books are more fascinating than those of Miss Harrison, Mr. Cornford, or Mr. Cook, when they burrow in the origins of Greek myths and rites." [9] His method of dealing with these literary traditions and his reasons for so doing can be traced to the influence of Sir James Frazer, whose work made such an impact on his poetry.

Frazer's facts suggest that archaic and contemporary behaviour are already juxtaposed in contemporary consciousness, and that a poet can further refine the juxtapositions . . . to disclose a ground of identity and to reveal the presence of a third entity, a metaphysical community of all men.[10]

By presenting the modern audience with ancient forms wrapped in a modern disguise, Eliot hopes to recreate, with all its archetypal resonance, a model for this community of all men.

Between the *Sacred Wood* essays and *The Cocktail Party*, Eliot assumed another major commitment—that to Christianity. While he uses the Greek ritual pattern in his play, he is not trying to convert the audience to the worship of Dionysus. Because it is part of his own avowed belief as well as a major influence on Western culture, Eliot fills out the regeneration pattern with Christian detail. Thus the community he envisions conforms to a model that is Greek in form and Christian in content. He uses his own understanding of Christian doctrine to specify and fill out the pattern he borrows from the Greek dramatists. The play, then, is a "comedy" in a number of related senses: a drawing-room comedy of marital misunderstanding, a proto comedy with ritual overtones, a *Divina Commedia*. We will begin by looking at the "crude form" that makes up the surface of the play.

The "crude form" that provides a starting point for *The Cocktail Party* is that hardy perennial which focuses on marital misunderstanding and the clandestine (or not-so-clandestine) affair. This comedy-type persists in Broadway shows like *Mary, Mary* or *Barefoot in the Park;* variations and gimmicks may disguise the formula, but essentially it holds on. This type is first-cousin to the sentimental romance, but it insists rather on the folly of love-making and the absurdities of social pretense. The lineage, in modern times, extends from the Victorial melodrama through the parodies of Wilde and the "idea" comedies of Shaw to the drawing-room sophistications of Noel Coward and Philip Barry. The basic device which moves the events of the plot is recognition or revelation, the discovery by one dramatis persona that another is not the character he or she appeared.[11] Thus the pattern emerges: a couple, after the first flush of the honeymoon, discover flaws that lead to separation. They often look elsewhere for comfort and support. A new liaison with another partner or partners generally leads to comic complications—abrupt intrusions, precipitous flights, embarrassing encounters. Further experience with the new loves leaves the partners unsatisfied; the comedy closes with a reconciliation of the original pair based on a new understanding. Often the rejected lovers pair off. This pattern—union, disenchantment and separation, reunion—is capable of infinite variation, but the essential structure is perennial.

In the opening scene of *The Cocktail Party*, the setting, the dramatis personae and the dialogue, are calculated to create the impression associated with the drawing-room formula. The cocktail party as an institution is emblematic of the frivolous sophistication of modern life—at once an escape from reality and a parody of communion. The characters are stock-types: Julia, a prying dowager with a scattershot mind and manner; Alex Gibbs, world traveler and gad-about who knows the modish shops and the fashionable psychiatrists; Peter Quilpe, the young artiste hanger-on; Celia Copelstone, a pleasant, self-possessed young woman. There is also, besides Edward Chamberlayne, the host, an Unidentified Guest who seems not to know what is going on and politely seems not to care. These stock characters in this stock environment—the aimless social vacuum of the cocktail party—converse with sophisticated polish about trivia. The patter is bright and inane, in stichomythia that recalls Wilde or Coward.

> *Alex.* You've missed the point completely, Julia.
> There were no tigers. That was the point.
> *Julia.* Then what were you doing up a tree?
> You and the Maharaja?
> *Alex.*　　　　　　　　My dear Julia,
> It's perfectly hopeless. You haven't been listening.[12]

This persiflage has the proper in-group, high-society air about it. The style has a familiar ring—for example, Coward's character who spends a dozen lines on Chuquicamata, a copper mine in Chile, and then discloses that he hasn't been there since he was two.[13] The

image is firmly established in the opening act—a contemporary sophisticated society at play; the audience is led to expect certain
marital complications.

The external events of the first and second acts—and, in a measure, of the third act also—follow the pattern of the drawing room
comedy faithfully, according to the established image. Eliot varies
the "crude" format by beginning *in medias res,* but all the essential
points of the pattern are included. Edward Chamberlayne's wife Lavinia has left him. Julia, "that tough silly old woman," picks this
information out of Edward. His wife, he avers, is down in the
depths of Essex visiting a sick aunt. Julia knows all about this aunt.
"And this is the first time/I've ever seen you without Lavinia."
When the situation becomes clear to the entire company, the party
breaks up. When the others—Julia and Alex, Peter and Celia—
leave, the Unidentified Guest becomes Edward's confidante; to the
confirmation of Lavinia's disappearance is added the information
that Edward wants her back. The Guest, who has assumed an air of
knowing more than he is telling, promises Edward that he will return Lavinia tomorrow. In a variation of the standard device of intrusions, Peter returns to confer with Edward about his love for
Celia—he wants the advice of the older man. The irony of this com-
plication appears when Celia returns, and it becomes clear that Edward has been having an affair with the younger woman. By the
middle of the first act the pattern of events has been established:
husband and wife who, up to this time, had been thought insepa-
rable, have separated; the young couple at the party are mistress to
the husband and lover to the wife, respectively. These affairs are
broken off—Edward rejects Celia for Lavinia, and Peter, Lavinia's
erst-while lover, is involved with Celia. In the third scene of the first
act, Eliot brings together all the members of the company—and Lavinia is returned to her husband. Peter and Celia decide to "go
away." Thus, by the end of the act all the components of the standard formula have been presented; the playwright has moved his
characters through the major stages of the marital-misunderstanding
formula. The husband and wife have taken lovers as antidote to a
hum-drum marriage; one partner finds the mistress unsatisfactory
and the lover deserts the other partner. Husband and wife are then
reunited. At this point, Eliot produces his own variations on the
formula.

The reconciliation of Edward and Lavinia—which is usually the conclusion of the formula—is here really an agon in which the husband and wife decide that they are, after five years of life together, strangers. The polished dialogue, which in the stereotyped marital comedy breaks down for comic purposes into railing and abuse, takes on a poetic intensity. The encounter is a commentary on the usual live-happily-ever-after conclusion and a preparation for the real reconciliation which takes place in the psychiatrist's office. Under the tutelage of the Unidentified Guest (revealed to be Sir Henry Harcourt-Reilly, Harley Street specialist), Edward and Lavinia make the final discovery—Edward's nature is unloving and Lavinia is unlovable. Their reunion has an uncharacteristically realistic tone—they choose to "make the best of a bad job." There is no joyous rushing together, but rather the cautious approach of two strangers who have a mutual interest in working out a *modus vivendi*. This development is an extension, then, of the pattern—the reconciliation is realized on a more personally realistic level than the admission of "true love" by the involved pair. Moreover, where the conventional plot might unite Peter and Celia as a counterpart to the Edward-Lavinia wedding, Eliot again employs a variation. Celia recognizes her destiny and moves into another dimension; though in the third act Peter discovers himself through Celia's love, Celia's love is not directed at *him*. The external action of *The Cocktail Party* is structured by the marital-misunderstanding formula; Eliot uses the conventional format to order his plot, and to create a surface around which he can draw out other, more complex, dimensions.

Eliot has also adapted the basic dramatic device on which the structure depends—anagnorisis or recognition. Often this device is used mechanically—as when the long-lost son returns incognito and at the crisis is "recognized" in time to rescue his imperiled family. In the Coward version what is recognized is often the "real self," the misunderstanding having arisen out of an opposition between the romantic and the real image. Eliot has desentimentalized this recognition and moved it out of the sphere of simple (either physical rapport or eccentric individualism) marital adjustment. He uses the discovery technique also with regard to the audience; the relationships are "discovered" to the audience, rather than enacted for them. The affair between Celia and Edward, for instance, is revealed

in its dissolution. The reason for the separation of Edward and Lavinia is not clarified until she returns to him at the end of the first
act. The comic formula and the devices of recognition and discovery
link the surface level of *The Cocktail Party* with an ancient tradition.

As we have hinted above, the "sentimental comedy" has a long
history reaching back to the New Comedy of Menander. This type
(called "sentimental" in comparison with the hard-nosed satire of
Aristophanes), with its abandoned hero who is recognized after
many adversities by his noble parents, thus acquiring wealth, happiness and a proper wife, has its germ in Euripidean satyr-drama like
the *Alcestis,* which builds to the Kômos, a wedding festival celebrating the ritual hierogamy of the Eniautos daimon and the goddess of fertility.[14] The basic plot of the *Alcestis* is the separation
and the reunion of husband and wife—the identical movement that
structures the comedy of marital misunderstanding. The significance
of this pattern, put in proper perspective, establishes a broader base
for the motivation and action of *The Cocktail Party.*

The satyr-play is said to have developed as a projection of the
worship of Dionysus, and its essential function was theophantic—
the revel of the half-animal satyrs in celebration of the wedding of
the Year-daimon with the goddess of fertility in the figure of a
young woman. The Kômos with which the Aristophanic comedy
concludes is the wedding-march remnant of this ritual. When, in the
development of dramatic forms, the tragic trilogy began to incorporate its own theophany, the satyr-play became superfluous. Euripides moved away from the strict satyr form and developed "a curious sort of pro-satyric tragedy, a plan in the tragic convention and
free from satyric coarseness, but containing at least one half-comic
figure and preserving some fantastic quality of atmosphere."[15] The
structure of the *Alcestis* follows the ritual pattern of the tragedy
with "satyric" variations: Agon, Death and Resurrection, Marriage,
and Kômos.[16] Eliot borrows elements of the *Alcestis* plot: the
"death" motif; "resurrection" by the Heraclean figure, Sir Henry;
the wedding of Edward and Lavinia "in spirit and in truth." These
details call attention to the Greek source of the modern plot and to
the ritual pattern underneath.

Eliot, be it noted, does not use a point-for-point approach to the
Euripidean play; he selects those features that fill out the surface

structure and point to ritual patterns. The *Alcestis* opens with an agon between Apollo and Death and proceeds to a vivid presentation of the death of Alcestis. Eliot omits both prologue and departure; when the play opens, Lavinia has already disappeared. The demigod, the Unidentified Guest, is already on the scene; his equation with Heracles, the proverbially gluttonous hero-god, is only faintly suggested by Reilly's drinking and by the song he sings on departure. More significant is the Guest's promise to return Edward's "departed" wife. Here the Heraclean function is clear and unequivocal. Besides the Heraclean figure, another parallel to the *Alcestis* is the agon between Edward and Lavinia. In the *Alcestis* Phares and Admetus dispute the culpability for the Queen's death; in *The Cocktail Party* Edward and Lavinia discuss the reasons for the death of their marriage. Also after the "wedding" in the psychiatrist's office, there is a sacrificial feast, a ritual symposium with invocations by Sir Henry and his accomplices, Julia and Alex. The cocktail party in the third act is a modified Kômos, a wedding celebration for Edward and Lavinia.[17] These analogues from the *Alcestis* introduce the motifs of regeneration and the renewal of society. The psychiatrist, like Heracles, brings Lavinia "back from the dead." (CP, p. 71.) In their toasting, the three conspirators declare that, for the Chamberlaynes, all is in order, and they drink to the "building of the hearth." The reunion of the Chamberlaynes involves a "rebirth" and a new order in society.

The format from drawing-room comedy and the *Alcestis* analogue account for salient features in Eliot's play; there are other components which they leave untouched. For example, Julia and Alex have puzzled and bothered some of the critics. "How can two such fatuous cocktail characters as Julia and Alex be translated between the first and second acts into Guardian Angels?"[18] In fact, in the second act it becomes clear that these two function in much the same capacity as Reilly-Heracles. Julia seems to have the same control over the "mysterious" (note that this word often recurs in the dialogue and that it has two senses—one profane and one ritualistic). She summons the psychiatrist to the party in the first instance, she sends the telegrams that reassemble the group the next day. She has knowledge as far-reaching as Reilly's and even operates as his critic-consoler. "You must accept your limitations." (CP, p. 148.) The "silly old woman" of the first act *is* hard to reconcile with the Guardian of Act II—it takes an understanding of the dramatic tradition behind the persona to manage it. Alex, the third guardian, is also a puzzle. That he should be a world-traveler is acceptable enough, for he can play Greek messenger and report Celia's sacrifice, but he is also an expert cook. This detail provides some witty dialogue and allows for a comic intrusion; however, it seems that entirely too much is made of such an irrelevant accomplishment. Here, too, there is the feeling that Eliot has some "underpattern" in mind, that these "irrelevances" conceal a deeper meaning.

Eliot's reference to Cornford provides the necessary clue to the "real" identity of Julia and Alex, and indeed to the identity of the entire cast in *The Cocktail Party*. Working out from his ritual base, Cornford describes the types that make up the protocomic cast of characters: Old Man and Young Man, Old Woman and Maiden, the Doctor and the Cook.[19] The "originals" of these types reflect the actors in the Dionysian ritual, as described in Cornford's study. The Old Man symbolized the Old Year, the character who must die and be born again before the cycle of life can go on. In his interview with Celia, Edward announces that he is beginning to feel old.

> *Edward.*   Only since this morning
> I have met myself as a middle-aged man
> Beginning to know what it is to feel old.   (CP, p. 65.)

He resembles the old King, bearing the name of kings, the Fisher King who has only barren property to protect (*Ead-ward*/guardian of property). In the ritual cast, the Young Man is the New Year who succeeds to the kingdom. He usually takes over the function and the role of the Old Man either through a fight or by guile. Peter Quilpe (whose name is an archaic variant of "whelp") has usurped Edward's place with Lavinia and desires to replace him in Celia's affections. Peter will plead *nolo contendere;* in this play (as in other versions of the ancient pattern) the battle is not joined. Instead the Old Man is rejuvenated, and the Young Man shares the Maiden with him. The Young Woman originated as the mute bride of the wedding, the fertile feminine principle.[20] This detail is carried out in the *Alcestis;* when the Queen returns from the dead, she is a mute. In *The Cocktail Party*, for reasons that become clear later on, the Young Woman (Alcestis) role is divided between Celia and Lavinia. Like Alcestis, Celia sacrifices herself for the community; like Alcestis, Lavinia becomes the bride of the wedding. These types fit the play neatly and their resemblance to the protocomic cast in Cornford is not surprising. The case is somewhat different when we turn our attention to the Guardians.

The personae who control the events of the play are Julia, Reilly and Alex. The full nature and significance of these characters appear and the puzzle about them is solved when we recognize, behind the cocktail types, the Old Woman, the Doctor and the Cook.[21] When the Old Woman appears on the Greek stage, she is the shrewish, drunken, amorous hag who dances the kordax. In the opening scene of Eliot's play, Julia remarks that she comes to the party for tidbits; she can drink at home. Celia refers to her as "that horrible old woman." Cornford argues that, though dramatic evolution turned her into a shrew, the original of this persona was the Mother who nursed the miraculous child, the young Zeus, in the ritual.[22] When the original function was wiped out, she survived as a grotesque. As *this* Old Woman, Julia's place in the plot becomes clear; she is the "mother" to the demi-god (hence her proprietary attitude toward Reilly) disguised in the role of "shrewish hag." Julia initiates situations, ferrets out those who need rebirth, and sends for the Doctor.

The ancient ritual function of the Doctor is to revive the slain hero; this persona and his capacities are most clearly realized in the English Mummers' Play, but the tradition goes directly back to Cornford's protocomic cast.[23] The Heraclean figure—the demi-god who has control over the powers of the underworld—is the Doctor of the *Alcestis*. Harcourt-Reilly (whose name reflects both "Harley Street" and "Heracles" phonetically) has a power that is immediately felt by the perceptive. On first meeting him, Celia says: "Who was that man? I was rather afraid of him;/He has some sort of power." His power is discovered to be resurrectional; Reilly promises to bring Edward's wife back to him and then startles him with: "It is a serious matter/To bring someone back from the dead." Edward considers this mode of expression a "trifle dramatic"; in view of the origin of Reilly's role, it is precisely "dramatic." He is only performing his traditional role as Doctor. As doctor to Edward, Lavinia and Celia, he "resurrects" them and sets them on the road to a new life.

Perhaps the most surprising of the trio is Alex; he too has an ancient ritual role which he announces himself: "You know, I'm a rather famous cook." (CP, p. 41.) What sounds like personal vanity is actually a broad hint about his character. Cornford has outlined his genealogy and the source of his fame: "The Cook is a magician, a dealer in enchanted herbs, a medicine man. As such he is not, in origin, distinct from the Learned Doctor." [24] His function is related to a purgation-mode of regeneration, what A. B. Cook has called the "cauldron of apotheosis." [25] We recall the rejuvenations of Pelops, Pelias and Aeson by boiling; this detail in the legends has led Cook to conjecture that the original Thraco-Phrygian ceremony of the death and resurrection of Dionysus involved a ritual stewing of the god, in the form of a kid, in milk as a preparation to the sacramental eating of his flesh. The Cook presides over this rite. Cornford cites a text that is peculiarly applicable to *The Cocktail Party* Alex:

An exponent of the art of cooking claims that the cook should be enrolled among the 'sophists', alike as professor of a learned subject and as artist. Others assert that the Cook must needs be a philosopher and a psychologist, and indeed that the culinary art embraces the whole catalog of human sciences. . . . He has an ancestor in the Maison of the Megarian farce, who must have figured in scenes of heroic travesty with the glutton Heracles.[26]

Here we have the connection between Alex the all-knowing and Alex the Cook and between the Reilly-Heracles character and Alex. Moreover, Eliot's choice of the name "Alex" is interesting in view of the fact that the passage above from Cornford is the summary of a fragment by *Alexis*.[27] Some of the dialogue, then, takes on an added set of meanings. While Edward and Peter are having their conference in Act I, Alex is working in the kitchen. He calls out for a "double boiler." Unfortunately the kitchen is not equipped with one and "there goes *that* surprise." The surprise that is left—a dinner for Celia and Edward—burns in the saucepan. A double irony in Celia's remark: "Anything that Alex makes is absolutely deadly" (CP, p. 57) underscores the Cook's role; he must kill to boil, and death precedes the resurrection. Edward needs "double boiling"; the ritual feast burns on the stove while Edward and Celia discuss their lack of rapport.[28] Alex represents a different kind of resurrectional figure who works in the sacrifice-feast context of the ritual pattern. This makes it fitting that he be the one to report Celia's sacrificial death at the second cocktail party. Thus he is at once, finally to answer Wimsatt's query (n. 18, above), a "cocktail character" and a protocomic figure.

Eliot has employed a set of characters with a pedigree reaching back to the ritual origins of comedy. Once these personae are discovered, other puzzling features of the play—the series of intrusions in the first act, the ritual incantation of the Guardians, the sacrifice-and-feast overtones of the third act—become intelligible. Eliot is drawing on the comic ritual that is at the roots of the Western comic tradition, as Cornford outlines it.

Some of the events in the first act must now be reconsidered. To begin with, there is the series of comic intrusions by Julia and Alex. One of the recurrent events in the second half of the Old Comedy play is the intrusion of the alazon, the "imposter." The alazontes, as the name suggests, wander into the feast and claim a part in the celebration. They are generally distinguished by some professional standing—the oracle-monger, the poet, the informer, the quack. They press their fraudulent claims, are ridiculed, and run off by the hero. This device of the intruder has been widely adapted through the ages—in such widely separated plays as *The Alchemist, She Stoops to Conquer* and *The Importance of Being Earnest*. In a sense, Reilly is the first alazon; presumably no one knows who invited him. Then there are the interruptions by Julia and Alex of Edward's private conversations. These two are alazontes; the man-about-town, the busy-body harridan mask their real identity as guardians. Eliot here adapts the "intruder" device to his own purposes. In Old Comedy, these intruders claim to be rightful sharers in the feast, but they are really imposters. In *The Cocktail Party* they appear as conventional "cocktail characters" whereas they are really Guardians. Moreover, their intrusions are not attempts to dispossess the hero, but to aid him. Alex does not claim a share in the feast, for instance, but prepares it for Edward. Eliot's inversion of the intruder device points to the underpattern by dramatizing the deception produced by appearances.

With this inversion it becomes clear that the first cocktail party is itself a pseudo-feast, an antimasque. The communion of gin and potato crisps emphasizes the isolation and desperation of the "communicants." The true feast follows the interviews in Reilly's office—the wedding of the Chamberlaynes and the rebirth of Celia. The Guardians gather alone—for they only know the full secret of their identity—and chant invocations and drink the communion. The secret community of Mother, Doctor, Cook cannot yet claim a complete victory, but they have set Edward and Lavinia and Celia on the right way. The prayers they utter reflect the model Eliot is using and the stage in which their clients find themselves. The two invocations, one for those "who go on a journey" and the other "for the building of the hearth," echo the two petitions in Alcestis' prayer before she dies. She prays to the hearth-goddess to protect her family while she goes on a long journey.[29] Edward and Lavinia must "build the hearth" and Celia must "go on a long journey." This "mystery" conducted by the Guardians presages the coming victory of the third act. Lavinia-Alcestis conducts her own wedding feast in Act III; Celia-Alcestis goes on to her sacrifice and apotheosis. Thus the ritual points to a Kômos-like celebration of the new union of Edward and Lavinia and includes the report of Celia's triumph.

The movement of the whole play, then, has this shape: the first act is a condensation of the marital-misunderstanding plot of union, disenchantment and separation, reunion. Here the modern surface is emphasized, and the "reunion" scene at the end of the act has an ironic flavor that stems from the couple's discovery that they are really strangers. The second act elaborates the reunion segment by revealing the basis for a true reunion. The set-pieces and details from the *Alcestis* throw a sharper focus on the ritual elements and on the regeneration motif. The ritual aspects of the personae are more clearly revealed, and the characters are incorporated into a new society.

These patterns, as we noted above, are filled out and specified by a doctrine (or, in Northrop Frye's terminology, a "dianoia") that is Christian. Eliot defines the mode of regeneration in Christian terms; from this point of view, the play is the Christian commedia whose purpose is, in Dante's words, "to remove those who are living in this life from a state of wretchedness and to lead them to a state of blessedness." (*Epistle to Can Grande.*) The "mystery" which is pure suspense and the Eleusinian arcane eventually emerges as the "mysterium salvificum" of Eliot's Christian tradition.[30] Though the

Christian references are neatly veiled in gnomic sayings and neutral exclamations, especially in the first act, their accumulation pushes this dimension of the play at the audience. Christianity is a positive force, a unique mode of rebirth toward which the characters move.

In the first scenes, where the drawing-room façade is thickest, the Christian dimension is adumbrated in small, indecisive allusions or resonances. After the other guests have departed, the Stranger asks for his gin "with a drop of water." This rubrical drop—on which he three times insists—faintly echoes the drop mingled in the offertory wine.[31] The "communion" image here, ironic in that it effects far more communion than Edward bargained for, is based on gin, not wine—the water of human nature without the wine of divinity.

Later the stranger offers the unlikely concept of "humiliation" to Edward; he will find that he survives humiliation. "He who humbles himself shall be exalted" sounds remotely in the mind. After Edward declares himself "in the dark," the Guest introduces "light." The "Light that shineth in the darkness" stays just out of focus. (CP, p. 32.) Julia's conversation is sprinkled with more explicit references. Intruding on Edward and Celia ostensibly (and therefore in another sense, really) to feed him, she remarks that he is lucky to have two Good Samaritans—Edward replies that he has three. (CP, p. 56.) Celia, the predestined soul, speculates on the identity of the stranger:

> Why should that man want to bring her back—
> Unless he is the Devil!

This archaism is nicely punctuated by a popping noise from the kitchen. Edward exclaims, "What the devil's that?" Eliot seems to be playing with the notion that the gods of one culture are the devils of the next. Or perhaps he is pointing to the curious doubling which reveals the antagonist of the drama to be a projected image of the god himself. In either event the playwright associates Reilly and Julia in a mysterious alliance. Though Celia does not understand their power and so attributes it to the adversary, she does recognize it, thereby showing herself superior to Edward who calls on the devil unawares. When Celia and Edward drink, it is to the Guardians—Edward's term for that "tougher self" who does not will but simply is. Celia, with her sharper sight, sees that the Guardian might be something outside the self: "It may be that even Julia is a guardian. Perhaps she is *my* guardian." (CP, p. 69.) Guardian here, besides its sense of legal protector, recalls both the Guardians of society in Plato's *Republic* and the "guardian angel" of Christian myth. Edward includes the angelic dimension also; in describing the current state of his soul, he uses a Christian analogy.

> What is hell? Hell is oneself,
> Hell is alone, the other figures in it
> Merely projections. (CP, p. 98.)

This reflection is only a scrap short of theological orthodoxy—hell as the pain of loss, isolation from love and fulfillment. These fragmentary allusions hint vaguely at the Christian orientation of the plot development; they take more explicit shape in the succeeding acts.

The whole context of the psychiatrist's office suggests that it is something more. Reilly strikes rather directly at the superstition of curative power concealed in the Freudian couch:

> I always begin from the immediate situation
> And then go back as far as I find necessary.
> You see, your memories of childhood—
> I mean, in your present state of mind—
> Would be largely fictitious; and as for your dreams,
> You would produce amazing dreams, to oblige me.
> (CP, p. 111.)

Edward is not afraid of the death of the body, but the "death of the spirit" terrifies him. Lavinia reiterates the characterization of Reilly as "the Devil." The Doctor refers vaguely and unprofessionally to several types of sanatoria and suggests that the patients must cure themselves. He assumes an omniscience that is surprising and renders judgment pontifically.

> When you find, Mr. Chamberlayne,
> The best of a bad job is all any of us make of it—
> Except of course, the saints . . . you will forget this phrase,
> And in forgetting it will alter the condition. (CP, p. 126.)

Celia's problem is put in terms explicitly theological: she suffers from an awareness of solitude and from a "sense of sin." The solution to her dilemma, as prescribed by Reilly, is "courage and faith." When Reilly sends these people on their separate ways, he uses the confessional formula: "Go in peace." The "learned Doctor" draws on the wisdom of Christianity to counsel his patients—their regeneration is a spiritual one. The ritual which the Guardian trinity celebrates is, as we have seen, the sacrifice and feast of the protocomic pattern, but the form of the words reflects the Litany and the Itinerarium of the Breviary. This syncretism (to which can be added the expression "Work out your salvation in diligence" addressed to the patient-penitents—a combination of St. Paul and Buddha) underscores Eliot's point by bringing the two dimensions, the Greek and the Christian, together.

The Christian dimension is unmistakable in the last act, which in Eliot's opinion, narrowly escapes being an epilogue, "if indeed it does escape." [32] This opinion of the playwright acknowledges the fact that the Kômos is in itself undramatic, that the reconciliation of husband and wife, along with Celia's decision, really complete the action as such. But this act does tie up loose ends, especially by making the content of the Christian dimension explicit. Edward and Lavinia are shown in a state of adjustment; they have accepted one another's limitations and so have altered their condition to a quiet (if rather clubby) rapport. Alex, acting the Greek messenger, arrives from afar to narrate Celia's eponymous "enskying." She has been crucified in a mission land as the result of a native uprising. This end scandalizes the company; she died for a handful of natives, who, as Edward observes, would have died anyway. The event is doubly shocking to Peter who, in the best sentimental comedy tradition, has been carrying the torch for Celia. Peter comes to recognize that Celia—his image of her—is a mirage and, to be saved, he must let her go.

> One thought has been going round and round in my head—
> That I've only been interested in myself:
> And that isn't good enough for Celia.   (CP, p. 179.)

By Celia's sacrifice, her self-donation, Peter is "saved," reclaimed from his unreal Hollywood world. Celia dies the Christ-death; she is the figure of the person with a religious vocation, the imitator of Christ. Reilly sums up the doctrine on her death: though she died for a handful of natives, the company cannot possibly know how much her death affected the state of mind in which they died. Lavinia is "willing to grant that." Reilly also points out that Celia paid the highest price in suffering—both at the end and in her journey toward it. Both Edward and Lavinia feel they share some of the responsibility for her death—they share the guilt, says Reilly, but not the triumph. However, their acceptance of this experience will renew them and alter the meaning of the past. The "faith and resignation" doctrine here is an application of Christian doctrine to the death-and-resurrection categories of the ritual structure. On this note the "words" are finally spoken for Peter; he must go on to Botwell to make his film and a beginning on creating a real castle in which to live. All the threads are drawn together, and the doctrine supplies the knot.

If the doctrine of the play is Christian, it is Eliot's own version. He has documented his position on the nature and function of a Christian society in his *Idea of a Christian Society*.[33] The dianoia of the play is a reflection of the ideas he develops in this essay. Its main point may be summarized as follows. The culture of modern society is mainly negative, but what positive aspects it has are still Christian. Vestiges of this heritage adhere in language, social conventions and mores.[34] Since the ordinary member of this (or any) society does not distinguish between cultural elements that are religious and those that are merely social, it is necessary only to integrate customs, conventions and ideals with a Christian vision of the world to revitalize the community. Within this society, however, there must exist an inner circle that is responsible for the creation and preservation of such a code. These selectmen are the "clerisy," the Church within the Church, "consciously and thoughtfully practicing Christians . . . of intellectual and spiritual authority." [35] They accomplish this integration of doctrine and practice and protect it from secular forces. This inner circle, though they live in the world, must respect the life of prayer and contemplation and encourage those who practice it.[36] The established hierarchy of this Christian society, based on knowledge, sets up three strata: the "ordinary" people, the spiritual elite who live in the world, the contemplatives who are called to a higher life and to greater union.

The community in the play is a dramatization of these ideas about Christian society. Reilly, Julia and Alex, the Guardians, are the "clerisy," people of intellectual and spiritual authority; though neither infallible nor omniscient, their work is to indoctrinate the others, to lead them out of the darkness into the light. The "sight" imagery is related to the "light-darkness" Christian allusion and to the function of the Guardians. Reilly is "one-eyed," Julia has single-lensed spectacles and Alex resembles the "one-eyed merchant of the Tarot pack." [37] The one-eyed Guardians are better than the ordinary people, Edward and Lavinia, who are "in the dark." In the kingdom of the blind the one-eyed man is king.[38] Because they are in the world, this trio is fallible and their knowledge is limited; because they are not of the world, they exercise a power that is prophetic. They can manipulate the rest of the company because of their knowledge of the Christian heritage.

Eliot's interpretation of Christianity in the play has raised the question of his orthodoxy. He has been accused of Manichean and/or gnostic tendencies.

Its [the play's] vision is not that of a humane . . . Christianity, but approximates to a radical division of existence into spheres of Nature and Transcendence sharply separated from each other; where the transcendent is not merely approached by way of the disclosure of Nature's essential imperfections, but finally embraced as a—literally—desperate alternative to the latter's graceless absence.[39]

Eliot does speak as if the natural and supernatural were discontinuous spheres: the ideal Christian society would be one "in which the natural end of man—virtue and well-being in community—is acknowledged for all, the supernatural end—beatitude—for those who have eyes to see it." [40] This statement, taken in conjunction with the sight imagery and the secret community in the play, has gnostic overtones. The Guardians (and presumably Celia after her conversion) perceive the full meaning of situations and live the complete Christian life. The ordinary members only redeem the time in a more or less golden mediocrity. Whether or not this position has theological validity, its inclusion in the play has a dramatic effect that is worth noting.

Eliot's gnosticism can be related to an accusation that critics have leveled at the heart of the play. They have called *The Cocktail*

Party "thin." [41] What the theologian calls "gnosticism" and the critic "thinness" focuses on a crucial area: Eliot's use of the ritual cast and of the basic device of anagnorisis. The protocomic personae are originally functionaries in a rite—their actions are prescribed and limited by their place in the ceremony. They move according to a prefabricated pattern; the ritual provides their sole motivation. Eliot attempts to "thicken" the characters, to make their personalities more complex, by a series of superpositions: Julia, for instance, as the prying dowager, the "Old Woman," the Christian conspirator. Each facet of the persona has a set of characteristics, but often they are the *same* characteristics. Her shrewdness serves both the prying matron and the Christian conspirator; matriarchal concern marks both the Old Woman and the Guardian. More important, these characteristics are determined *and* delimited by her function, in Julia's case, her office as an associate to Reilly. The more she is assimilated to her ritual role, the less real she becomes. The outstanding comic characters in drama have an autonomy that cannot be encompassed by their function. Falstaff, for instance, is at once a fat knight, the Lord of Misrule, the Vice of medieval moralities, the tavern roisterer, the braggart soldier, the ancient alter-ego of the hero—Captain Bluster. But these traditional roles do not constitute the character; we feel that they are aspects of a richer reality, the personality that is Sir John. Although Eliot has chosen to cast his drama in a relatively realistic mode, his characters seem to suffer from a lack of reality. This proceeds from the ritualistic limitations of their roles.

The gnostic impact on the reality of the personae is most evident in the doubling of the Alcestis figure. In *The Cocktail Party* the sacrificial death is given to Celia, the role of the bride to Lavinia. This inevitably "thins out" the role of the Young Woman. Eliot makes this division to insist on a doctrinal point: the distinction between the person chosen for a life of complete sacrifice and the common ordinary Christian. Lavinia's "resurrection" is accomplished, not by sacrifice, but by an acknowledgement of her limitations. Thus the Christian dimension, as Eliot presents it, also limits the potential of the personae. It is this limitation of character by function, either Christian or protocomic or both, that produces what the critics have labeled "thinness."

In considering, then, the motivation of the action, we see that what moves the characters is not an interior élan, a psychological pressure from within, but rather the demands of their role in the ritual. The basic psychological action is the recognition and acceptance of their role in society. The playwright warns his characters (and the audience) that the ritual is in control.

> *Unidentified Guest.*   To approach the stranger
> Is to invite the unexpected, release a new force,
> Or to let the genie out of the bottle.
> It is to start a train of events
> Beyond your control.   (CP, p. 28.)

Progress in the play amounts to a greater self-knowledge, always within the prescribed limits of function. Edward and Lavinia come to know their own condition, an inability to love and to be loved respectively, and they operate on the mundane level of the cocktail-party world. As the embodiments of the Year-daimon and his bride, as the representatives of the majority party in the ideal Christian society, they can arrive at a renewal of life without understanding the principle of this renewal. They must simply accept the pattern and their place in it and work to realize its potential. Celia, as the immolated and resurrected Alcestis, and, in the Christian society, the model of "religious life," can move into another world of complete vision and greater union. The Guardians watch over the mundane world while participating in it because they are the demi-gods and the "clerisy." [42] All these characters have a fixed status, and their motive force is outside themselves—in the ritual pattern. The feeling that Eliot reveals a "contempt for reality" results from a perception of this static quality.[43] The personae are being manipulated according to the prescriptions of the ritual.

Behind the structure of the play, then, is a paradigm—an ideal model for society. The drawing-room surface, the realistic settings and conversational verse, is a pale shadow of the "basic realities" underneath, like the projections in Plato's cave. Eliot is trying to tap tradition for a viable myth and to revitalize it by "juxtaposing archaic and contemporary behavior" in the audience's consciousness. The use of the "model" looks back to the "primitive mentality" which founded "reality" in this kind of archetypal model:

An object or an act becomes real [for the primitive] only insofar as it imitates or repeats an archetype. Thus reality is acquired solely through repetition or participation; everything which lacks an exemplary model is "meaningless," i.e., it lacks reality. . . . Hence it could be said that this primitive ontology has a Platonic structure; and in that case Plato could be regarded as the outstanding philosopher of "primitive mentality," that is, as the thinker who succeeded in giving philosophical currency and validity to the modes of life and behaviour of archaic humanity.[44]

This vision of the world puzzles the modern observer, for it contains what modern man accounts a paradox: the man of the traditional culture sees himself as real only when he is imitating the actions of the archetypal figure—god, demi-god, hero. His actions are significant because they conform to an archetypal gesture which takes place *in illo tempore,* the mythic dimension that is coextensive with chronological time and yet is "outside" it. Plato, while formulating this vision into a philosophy, destroyed the unity of the vision by insisting on the distinction between the archetypal model and its mundane copy. The primitive, when he was performing his ritual action, considered himself actually united to the exemplar, at once in time and outside it. The Eleatic insistence on the Logos, the separated world of Ideas, disjointed these dimensions.[45] The Greek dramatic form, however, preserved the primitive vision; the finite representation in time existed simultaneously with the ritual structure. Comedy, while preserving the ritual pattern, affirms the reality of the finite particular. In *The Cocktail Party* Eliot uses the finite particular to affirm the reality of the archetypal model. This reversal of emphasis calls into doubt the reality of both dimensions.

The epiphany of *The Cocktail Party* is the discovery of an archetypal model with Christian specifications for modern society. Each component of the structure leads to this epiphany. The reconciliation to which the comedy of marital misunderstanding moves is realized as the ritual wedding of the *Alcestis.* This wedding, in turn, "imitates" the hierogamy of the Dionysian rite. The new society that is formed at the conclusion of *The Cocktail Party* is based on two main streams in Western tradition, the Greek and the Christian. The assumptions that underlie Eliot's society are, in many ways, diametrically opposed to the assumptions that underlie contemporary society. In Eliot's play, as we have seen, the status of any given member of the group is fixed; the individual is not free to pass from one level to another. Edward and Lavinia are essentially ordinary, run-of-the-mill citizens who must "make the best of a bad job." They can never become Celias or Julias. There is no vertical freedom available to them. This position seems offensive both to the contemporary democrat who holds for "rugged individualism," and to the Christian who does not accept the gnostic doctrine of an "inner circle." Moreover, the play denies in effect what many moderns take to be a fundamental postulate of civilization, that indefinite progress is desirable and possible. "Progress" in the play means recognizing and accepting a permanent status in society. Even though it might be recognizable to the audience, this model does not correspond to the ideal of the majority in many of its fundamentals.

Granted that Eliot has artfully concealed his design and his purpose and that he has attempted to use a crude form to woo the audience, still he must establish his premises at the same time that he is communicating his conclusion. The tradition that provides the grounds for communication here exists largely in the academic community, and perhaps it is not really vital even there. Eliot does not create a taste for his kind of community; his characters are too limited to be very appealing. If, on the other hand, he is saying that, whether we like it or not, this kind of society is ideal, "salvific," we want proof more relative than its correspondence to a Greek ritual. As the mythical world of regeneration ritual grows, the world of the cocktail party (the world *we* live in) diminishes; the society of Harley Street and Shaftesbury Avenue fades into unreality as the society of the Guardians grows clear. To create a vital model, both the world of reality and the world of myth must remain in focus. In short, the archetype cannot destroy the particular which dramatizes it. Because, in Eliot's play, the realistic surface gives way before the ritual underpattern, the critic feels a dissatisfaction with Eliot's art:

I am trying to suggest that the ontology of Eliot's poetry and his own special version of Christianity is dramatically doomed from the start: the stage, as Plato himself suggested when he destroyed his own tragedies, is no place for Platonists, or for gnostics, or for the theologian of the *Four Quartets*.[46]

In his endeavor to lead the modern mind back to its cultural heritage, Eliot runs into an impenetrable barrier. History is irreversible, and the artist cannot, by establishing a series of literary references and resonances, take the audience back to other days, other times. He cannot, like the magician-cook, boil life into the bones of a society pronounced dead at the start.

4

Who Knows Not Patient Job:
J.B.

Even in its most secularized phases, contemporary Western culture continues to be shaped by the Judaeo-Christian heritage. As Eliot has pointed out, Christian attitudes towards manners and morals are embedded in the proverbial wisdom, the thought patterns and the language habits of modern man. Most of these attitudes can be traced, directly or indirectly, to the influence of the Bible. When a contemporary writer becomes interested in the religious implications of the modern situation, he has available this tradition and *the* Book as a source for plot materials and doctrine. Thus with the inevitability of a trip upstream, the search for a literary model has led one poet-playwright to a portion of the Bible that has exerted a fairly constant influence on Western literature and culture. In order to present his version of modern man's predicament, Archibald MacLeish set out to adapt the Book of Job to the contemporary situation. It gave him a starting point, an approach and the components of a structure:

When you are dealing with questions too large for you, which, nevertheless, will not leave you alone, you are obliged to house them somewhere—and an old wall helps. Which is perhaps why so many modern plays have proved, on critical examination, to be reconstructions of the myths of Greece.[1]

Where O'Neill turned to Greek tragedy and Freud, and Eliot to Cornford's analysis of Greek comedy and his own idea of Christian society, MacLeish goes to the Bible for his materials and his dramatic framework.

MacLeish, like Cummings and Jeffers a clergyman's son, was fascinated, from the outset of his poetic career, with modern man's religious dilemma. What is man to do, when faith wanes, with the big problems: time and eternity, a Nature that conceals the secret of life, man's fragility and instability in an expanding universe? In *Streets in the Moon* (1926), his first critically acclaimed collection, he sees man caught between his consciousness and his ignorance. The world is swept by wind and water, man waits for answers, but the voice he thinks he hears fades on the wind. Life ends abruptly, and only the ignorant do not fear the abyss. The poems in *New Found Land* (1930) elaborate the same problems: "You, Andrew Marvell" is a commentary on "time's winged chariot" that passes quickly over dead civilizations to the new world; even in the sunlight of democratic optimism and new institutions the shadow of night comes quickly on. For MacLeish, time is linear and unredeemable, and the Hamlet of today cannot set this disjointed time aright —he can only endure. The early poems show these preoccupations and a consistent stoic bent.

When, in 1936, MacLeish turned from his metaphysical problems to public issues, he did so without really laying aside his original concern. Speculations on man's destiny ceded to the demands of the moment; if tyranny and genocide were allowed to flourish, there would be little point to man's endurance. So during the triumph of Nazism in Germany and the cataclysm of World War II, MacLeish celebrated the democratic spirit in his poetry, the affirmation of man's dignity and worth, and actively participated in government as aide to the President. (*Public Speech* [1936] and *The Fall of the City* [1937] a radio drama, are typical of his work during this period.) But his message, even in the propaganda pieces, remained consistent with his earlier views:

> And voices in the dark of air
> Cry out Despair and fall and fail—
> . . . .
> And know the part they have to bear
> And know the void vast night above
> And know the night below and dare
> Endure and love.[2]

In 1954, about the time he began work on *J.B.*, MacLeish published a book of short poems based on Biblical themes, *Songs for Eve*. The leading ideas of his early and middle work recur, couched in much the same image-patterns. In the first poem of the "Eve" series, the woman hears intimations of immortality ringing in the greenwood tree; she reaches out to touch and climb "in spite of space, in spite of time." At the end of the poem, however, the wind tells the water that man is eaten by time, that life is luck and death random. From *Streets in the Moon* through *Songs for Eve*, over three decades of writing, MacLeish worries the problem of order and meaning in man's life. He concludes uniformly throughout that this meaning always eludes men. This does not, however, mean that we should despair, rather we should gather our dignity together, endure our lot and love our fellows. These motifs from the poetry establish MacLeish's point of view; they are incorporated into the argument of his version of the Job story.

MacLeish gravitated to the Book of Job for his dramatic material because "the structure of the poem of Job is the only one I know of which our modern history will fit." [3] This Book has much to recommend it to the troubled seeker after meaning in life today or in any age. The poet of Job has selected the most enigmatic element in human experience, innocent suffering, and has explored its meaning. For the first time in Jewish history—and perhaps in the history of civilization—the orthodox doctrine that suffering is a punishment for personal sin is called into question. By God's own testimony, Job is a just and upright man, yet he is hurled from prosperity to the ash-heap, from health to running sores. He cries out his momentous question in the face of Yahweh: SHOW ME MY GUILT, O GOD! To the man who has seen two World Wars and who now lives in the shadow of the bomb, this question seems especially pertinent.

As the subject matter of the Book of Job is relevant to the modern predicament, the literary form is attractive to the artist. The central issue is dramatized by the poet, rendered in dialogue form. The dramatic action consists of two sets of encounters, debates between God and Satan and between Job and his Counselors. A critical examination of the text shows that this drama, the poem of Job itself, was inserted into the framework of a traditional story, one which probably presented the orthodox message that God rewards his faithful servants with material blessings. The Book opens and closes with prose narratives, five verses (Job, 1:1–5) at the beginning and nine verses (42:7–16) at the end. The frame story summarized in these sections recounts Job's original prosperity and his final restoration to health, wealth and security at the end. Within this framework the poet presents a struggle of minds and wills that has nothing to do with rewards and material blessings. The issues at stake are God's providence and Job's destiny. After Job is stripped of his wealth, his family and his health, he is visited by three sages who argue that his sufferings must be just punishment for his sins. He refuses to accept their arguments, affirming his innocence and demanding vindication from God. A theophany resolves the struggle when the Voice from the Whirlwind answers Job. It is the wisdom of God that sends his suffering, and he is not wiser than God. Job responds to the Voice with an act of faith. Though the speculative problem is left hanging in the air, his personal problem is resolved by this confrontation. The poet has shaped his material dramatically and presented it in terms of personalities and action.

MacLeish's use of this model, his exploration of its dramatic possibilities, is part of a long tradition in Western literature. Earlier ages interpreted the form and the issues according to their own lights. John Milton, who considered Job a "brief epic," used the structure as a model for *Paradise Regained*. He saw, in the testing of Job, a parallel with the testing of Christ; in both works Satan fails to subvert the fidelity of God's servants. Job's perseverance overcame "Whate'er his [Satan's] malice could invent." [4] Puritan popularizers of the seventeenth and eighteenth centuries, like Richard Baxter and the Methodists, found in the Book a good illustration for one aspect of their doctrine:

On the one hand, it [Job] contained a grand conception of the absolute sovereign majesty of God, beyond all human comprehension, which was closely related to that of Calvinism. With that, on the other hand, it combined the certainty which, though incidental for Calvin, came to be of great importance for Puritanism, that God would bless his own in this life—in the Book of Job only—and also in the material sense. [5]

This view of Job continued into the nineteenth century in American tradition, spurred by the commendation of Ben Franklin and the business-oriented preaching of divines like Russell Conwell. [6]

After World War I the balance of emphasis shifted from the triumphal aspects of the story to the tragic aspects. Because the speculative problem does remain unsolved, man rests his dearest hopes on a faith that the modern temper finds wanting. H. M. Kallen wrapped his suggestion that Job has something to say to the modern in literary guise; in 1918 he advanced the thesis that the Book of Job is literally a Greek tragedy, written by a Hellenized Jew of the fourth century B.C.[7] Since then, the tragic vision at the heart of the work has received a good deal of attention; Job expresses, in Unamuno's term, the "tragic sense" of life—man must live by faith on the brink of uncertainty. Richard B. Sewall analyzes it from this point of view:

The sense of frustration is largely eliminated by Job's rewards. God is good; justice of a sort has been rendered; the universe seems secure. . . . But only to those who do not question too far. Can a new family make up for the one Job lost? What about the faithful servants who fell to the Sabeans and Chaldeans? These questions the folk story ignores, and its reassuring final picture also makes it easy to forget Job's suffering and his unanswered question.[8]

His study points out that, though the poet does not deal in physical action, he presents inner realities that function like actions, and "although Job and his Counselors do not budge from the ash-heap, they are actually at death-grips." [9] The modern artist or critic, then, generally takes this view of Job; he sees it not as a mine for theological doctrine or as the triumph of God over Satan, but as the tragedy of unaccommodated man who must live with unanswered questions.

This concentration on Man's plight coincides with corresponding changes in the idea of God as the Book of Job presents him. The absolute sovereign of the Calvinist and the Puritan bestower of blessings has retreated before the advance of science and psychology and the prospect of universal annihilation. As his early poetry reveals, MacLeish fits into the modern trend; he is at best uncertain about the existence of such a deity. The object of faith, so clear in Job and to the Biblical author and taken for granted by the interpreters of the Book in preceding centuries, dissolves before the atomism of science or fades into the mists of psychology. In approaching the Job story MacLeish brought with him a theory about the God of Job, one that he found ready-made in the writings of Carl Jung.

In an interview after the opening of *J.B.*, MacLeish said that he "had been influenced in his own thinking by an analysis of Job written by the psychologist Carl Jung." [10] In this analysis, called *Answer to Job,* Jung treats God as a projection of the unconscious, an expression of the numinous archetype that is impervious to critical analysis.[11] Jung's God is characterized by a lack of consciousness; he is a primitive who jealously protects his own prerogatives from his "son," Satan, and his servant, Job. He resembles, in short, the theologians who argue for his prerogatives. Therefore, any attribution of omniscience or absolute goodness is unthinkable. Jung holds that the problem in Job is God's flight from his own growing consciousness; Job by questioning forces him to face himself. Thus God must measure up to man, a feat that can only be accomplished by taking a human nature. Jung can speak of God in this "objective" way because God comes out of the autonomous unconscious and so has validity for the psychologist. MacLeish's understanding of the case locates God in this same order, in man's love for man; the reality of God's existence in any objective sense is, if not denied, at least irrelevant. For "love creates even God." [12]

MacLeish's adaptation differs, then, from O'Neill's approach to the *Oresteia* or Eliot's to the *Alcestis.* Whereas they use the source for the structures it contains, MacLeish sets out to reshape the source to fit the theses he wishes to prove: first, that the crucial incident in the story is not, as the Bible seems to insist, Job's repentance, but rather his courage in taking up his life again; second, that the image of God in Job contains a contradiction and must be replaced with a proper image of Man. MacLeish builds his drama to illustrate the first thesis and to argue the second. He wants to replace the traditional idea of Job the faithful servant dutifully rewarded by God with the modern picture of Job the unaccommodated man. To accomplish this, he must unseat the sovereign Deity of the Bible and exalt his hero to self-sufficiency. His adaptation proceeds on these grounds.

Because MacLeish is trying simultaneously to tear down one tradition and to create another, he cannot simply retell the Job story in modern terms. He has to reshape his source so that the message he finds there is translated into dramatic terms for the audience. This leads him into a labyrinth of theatrical devices which almost defy analysis. There is an expressionistic "circus-tent" setting that disappears halfway through the action, a "play-within-the-play" treatment of the Job story, and two actor-stage managers who com-

ment on the action. These devices help to give an over-all shape to
the play. It breaks roughly into two major parts: in terms of the
theses outlined above, the first half is a refutation of the traditional
views about the relations between "God" and man; the second half
is an affirmation of man's self-sufficiency. This division—by no
means as hard and fast in the play as it appears from this statement
—is accomplished visually by the collapse of the circus-tent. While
the tent covers the acting area, there is a line of demarcation between the stage manager-commentators, Nickles and Zuss, and the
situation of J.B. and his wife in the "play-within-the-play." Once
the tent falls at the drop of the bomb, the two situations begin to
merge into one. The protection of traditional rationalizations is
taken away; the play-within-the-play dimension merges with the
Zuss-Nickles dimension; actor, commentator and spectator are all in
the same boat.

Within the framework of these situations and using the format of
Job as a model, MacLeish arranges a series of debates that are
geared to establish his doctrine. Zuss and Nickles, the stage managers of the performance, engage in an intellectual duel about the
nature of God. Zuss represents and argues for the Calvinist God of
absolute Will; Nickles represents "the Adversary" and argues for
total rejection of this God and of a universe that reflects his pitiless
qualities. This debate is conducted as a commentary on the Job
story that is being played out at their behest. Within the dimension
of the "play-within-the-play," another series of debates is carried
on, between J.B. and Sarah, between J.B. and the three Comforters.
Sarah represents the Puritan position that views God as responding
to the actions of men, with rewards when man obeys and with pun-
ishments when man defects. J.B. holds on to a blind confidence in
God's goodness as long as his situation allows. He argues with the
Comforters, who present three deterministic positions, the Marxian,
the Freudian and the Calvinistic. These debates, on both levels, lead
to J.B.'s final rejection of the Comforters, and of both Zuss and
Nickles. His dialectical stand at the conclusion of the play coincides,
predictably enough, with MacLeish's humanistic solution to modern
man's dilemma. These debates make up the dianoia of the play: if
the drama were only debate, the ultimate meaning of the play would
be identical with the argument.

What the dramatis personae say, however, is related to what they do; that is, under the dialectic surface, the plot makes its own statement. We have pointed out the two dimensions that are established at the outset; each has its own plot-line. Though these plot lines intersect at the conclusion of the play, the Zuss-Nickles plot and the J.B.-Sarah plot have their own characteristics and operate on their own principles. By establishing these different movements, MacLeish effectively (if unconsciously) provides a commentary on the explicit doctrine of the play, a commentary which contradicts his humanistic affirmation. The level of action in the play reveals a set of attitudes which the level of argument does not recognize.

The main plot of the play is MacLeish's recasting of the Job story. The most significant change that he made in the Biblical source was the elevation of Job's wife to the status of a main character. In the Book of Job she is a supernumerary who presages the advice of the Counselors, then disappears into the wings. In *J.B.* she plays a pivotal role. The reason for this addition is MacLeish's switch from the traditional focus:

What attracted me to the story of Job in the first place was the end of the *Book of Job*—a part of the myth that the theologians, for obvious reasons, neglect or disparage. And what excited me about the end was something that is obviously there but is omitted from the Biblical account—*Job's* action. . . . Job, who, like all human beings, had dared to ask his Why of life, of the universe, has been answered, as men are in fact so often answered, by new and greater questions. Which means that he has not been answered at all—he has merely been silenced. . . . And nevertheless, and in spite of all this, Job accepts the chance to take up his life again—risk his heart and his hopes again.[13]

To start over again, J.B. needs someone to love, he needs a life to take up, and so MacLeish focuses on husband *and* wife. By making this adjustment in the plot, however, the playwright adds a new element to the Job story, one that we will recognize as the conventional comic plot-structure. The husband and wife, happy but untested lovers at the beginning of the story, are gradually alienated from each other by the catastrophes and their respective reactions to them —by J.B.'s acceptance of "God's Will" and by Sarah's revolt at God's injustice. In the end, Sarah returns and the lovers are reconciled. This pattern of union, disillusion and separation, reunion is the comic structure that underlies the sentimental comedy, the satyr-play, the fertility ritual. Thus the J.B.-Sarah plot—which is meant to illustrate man's essential isolation—progresses to a wedding.

The Zuss-Nickles plot has a different structural pattern. While they represent two irreconcilable intellectual positions, they also clash, in their private identities as vendor-actors, on the emotional level. Zuss and Nickles are not only involved as spectators to J.B.'s story (though this is their primary function), they are also involved with one another. By the time they step into the J.B.-Sarah plot, they are arguing a personal cause, and their reactions to the disasters, to the isolation of the hero, to the arguments of the Comforters have developed into personal commitment. As individuals, their debate is an agon that reflects Job's struggle with his Counselors. As the Voice from the Whirlwind judges the dispute between Job and his friends, so J.B. judges between Zuss and Nickles. That is to say, their descent into J.B.'s dimension resembles, in function, an epiphany. They put their cause in J.B.'s hands so that, when he renders his decision, he is judging both the argument and their personalities. This tragic pattern of agon and epiphany runs parallel to, and at the end of the play meshes with, the comic structure of the J.B.-Sarah plot. The presence of these two structures in the play is as important to the over-all dramatic meaning as the explicit humanistic doctrine that characterizes the dianoia. As we shall see, the clash of these two levels results in a most peculiar dramatic effect—the plot effectively contradicts the dianoia.

With these general remarks as preface, we may now look at the play in detail. MacLeish tries to keep a good many balls in the air through the course of the play; the critic has to struggle to keep everything in focus. He is aided by the fact that the play passed through a number of revisions, from the production at Yale to the final Broadway acting version. The evolution of certain techniques and ideas are evident from version to version. For instance, in the Yale production (April 22, 1958) the division between the Zuss-Nickles sequences and the J.B.-Sarah plot was more pointed than in the printed version. The Zuss-Nickles scenes were played exclusively on the platform "heaven" as discrete dramatic units; the J.B. scenes were acted in the arena below. The interlocking of these scenes and other adjustments that resulted in a more unified production resulted from MacLeish's collaboration with Elia Kazan who staged the Broadway version. Kazan made the following suggestion about the Yale script:

Let me say first that there is something underdramatic [sic] to me about staging which alternates between action and comment on action. The marvelous thing about your play to me is that *in time* Zuss and Nickles become emotionally involved in what's happening and become partisan. I would try to involve Nickles particularly from the very *beginning*. (Letter to MacLeish dated "Spring, 1958".) [14]

Later Kazan voiced some misgivings about the ending of the published version (Boston, 1958). Even after the play opened on Broadway in December, 1958, MacLeish continued to work on the conclusion. The final result of these revisions was published as the "acting version" in *Theatre Arts* for February, 1960. The differences between the published version and the acting version do reflect progress in MacLeish's thought; they are equally a tribute to Kazan's sense of good theatre. The changes give the critic an insight into MacLeish's methods and intentions; the "acting version" represents a final text and will be the basis for our discussion of the play.

MacLeish, as we noted above, situates his drama in a circus tent, "the interior of a traveling circus, once splendidly gilded and painted but now worn, tattered and patched from year after year on the roads of the world." [15] This setting is at once a spatial context for, and a commentary on, the action. The circus is a world that man has made but cannot altogether control. The perils of the high-wire and the animal cage are very real for the performers; the spectators enjoy vicarious thrills without undergoing the danger. The Job story takes place in the center ring, a fiction which, for all its unreality, still involves real peril for the performers. While the circus tent covers the sky, Zuss and Nickles (and presumably the audience) can watch the spectacle philosophically, from the safety of their seats. For this period the Zuss-Nickles debates have the air of a speculative theological squabble, interesting but of no special moment. J.B.'s trials are play-acting, even if the principals do not know it. This "circus tent" world is the secure world "before the bomb" where someone is "always playing Job," but fortunately it is not you or me.

At the end of Act I, when the bomb falls, the tent-covering collapses to reveal "a black sky streaked with smouldering light like the horizon of a stormy sunset or a burned-out city far away." The dimensions of the circus are converted into a world of infinite space. Performers and spectators are no longer sheltered even by the thin fabric of a circus tent. J.B. and Sarah, the bombed-out women, Zuss and Nickles are all unaccommodated; they share the same situation.[16] The setting situates the action first in a man-made, make-believe world, then in a world of empty spaces behind the circus tent. This change of situation underscores the plight of modern man —he can no longer be protected from ultimate concerns even by his own determination. The scenic device is closely related to a plot device—the inclusion of the Job story as a "play-within-the-play."

The Job story is not presented in the direct fashion of the Biblical narrative; it is included in a theatrical frame. The J.B. performance is set up and stagemanaged by Zuss and Nickles, two vendor-actors who bridge the gap between the circus setting and the play-within-the-play. They are at home in the circus tent though they are not part of the show. They live by the performers' daring, selling balloons and popcorn. Their merchandising is a commentary on their function as entrepreneurs; Zuss peddles miniature air-filled globes and Nickles sells insubstantial stuff that feeds without filling. Presumably the doctrine they elaborate is imaged by what they sell. Within the empty tent they have control and decide to "play the play." [17] So they set the stage within the tent and circumscribe the Heaven and Earth: "That platform's Heaven." MacLeish indicates here that Zuss and Nickles do not have complete control even at the outset; they are concerned about "those that own the show." The "hidden gods" have not conceded them absolute power; when the tent collapses, the two stage managers become uncertain about the accuracy of their script.

The Zuss-Nickles personae are ambiguous; they are vendors, actors, Godmask and Satanmask. Their precise identity fluctuates through the drama.[18] The constant features, in whatever role, of these personae dramatize their doctrinal positions. Mr. Zuss, whether he speaks through his mask or *in propria persona,* is the orthodox authoritarian who looks to the abstract principle rather than to the concrete instance. The God he represents is an image of himself, a God of power and will:

> Enormous pattern of the steep of stars,
> Minute perfection of the frozen crystal,
> Inimitable architecture of the slow,

Cold, silent, ignorant sea-snail:
The unimaginable will of stone:
Infinite mind in a midge of matter. (TA, XLIV, 47–48.)

The power of this God comprehends the infinite reaches of space and the perfection of animalcula. It is embodied in God's will—"in his Will is our peace." The universe, man, Job's suffering are justified simply by God's willing it. Zuss is confident, calm, quasi-omniscient; his confidence is bolstered by his knowledge of the script. He need not worry about the outcome; even Nickles knows that "God always wins." Zuss and Godmask speak with one voice so that his image and God's meld together.

Nickles' persona is determined by his attitude toward Zuss-God. To him this God is the God of the animals, of blind power and inhuman will. His eyes are blinded; his justice has a face like "skies of stone." The mask of God wears a look of cold complacence—no great intelligence, no humanity, no mercy. Nickles believes with a great unbelief:

> If God is God He is not good,
> If God is good He is not God.[19] (TA, XLIV, 37.)

The creator of the animals can manage an unconscious universe mechanically, but with self-conscious, reflective creatures he is inept. "His Will our peace" is an equation which works only for the unreflecting sea-snail and the remote stars. Though Nickles, like the existential philosopher he resembles, believes in this God of will and power, he does not have to like him.

The personae of Zuss and Nickles express their positions in the debate. Mr. Zuss both defends and represents the absolute ruler who dispenses salvation and suffering as he pleases. He has no qualms about his position; it is the only answer to the human situation; man must capitulate or be lost. His opponent is the antitype, the young, defiant nihilist. If suffering had any point at all, Nickles would be sympathetic. He is the "father of lies" only in that he doubts if anyone knows enough to recognize truth.[20] The futility of their debate is anticipated from the outset of the drama for they agree on two points. Their image of God is identical; both advocate a return to unconsciousness, Zuss through blind acceptance of God's will and Nickles through a suicidal rejection of existence. The dianoia of the play, an affirmation of the humanistic Weltanschauung, dictates that both must go down to defeat; MacLeish stacks the deck against them.

The Zuss-Nickles debate and the "play-within-the-play" device is further complicated by the intrusion of the "Distant Voice." The Voice breaks into the action always with Biblical lines; it has no identifiable source or clear identity. When it first echoes through the empty tent, urging Zuss and Nickles to get on with the play, Zuss uneasily identifies it as "Prompter probably. Prompter somewhere." (TA, XLIV, 40.) It is not heard by all the personae—at least some do not admit hearing it. The chorus of women, whose foremost concern is food and a place out of the cold, do not hear it. The Comforters are not sure—"The wind's gone round." Zuss, Nickles, J.B. and Sarah hear it clearly; at the crisis, when J.B. is completely alone, Zuss-Godmask is silent and the Distant Voice answers J.B. with the "whirlwind" speech from the Book of Job. The "Distant Voice" adds a dimension of mystery to the drama; the Unknown, the numinous, is also playing a hand. But it comes out of an "empty" sky, from those infinite spaces that bound the action. Like Nickles and Zuss, the status of the Voice is ambiguous. It sounds like God, but to be consistent with the logical scheme of the play it cannot be "God" in any objective sense. One reasonable explanation, in view of Jung's influence on MacLeish, would make it the expression of man's primitive experience, that experience which generated the Bible. This experience of the race—dimly remembered, never quite forgotten—speaks in the void when the conscious mind falters before ultimate problems. It is then, perhaps, that numinous archetype which the primitive experience of the race, and the childhood experiences of the individual (in Bible school, at the parent's knee) create and preserve.

This rationalization explains the Voice logically, not dramatically. It cannot be God, and yet the overwhelming impression announces that it is. The Biblical text and the dramatic context indicate that something or someone beyond the sky is speaking; the audience hears it and has to cope with its presence. In the medieval morality or cycle play, the Godmask is simply God; this convention was (and is) accepted, and the line of action is kept clear. In *J.B.* the audience must attempt to reconcile Zuss-Godmask with the Distant

Voice against the empty-sky background. Whatever the audience may make of it, the Voice functions to show that Zuss and Nickles do not have complete control of the performance. It is "Prompter somewhere," the voice of the unconscious—an a-rational element in the texture of the play.

This situation, the Zuss-Nickles stagemanager device, makes a framework for the Job story. In the first scene, J.B. is presented as a "typical" American business man with a typically American family at an American feast. He has all the earmarks of the successful man: a prosperous bank, an attractive wife, a brood of blond children. He had been "lucky." In fact, he has been accused of being merely lucky. The composite picture is the familiar one of the elect, blessed by God with the sign of material success, who in turn uses his wealth faithfully as becomes a good steward.

> *Sarah.* Us he [God] has rewarded. Wonderfully.
> Kept us from harm, each one—each one.
> And why? Because of you—your . . . faithfulness.[21]
>
> (TA, XLIV, 43.)

J.B.'s success is a corollary of his moral rectitude; he is, as the Book of Job affirms, a "just and upright man."

His religious beliefs, also intended to be typical, are not codified, dogmatic, formal. He does not stand on ceremony. The prayer which opens the Thanksgiving dinner is hurried through for the sake of the children who are anxious to get at the turkey. Informal fiducial trust is characteristic of J.B.'s piety; he trusts "my luck—my life—our life—God's goodness to me." "Luck" is his self-effacing term for God's favor; from the first God was "on my side helping me."

> I never thought so from the first
> Fine silver dollar to the last
> Controlling interest in some company
> I couldn't get—and got. It isn't
> Luck.
>
> (TA, XLIV, 42.)

This attitude is enshrined in a family myth—"the lucky story"—which emphasizes the Protestant ethic. A "new-come man" accosted J.B. in a restaurant and demanded to know why he gets the best of the "rest of us." J.B. tells him that his success comes because "It's

God's country, Mr. Sullivan." The story is chanted antiphonally by
J.B. and the children. The point is clear: a newcomer (an Irishman)
couldn't be expected to understand that J.B. is led by God. J.B.
trusts in this luck; the object of his trust remains as yet undefined
—luck, life, the goodness of God. The image of the protector has
not yet taken shape.

If the image of God is vague, the content of J.B.'s religious experience is not. Nature is the medium through which J.B. objectifies
the deity. His approach to nature is simple, instinctive, reverential.

> *J.B.* Children know the grace of God
> Better than most of us. They see the world
> The way the morning brings it back to them,
> New and born [sic] and fresh and wonderful.
>
> (TA, XLIV, 42.)

J.B. himself has not lost this view of the world. He counts on God
because of the order of Nature and "the certainty of day's return." [22] Though Sarah has some reservations, the family community
shares this view. They finish the feast with another chant celebrating the passage of time and the permanence of Nature.

> *The Whole Family.* I love Monday, Tuesday, Wednesday,
> Where have Monday, Tuesday gone?
> Under the grass tree,
> Under the green tree,
> One by one.
>
> (TA, XLIV, 44.)

Whatever one may think of the poetic quality of this verse, it fixes
the image of Nature's cycle in the mind. The green tree stands firm
in the middle of time's flow; though it is time's tree, it has the permanence of Nature's annual renewal.[23] In Nature J.B. finds the
reason for trusting God's favor. Its cycle of death and rebirth is a
guarantee of goodness and a constant in experience.

This "natural piety" of J.B.'s is not exactly equivalent to either
the experience of nature in the Bible or the mild pantheism of the
Romantic. In the Book of Job the majesty and grandeur of creation
is not a medium through which the individual acknowledges the existence of a beneficent creator; it is part of the challenge which Yahweh throws at his faithful servant. That is, the I-Thou relationship

comes first and the mystery of nature expresses the power, the wisdom, the providence of Yahweh.[24] Thus nature is not represented as an object of aesthetic delight; it is mystery, full of raw power and awe-inspiring élan. The soaring hawk, the bronze-boned hippopotamus, the Leviathan range far out of Job's control. When he can create such a cosmos or even penetrate its secrets, then he has the right to question the providence and fidelity of his God. The Romantic Nature-worshipper, in contrast, finds God-in-nature, the divine in things. Nature is a Platonic looking-glass by which man can conceive the ideal; by contemplating Nature, man can lift himself to a higher reality. J.B.'s vision is neither a "mystery" nor a pananimist transcendence.

J.B.'s experience is of the "green world"—the gentle, fertile, light-filled force which supplies the sunrise and the turkey dinner. His trust is not directed at a person or a transcendent ideal, but to the certainty of day's return. His commitment is the commitment of the contemporary American—a trust in the continuance of the good that he possesses.[25] This trust is related to that complex of attitudes which we have explored as the "myth of the garden" and the search for a lost paradise. The American experience (or the image of the American experience) included the freedom of the frontier, the simple life of the farm and of Walden. The conquest of the wilderness in the name of progress did not obliterate from consciousness the "innocence" of that primal culture. Nature communicated—in the eyes of the city-dweller who could avoid the blighted harvest and the barnyard smells—her gentle virtues to the contented tiller of the soil, the free-ranging scout on the plain. No reflection on the author of this Nature was necessary; the outdoor life had a virtue of its own that was immediately communicable. J.B.'s God is the vague figure who blesses a fertile America; as long as the land is fertile and its people prosperous, God can remain quietly in the background.

J.B.'s wife has some reservations about this picture. Sarah, as the stage direction has it, is "all New England in her look and carriage" and in her theology. She deals anxiously with a God who rewards *and* punishes. He will do his part only if the believer does his. The covenant still holds good—

> If we forget him,
> He will forget. Forever. In everything.   (TA, XLIV, 42.)

J.B.'s faithfulness may account for the family's prosperity, but the children must not forget that faithfulness is prerequisite to reward. Sarah envisions an anthropomorphic God who reacts to man's performance. Though both Sarah and Zuss are in the Calvinist tradition, Zuss does not make the mistake of confusing God's absolute will with a knowledge of man's merits; he knows the script too well for that. Sarah's fear is muted by hope because she does not know the script. Her faith is more orthodox than her husband's, less consistent than Mr. Zuss's. She accepts the popular view that God protects his own as long as they serve him. This difference in Sarah's attitude toward God is the knife-edge that will sever the bond holding her to her husband.

In the calamities episode and the Comforters episode, the beliefs of Sarah and J.B. are tested. On the level of debate, these sections stand as illustrations of the plight J.B. is faced with and, as such, they are the practical experiences which educate him to his real situation. The disasters are tailored to provide this instruction. All the blond children of the Thanksgiving scene are destroyed in pathetic circumstances: in a skirmish after the Armistice, in a highway collision, at the hands of a dope-addicted rapist, with the fall of a bomb. Invariably two messengers—one who realizes the horror of the event, the other oblivious to it—report the disasters to J.B. and Sarah. In each scene pathetic instances pile up to underscore the innocence of the victims and the senselessness of the loss. The oldest son is buried in a too-short coffin with feet exposed. The teen-age pair, "just kids," die

> Screaming when they hit the wall.
> —Then silent . . .
> Blonde in all that blood. (TA, XLIV, 48.)

Two police officers bring a toy parasol belonging to the youngest, a red umbrella "she used to take to bed with her even." (TA, XLIV, 50.) In place of the economy of the Biblical account, MacLeish elaborates, with pathetic detail, the innocence of the victims and the shocked incredulity of the parents.

The calamities advance the argument on both plot-levels. Zuss insists that the disasters will teach J.B. to praise "no matter," that the experience will teach him to see God, that God is seen (as absolute master) only from the ash heap. Nickles also holds that God will teach J.B.—to wish he had never been born. The Sarah-J.B. debate revolves around the question of God's justice and goodness. Sarah will not accept any explanation of their suffering; to her, it seems that God himself is abandoning the covenant. J.B. holds on to his blind trust; he accepts the evil because of the good. The existence of evil, he argues, does not prove there is no good. But the chink in J.B.'s theological argument appears at this point:

> Sticks and stones are chances
> There's no will in stone and steel . . .
> It *happens* to us . . . (TA, XLIV, 48.)

Somehow, for J.B., God is not responsible for evil—it just happens. Accidents are outside the order of nature, outside the cycle of events on which man can count. J.B. tries this gambit like a gambler waiting for his luck to change. Sarah cannot accept this position; her theology has no room for this concept.

This calamities segment is separated from the next section on the Comforters by the fall of the bomb. The circus covering is stripped away, revealing the black sky. To emphasize this change in the situation of the play, MacLeish brings on a chorus of women, the ragtag of the bombed-out city. Of various backgrounds and nationalities, the little people caught in the maelstrom of war, they are concerned with survival, not metaphysics. Though they had less to lose in the bombing than J.B., they lost what they had. But, because they can ignore the Why of their plight, they are able to deal with isolation and desolation by huddling together against the cold and making the best of their lot. The universe of the little people, J.B.'s universe and that of Zuss and Nickles are all coincident now. This leveling-out is effected by the screaming sirens and falling walls—by the advent of the bomb, the threat of universal annihilation. Whether the personae are conscious of the ultimate questions or not, all share the same cosmos.

After J.B. loses the rest of his blessings—his bank, his last two children, his health, he has an opportunity to reflect on his experience. He is beginning to learn, the balance has shifted from God the giver of good things to God the destroyer, and J.B. begins to move in the direction of Sarah's God-image. He finds that God's will is everywhere against them, even in dreams. He can no longer look to his luck; if he suffers, then God is somehow involved in that suffering. But he is as yet unwilling to give up the author of good, order and "reasons" because of the existence of evil. Suffering must have a reason:

> *J.B.* God will not punish without cause.
> God is God or we are nothing—
> Mayflies that leave their husks behind—
>
> . . . .
> God is unthinkable if we are innocent.   (TA, XLIV, 53.)

Sarah accepts the principle of guilt, but not J.B.'s application of it. "Must we be guilty *for* Him?" For the first time in the play, the possibility that he himself might be guilty is presented flatly to J.B. He responds to this situation by hanging onto his wife's hand and asking her to make a profession of faith with him: THE LORD GIVETH . . . Sarah refuses; for her, the Lord does not "take away," he kills. He has killed her innocent children. J.B. will not take his wife's advice to curse God and die; he completes the formula: BLESSED BE THE NAME OF THE LORD. At this Sarah leaves him. This portion of J.B.'s education is now complete. His experience has led him from his vague commitment to a God of blessing to a consideration of a God who can curse without cause. Now he can cry the traditional cry: SHOW ME MY GUILT, O GOD!

In answer to J.B.'s challenge, the Comforters come. They represent three current interpretations of J.B.'s sufferings: historical determinism, psychological determinism, theological determinism. The first two Comforters, the socialist and the doctor, maintain that guilt is an illusion, a subjective projection on historical necessity or a symptom of mental disorder. To their arguments J.B. replies that guilt is a reality. Zophar, the cleric, holds the omnipresence of guilt and makes it the only reality. To his argument, J.B. opposes the consciousness of his innocence. Guilt may be real, but J.B. cannot see that he is guilty.

The arguments and the attitudes of the Comforters are, in large part, extrapolations of the positions of Zuss and Nickles, elaborated and justified by current argument. The socialist is a cynic, the psychiatrist cool and detached, the cleric is pompous and preachy.

In their various encounters Zuss and Nickles have encompassed all these postures, but without the jargon, the self-justification and the total lack of sympathy. All three Comforters take a deterministic stance that keeps them from relating to J.B.'s human situation. For them, Man is not in control at all. He is born bound to a certain destiny by history or his unconscious or his corrupt nature. As Zuss and Nickles argue about the nature of God, the Comforters argue over the nature of man. In answering them, J.B. moves definitely toward the humanistic position. He affirms man's responsibility without admitting universal guilt. "Guilt matters," but Zophar's position puts the source of the evil squarely in the Creator's will.

> *J.B.* Yours is the cruelest comfort of them all,
> Making the creator of the Universe
> The miscreator of mankind—
> A party to the crimes he punishes.   (TA, XLIV, 58.)

Bildad and Eliphaz represent a god who masquerades as History or Psychology; Zophar represents (rather badly) Mr. Zuss's God. Ultimately, these positions lead their advocates to despair of man's condition. Man is a fly crawling across the wall, their choral conclusion states, he shrieks into the night and "that is all." This linking of the Comforters mirrors the three sages of the Book of Job, but their common ground is not the theological unanimity of Job's counselors, but a mutual determinism that leads to despair.

The dismissal of this trio clears the ground for the argumentative conclusion of the play—the triumph of Man. By rejecting their arguments, J.B. establishes himself as the humanist hero, a responsible free agent. But before he can achieve his full stature, the Job story must be played out. After the departure of the Comforters, he cries out to God, demanding an answer, "his voice a challenge thrown against the door of the ultimate mystery." (TA, XLIV, 60.) The Distant Voice then answers him with the whirlwind speech. Presumably, even with the canvas down, the Comforters vanquished, and man alone in a smashed cosmos, the Voice from the past is heard in the consciousness of the religious thinker—and the child. (Jolly, the child among the bombed-out women, hears the Voice; he tells his mother that "under the wind was a word.") J.B. answers the Voice like the primitive over-awed by the vision of God's majesty and excellence: he is not like to God; WHEREFORE I

ABHOR MYSELF AND REPENT. The Distant Voice is the last apologist for the traditional view of God; once the Job story is finished, the Distant Voice will not be heard from again. The "play-within-the-play" is over (what was left of it) and J.B. can fend for himself.

At this point in the play the Zuss-Nickles plot-line converges with the J.B. plot. Though the drama seemed out of control for a while, Zuss is satisfied by J.B.'s repentance: "That's . . . *that.*" Nickles seems to accept this much of the situation; though he damns J.B. for a "contemptible goddam sheep," he concedes the victory to Zuss. (TA, XLIV, 60.) But he also introduces a sour note into his capitulation: God has triumphed only because J.B. was able to swallow his vomit. This implies that, by his repentance, J.B. has forgiven God.[26] At this point the debate reverts to its original premises, Zuss reiterating that man can only be happy by accepting God's Will, and Nickles that man's most logical move is to reject the universe. Here we see that the argument has not really progressed; each remains entrenched in his own rhetorical position, but, on the level of plot, there has been a change. Now Zuss and Nickles clash man to man, without their masks. When J.B. begins to reconsider his repentance: "Is that my wickedness—/That I am weak?" (TA, XLIV, 61), the outcome of the debate hangs in the balance. The argument will be settled, not by the Book, but by J.B.'s decision. Together Zuss and Nickles descend into the arena to plead their respective cases before J.B.

When they enter J.B.'s universe, not as Godmask and Satanmask, but as individuals, the personal-agon aspect of their plot-lines comes back into focus. Their destiny is at stake. In the Job story the Distant Voice judges between Job and his Counselors; MacLeish has shifted the main issue to J.B.'s acceptance or rejection of "life," and so he must choose between Nickles and Zuss. On the level of plot, this sequence culminates in an epiphany, and it is J.B. who exercises the god-like function of judgment. That this scene does involve an epiphany is confirmed by the playwright's own testimony. MacLeish added this confrontation episode at Kazan's suggestion after the play had been running for some months. Kazan describes how he hit on a solution to the problem of an effective solution:

Wednesday morning I woke up early and I knew at least where the trouble was. We had left out Aristotle's "recognition scene." The very turning point of our protagonist has been left undramatized. . . . I had studied the play all summer and hadn't seen till almost too late, that the one scene the audience must have was that one: the moment when J.B., having accepted his insignificance and impotence in the face of the scale and majesty of the universe, passes from dependence and humbleness to independence and dignity and pride in his own manliness.[27]

This anagnorisis, omitted from the book version, reveals J.B. determined to stand on his own feet and confronting both Zuss and Nickles. He turns his question: "Is that my wickedness . . ." into an answer by assuming control of the situation. He can cut the Gordian knot by rejecting both arguments.

> *J.B.* [to Nickles] Life is a filthy farce you say
> . . . . Men
> Must have ironic hearts and perish
> Laughing. . . . .
> Well, I will not laugh. (He swings on Mr. Zuss)
> And neither will I weep among the silent
> Who lie down to die
> In meek relinquishment. . . .
> Neither the Yes in ignorance
> The No in spite. . . . . . .
> Neither of them! (Mr. Zuss exits to ramp left)
> Neither of them! (Nickles crosses to right ramp)
>
> (TA, XLIV, 61.)

J.B. thus summarily dispatches the antagonists; he saws off both horns of the dilemma. Now he possesses the stage alone—the platform heaven is vacant, the skies above are empty, the Distant Voice is silent. J.B. achieves the status of sole inhabitant of his cosmos. The implications of his decision are important: by resolving the Zuss-Nickles plot, he functions as a god. Zuss and Nickles represented (along with the Distant Voice) the traditional Deity—or at least belief in him; J.B. sends them away. J.B.'s triumph deifies man for the moment. This dramatic statement of man's position in the universe supports the rhetorical bias of the play's dianoia.

One should make clear to oneself what it means when God becomes man. It means nothing less than a world-shaking transformation of God. It means more or less what creation meant in the beginning, namely an objectivization of God. At the time of Creation he revealed himself in Nature; now he wants to be more specific and become man.[28]

In this moment of epiphany, the culmination of the Zuss-Nickles structure, J.B. does become a god because his function is god-like. Like the Voice in the Bible or Athena in the *Oresteia,* he orders the cosmos.

J.B. stands in this role only momentarily; the structural statement that deifies him takes away with one hand what it conferred with the other. The play does not end with the dismissal of Zuss and Nickles; there is more to come. In the opening scene and throughout the Job story MacLeish focuses on the relationships between Sarah and J.B. This plot-line demands resolution, and what MacLeish does with it changes the meaning of the entire play.

In order to make clear how the J.B.-Sarah plot functions, we shall have to draw its threads together. On the level of structure, the events that contributed to J.B.'s education also separated him from his wife. The Thanksgiving dinner concluded with a visual image of marital communion: "J.B., yawning luxuriously, puts his arm around Sarah. She leans lovingly against him. They kiss each other." (TA, XLIV, 44.) Their separation, the result of their dispute about innocence and guilt, is symbolized by Sarah's refusal to embrace him. "No, don't touch me." (TA, XLIV, 48.) As the symbol of their mutual love, the children, have been destroyed, so their physical union is broken off. The separation is complete when Sarah leaves him to "curse God and die." Here the family is totally dissolved and J.B. is left alone.

The theme of physical union is introduced into the main issue when Zuss and Nickles discuss J.B.'s "taking up his life again." Nickles says that J.B. will not want to touch his wife, to "take the seed up of the sad creation/Planting the hopeful world again." (TA, XLIV, 61.) Nickles holds that J.B. will reject marriage, life, and the creation of a new life. Mr. Zuss points to the fact—generation after "blessed generation" people begin again. In the middle of his scene with Nickles and Zuss, J.B. is distracted: "There's someone standing at the door." Though he declares that he will carry on alone, the presence at the door persists throughout the argument. When Zuss and Nickles depart, Sarah enters, holding a petaled branch.

The resolution of the Sarah-Job relationship is the resolution of the whole drama. Her return, on the level of dianoia, implies a rejection of Nickles' position—she cannot bring herself to the act of self-destruction. More important to the structural resolution is the *reason* for her return. It is Nature that keeps her from self-destruction:

> *J.B.* Sarah!
> Why have you come back again?
> *Sarah.* (confused, holding out the small green branch like a child)
> Look, Job,
> The first few leaves . . .
> Not leaves though—
> Petals. I found it in the ashes growing
> Green as though it did not know . . .
> All that's left now is ashes. (TA, XLIV, 64.)

Sarah, the woman, returns with the sign of rebirth, of fertility in nature. Her return and her declaration of love for J.B. establish the dramatic relationship of husband and wife. "Love" here is, in effect, the society of the family; man and woman form a new society based on the fertile cycle of Nature. This reunion rounds out the comic pattern begun in the Thanksgiving Day scene; a society dissolved and reformed on a new understanding. The completion of this comic pattern conceals the establishment of a new divine hierarchy to replace the old gods.

In the end the tragic pattern of the Book of Job and of the Zuss-Nickles structure yields to the comic pattern. Though its use here is even less "funny" than in *The Cocktail Party,* it functions in the same way toward the formation of a new social organism. Through the fertility references, the Nature imagery, the return of the woman, the "high gods" of the sky give place to the *magna mater.*

It must always be remembered that it was the sanctifying of life, in the first place, of the magico-religious powers of universal fecundity, which displaced the Supreme Beings from worship and from religious primacy. . . . The substitution of "strong" and "potent" gods is accompanied by another phenomenon of no less importance; the god of fertility becomes the husband of a Great Goddess, of an agrarian Magna Mater; he is no longer autonomous and all-powerful like the ancient gods of the sky, he is reduced to the status of partner in a divine marriage.[29]

Thus the reunion of Sarah and J.B. is a modified hierogamy. In dispatching the "old gods" of the sky, J.B. himself is deified. Sarah comes bearing the sign of fertility, like the "mute" bride of the ritual, and is wedded to the god. Children will follow in the natural course, as Mr. Zuss has indicated, and the new society will be fully established.

The establishment of this pattern creates a serious problem because it clashes sharply with the dianoia of the play. Just as O'Neill gives us a Puritanism without God in *Mourning*, MacLeish pretends, in his argument, that this new society has no celestial archetype, that is, that J.B. and Sarah must depend solely on their own resources. The comic structure is itself a denial of this assertion. The "sacred marriage" on which this structure is modeled is a celebration of an extrinsic power—the power of Nature. Dispatching the God of the theologians, of the Book of Job, of traditional Calvinism out the front door in the epiphany scene, MacLeish slips the "strong" gods of fertility in through the kitchen. The petals from the ashes bring back the wife; this use of Nature recalls a passage in Jung:

The enchanting and springlike beauty of this divine youth [Tammuz, Adonis, Balder] is one of those pagan values which we miss so sorely in Christianity, and particularly in the somber world of the apocalypse—the indescribable morning glory of a day in spring, which after the deathly stillness of winter causes the earth to put forth blossoms, gladdens the heart of man and makes him believe in a kind and loving God.[30]

Nor is this view of Nature introduced only at the end; it moves through the entire play—even Nickles is not immune. During the Prologue, before he understands which mask he is to wear, he sings:

> If God is God He is not good,
> If God is good He is not God;
> Take the even, take the odd,
> I would not sleep here if I could . . .
> . . . .
> Except for the little green leaves in the wood
> And the wind on the water.   (TA, XLIV, 38.)

The chorus of women accept the vitality of Nature also and keep the imagery of the Thanksgiving scene alive:

Mrs. Bottecelli. Know what humanity is? A potato.
Tramp it deep enough it . . . grows.
Miss Mabel. Even old and dry, it flourishes.   (TA, XLIV, 56.)

The proverbial wisdom of the "little people" contains fertility references; the women know how the world operates. So when Sarah
enters with her flowering branch, she climaxes a subterranean
progress toward a Nature religion. The "high gods" with "bullwhip
and thunder" (TA, XLIV, 62) have departed the cosmos; with their
dismissal MacLeish declares that all deity has been banished. The
overt meaning of the play is a declaration of man's supreme isolation; the J.B.-Sarah structure affirms a cyclical rebirth in Nature
which itself implies a deity.

In order to retain the relevance of this conclusion to the Zuss-
Nickles structure, and to resolve the tension between man's isolation
and the comic model, MacLeish splits the attention of his audience.
In the final scene J.B. looks back to the moment of his apotheosis;
Sarah looks forward to the new life of the new society.[31] Sarah goes
about straightening up the stage while J.B. discourses on the lesson
he has learned: "Nothing is certain but the loss of love." Then he
affirms the new faith: "Yet you say you love me." In the dialogue
the balance is maintained between past suffering and present union,
but the dramatic structure emphasizes the comic celebration, the
wedding.[32]

The problem of rhetorical pattern versus dramatic structure, most
clearly exemplified in the final scene, runs through the entire play.
MacLeish is using his drama to make a point, to instruct the audience about his humanistic philosophy. From the comment which the
staging makes on the action, through the drawn-out discussions of
Zuss and Nickles to the ultimate vindication of Man alone in an
alien cosmos, MacLeish is building his case. J.B. is Man, and Man
must learn to live armored by his own dignity.

If the world can be taught to believe in the worth of man, it can be
taught not only to survive but to live. If the world can be governed by
belief in the worth of man, in the dignity of man, it can be governed in
peace. These propositions need no proof. They speak for themselves.
. . . It is necessary to believe in man, not only as the Christians believe
in man, out of pity, or as the democrats believe in man, out of loyalty,
but also as the Greeks believed in man, out of pride.[33]

In order to demonstrate this proposition, the ground must be cleared. All the Gods of modern man must be demolished—Zuss's God of absolute will, Sarah's covenanting God of reward and punishment, the amorphous God "Luck" of J.B.'s trust, the God Determinism in whom Bildad and Eliphaz put their faith. The pattern of events is manipulated so as to illustrate these points; J.B. (and the audience) are educated to the problem and then to the solution as MacLeish sees it. Because of the religious implications of the play and because of its Biblical source, much of the critical discussion tended to concentrate on theology and/or philosophy.[34] On the other hand, no matter how tempting it may be, the critic misses the point if his comment is directed solely to the dianoia and its implications. The structure of the play makes its own comment on the author's meaning; J.B. is, in fact, not isolated at the end of the play and while Nature works in the cosmos, all the gods are not dead. The dissatisfaction that the critic feels is traceable to this contradiction between MacLeish's message and the message of the dramatic structure.

Perhaps the ultimate source of the problem which MacLeish and Kazan were pondering is an ambiguity in American culture between our anthropomorphic view of God and a nostalgic view of Nature. These two influences have never been reconciled in the popular mind. The acceptance of God as absolute Will and suffering as an expression of subjection to that Will does not really fit into the vision of primal innocence and liberal living associated with "Nature." The formal concept of God does not include the pastoral qualities of the Old and New Testament images. "God," for the American, remains a God in the sky and of the sky who never descends to inhabit the green earth. The humanistic gloss which constitutes the dianoia of the play is an attempt to destroy this sky-God and to establish man's dignity and worth in a Godless universe. This attempt results in a rhetorical bias toward Nickles' position without accepting his conclusions and in a gratuitous affirmation of man's self-sufficiency without discovering a form that would support these assertions. MacLeish concludes by offering an alternative that reflects the old nostalgia for a pastoral existence. In spite of the bomb, in lieu of fruitless questing after answers, man is to rely on the cycle of Nature and love for his fellow-man.

The confusion that stems from the clash of dianoia and structural pattern leaves one dissatisfied with the play as a whole. MacLeish does not really find an integrating principle for reshaping the Job story; his "old wall" becomes part of a maze that winds intricately about and leads back to the point of entrance. It is ironic that the playwright's addition to the story—the focus on Sarah and "starting life over again"—establishes the comic pattern and concludes by celebrating a divinized Nature. This attempt at resurrecting a nineteenth-century myth seems hardly worth the rhetoric MacLeish has lavished on it, especially since the structure, simply by exerting its own subtle pressure, destroys his argument. Perhaps ultimately the most affecting sections of the play are the speeches of the Distant Voice, those moments borrowed from the past when Job chides his God and God answers him.

5

Tragedy and the Private Eye:

Detective Story

In his search for dramatic forms the playwright has at hand a source comparable in dramatic potential to traditional literary models: popular "subliterary" forms. Contemporary popular genres —western fiction, the detective story, the slick romance—have this potential, first and foremost, because they *are* popular. The public puts in millions of reading hours on the paperbacks, the pulp magazines, the slick-paper journals. Like the Greek dramatists who drew on their audience's acquaintance with ritual to establish rapport, the modern playwright can assume that his audience is familiar with the general outlines and the leading character-types. As a genre develops, it acquires a predictable structure and stereotyped characters, e.g., boy-meets-girl, boy-loses-girl, boy-gets-girl. These structures become canonized into formulae. They are usually described as "conventional" and considered to be superficial, trivial, "subliterary." Such description conceals a very real issue. Why does one popular genre gain widespread acceptance while another fails to make a lasting impression? Clearly the successful formulae endure because they satisfy deeply felt, vague and unformulated needs in the audience. In this sense the popular formula is one contemporary equivalent of ritual.

Another rationale for the use of these formulae by the dramatist, related to the ritualistic aspect, is their function as "escape" literature. Like "subliterary," "escape" covers an area of considerable complexity. How do popular formulae provide escape? What does the reader want to escape *from* and what does he escape *into?* These questions can lead the critic into deep water. Sociologists, anthropologists, moralists, aestheticians, metaphysicians have answered them in different ways. The popular formula has many characteristics of the myth; it performs some of the functions of myth.

Reading replaces not only oral folk traditions, such as still survive in rural communities of Europe, but also the recital of myths in the archaic societies. Now, reading, perhaps even more than visual entertainment, gives one a break in duration, and at the same time an "escape from time." Whether we are "killing time" with a detective story, or entering into another temporal universe as we do in reading any kind of novel, we are taken out of our own duration to move in other rhythms, to live in a different history.[1]

Whether literature can be built into an explicit myth that would provide a "real" escape from time, as critics like Richard Chase and Leslie Fiedler insist, is an open question. In any event, the popular formula provides a link between the desire to escape present reality and the kind of ideal universe that the reader envisions. Popular genres create a world into which the public is happy to escape. Thus in the popular hero, cowboy or detective or lover, are realized the attitudes, ideals and aspirations of the culture that supports him. Through the formula, then, the playwright can get at those vital attitudes which animate a culture, inform the actions and set the objectives of the audience. The formula provides, in Eliot's phrase, a "crude form" that may be refined into a vehicle of dramatic expression.

Among popular genres the detective story, in all its phases from Edgar Allen Poe to Mickey Spillane, has retained its hold on the reading public. Detective fiction concentrates on one aspect of experience, crime and punishment, in a simple black-and-white Cartesian pattern. While real standards of guilt and innocence wax and wane, the formula of detective fiction maintains a clear criterion. The questions of motivation versus motive, or moral versus legal guilt, are not at issue; the criminal becomes so by virtue of his crime, usually murder—this is virtually all we know about him and all we need to know. The detective then tracks him down by a series of logical deductions or (in the case of the hardboiled private eye) by intuitive leaps. In the revelation of the identity of the murderer justice triumphs and the world is set right again, as right as it can be set. The pattern can be complicated by ambiguous motives, a sympathetic murderer, or by a criminal milieu in which the murderer is simply the worst of a bad lot, but there is always a clear reference point for the reader by which he can measure the triumph of justice.

The formula *qua* formula does not vary: the commission of a crime, the search for the criminal (which involves attaching suspicion temporarily to innocent parties), the discovery of the real criminal. Whatever the basic appeal of this pattern, it has proved very durable over the past hundred years.

There does seem to be considerable agreement among critics and reviewers of detective fiction that the conventional or formulaic element in the story is a major source of satisfaction to the reader. The thesis that the fascination comes from trying to solve the mystery with the detective is largely exploded, since some of the greatest mysteries cannot possibly be solved on the evidence presented. Haycraft's assertion, that the detective story flowers in a democracy and somehow embodies the democratic way of life, was conceived in the midst of World War II. It has since come in for rough handling because of the totalitarian qualities of the detective-hero and the scapegoat characteristics of the criminal.[2] While granting that the reading of detective fiction is fun, the theorists cannot resist speculating on the effect of the formula. All tend to agree that a purgation ritual is involved: "We all aspire to crime, we are all guilty, we hunt ourselves down and punish ourselves in expiation." Or "in the mystery story we try to appease death and make ourselves emotionally safe from its horrors."[3] In a more comprehensive view, it is suggested that the mystery story is a microcosm which mirrors present-day confusion. The hero "heartens us" because he can find his way out of the dark wood of evil into a patch of temporary light. Auden, in perhaps the most interesting study of the English mystery, finds purgation in the illusion of being "dissociated from the murderer."

The magic formula is an innocence which is discovered to contain guilt; then a suspicion of being the guilty one; and finally a real innocence from which the guilty other has been expelled, a cure effected, not by me or my neighbors, but by the miraculous intervention of a genius from outside who removes guilt by giving knowledge of guilt. The detective story subscribes, in fact, to the Socratic daydream: "Sin is ignorance."[4]

All of these suggestions emphasize the ritual aspect of the form as making the primary contribution to reader satisfaction. The strategy employed falls into the category of purgation.

Given this perspective on the detective story, the critic is drawn to make a comparison with tragedy. Auden calls attention to this analogue. In its pattern of events, *Oedipus Rex* resembles a detective mystery.

There is Concealment (the innocent seem guilty and the guilty seem innocent) and Manifestation (the real guilt is brought to consciousness). There is also peripeteia, in this case not a reversal of fortune but a double reversal from apparent guilt to innocence and apparent innocence to guilt.[5]

The resemblance may be only skin-deep, but it is definite. Even though the "crime" in *Oedipus* stretches past the event into the dimension of fate and the gods, the formula is identical: the crime, the search for the criminal, the discovery of the criminal. Like Greek tragedy, the formula is self-limiting; it has the celebrated beginning, middle and end that Aristotle called for. This definitive pattern, the ritual overtones, the plot-devices of classical tragedy give the formula a large dramatic potential.

At the most refined level of articulation as well as at the crudest level, the detective story formula provides only a generic structure; the content is determined by the character of the detective-hero and the situation in which he works. Frequently the type of hero determines the type of situation. The detective can be a professional policeman (Dupin, Maigret, Alleyn), an amateur sleuth (Nero Wolfe, Sherlock Holmes, Lord Peter Wimsey), or a private investigator (Sam Spade, Philip Marlowe, Mike Hammer). The amateurs range from little old ladies (Miss Marple) to clerics (Father Brown) to members of a profession (Perry Mason); any logician qualifies. The hero brings his own situation with him into the story. Agatha Christie's sharp-eyed spinster operates in a world of country homes and flower shows, Father Brown in the common-place parish world (with clerical excursions to the continent), Perry Mason in the upper-middle-class society of a large city. Whatever his particular milieu, the hero is in control and renders his universe "safe" for the innocent members of its society. In this type of detective fiction, the omniscient hero operates in an ordered, disciplined, well-lighted universe which goes well with his ordered, disciplined, well-lighted mind. The murder and the murderer do not belong in this world and, once the murderer is discovered, all returns to normal. In the fiction of the hardboiled American school, matters are, like the detective-hero, darker and bloodier.

A late development in detective fiction and still currently popular, "the private eye"—Sam Spade, Marlowe and Mike Hammer—is a uniquely American version of the detective. Their world is not the country house or the secluded vicarage or even the bourgeois suburb; they are at home in the chaotic and sinister big city. "If the universe of the transcendent detective has all the elements of a daydream [closed, controlled, static], the universe of the private eye has all the naked intensity of a nightmare. It is preeminently the place where beams fall." [6] The hardboiled sleuth is tailored to deal with this kind of milieu; as Auden disparagingly points out, the detectives of the hardboiled school are difficult to distinguish from the criminals.

Whether or not the critic likes it, the hardboiled hero has a long pedigree in American fiction. His individualistic tendencies are suggested by Washington Irving's Brom Bones, that "burly, roistering blade," in the frontiersmen of A. B. Longstreet, Charles Webber, Joseph Baldwin, and the desperadoes of Alfred Arrington. In 1860 he passes into the Beadle and Adams dime novels so that he was ready-made for early writers of the western novel like Zane Grey. He remains the model for the western hero. As a detective he first appeared in the pages of *The Black Mask,* a pulp magazine which came out in the early 1920s. This magazine popularized the tough detective in the stories of John Carroll Daly (Race Williams) and Dashiel Hammett (Sam Spade). In the early 1930s Raymond Chandler contributed the character that was to become Philip Marlowe; his work set the pace for the hardboiled school and comes closest to having literary qualities. His hero, moreover, is the epitome of the qualities which characterize the "private eye": courage, physical strength, indestructibility, indifference to danger and death, a knightly attitude, celibacy (not, however, chastity), a measure of violence, and a strict sense of justice.[7] Because both are born of the same stock, the similarities between the western hero and the tough detective are striking. Both are isolated in a savage world, both carry their own law with them, both are fierce defenders of justice as they see it. Together they help to make up the image of the American popular hero.

The tough detective, then, has those features with which the contemporary American can identify. He moves in an environment like that described on the front pages of the big-city tabloid. Crime is an everyday occurrence and any citizen can be involved. The private eye acts on the assumption that society is decadent and evil and that he can handle it on its own terms. This attitude is reflected in Chandler's response to Auden's charge that he was writing about a criminal milieu: "Is this [the world of Philip Marlowe] a criminal milieu? No, just average corrupt living with the melodramatic angle over-emphasized." [8] The "average" condition of society is corrupt; Chandler's view is also the view of his hero. In the midst of this corruption the detective moves untouched, or at least as untouched as the world will allow. Often he must fight crime and corruption with their own weapons and assume the protective coloring of the underworld, but he never succumbs to the principles of this corrupt society. He represents that character which the average man would like to fancy himself were he in a comparable situation: "the glorification of toughness, irreverence, and a sense of decency too confused and almost half-ashamed to show itself." [9] The public recognizes this milieu and identifies with the ideal qualities of the hero who can control it.

Thus when the playgoer approaches a drama entitled *Detective Story,* he brings a positive, if unformulated, set of attitudes with him. Sidney Kingsley's play opened on Broadway in March, 1949, the same year in which Mickey Spillane's *I the Jury* appeared. The title is ambiguous in Empson's sense of the term. It can be construed literally, the story of a detective. It is also a story of detection; the play includes a mystery, a modified "whodunit." In a broader context, the title describes the world of the play, which takes place in the squad room of a New York police station. Finally it is fraught with ironies since the detective himself turns out to be guilty. It is possible to leave the analogy with detective fiction right here with a consideration of the title, as most of the reviewers did. However, the conventions of the drama, the character of the hero, the structure of the events owe a great deal to the tough-detective formula, and an investigation of their function in the play sheds a good deal of light on the meaning of *Detective Story.*

Just before opening, Kingsley gave an interview to a *Times* reporter in which he discussed his problems as author and director.

With a "sardonic nod toward a favorite product of the fiction mills," he talked about his play as a model of the police state. He saw, within the walls of the squad room, a microcosmic society with his detective-hero as the incarnation of abusive police power, a totalitarian with a badge:

> The police power is a symbol, or you might say one of the measuring rods, of freedom in a society. When the police power answers to a democratic code of human rights, you have a free society. . . . McLeod [the detective] has a medieval attitude—just as the Communists have—that he has a mission to make people abide by the right as he sees it or personally bring them to account if they don't.[10]

This view highlights the dianoia and converts the play into a thesis drama with a message. The reviewers and critics took Kingsley at his word, but found the message incidental to the entertainment value of the representational details.

Detective Story is a typical piece of Kingsley realism, in which an environment is recreated with striking fidelity and then translated into vivid theatre while the well-paced and tense action carries a significant theme— namely, the dangers of extreme righteousness in a world of fallible human beings.[11]

The realism overpowers the thesis, often to the point where the message is taken to be straight hokum: "Aside from the psychological arbitrariness with which the characters are maneuvered, nothing in the events of the play proved that McLeod's point of view is necessarily wrong. One does not have to be tainted in any way to believe in fierce justice." [12] The "police state" allegory failed to impress the critic because he did not find the detective's attitude toward strict justice wholly unsympathetic. Kingsley's bias toward this message about totalitarianism is apparent in the rhetoric of the play, but the structure of the events and the character of the hero take a different direction.

Kingsley situates his drama in the chaotic world of "average corruption," that world in which "beams fall." The setting is a realistic police station with stained walls, cage-wire on the windows, dark woodwork and litter on the floor. It also includes an electric wall clock that runs concurrently with the time of the action. The world of the play is strictly delimited in space and time, according to the best slice-of-life tradition. This use of setting and time follows the convention of detective fiction, realism in the situation and confinement to a short period of time.

A sense of reality is essential to the detective novel. The few attempts that have been made to lift the detective story out of its naturalistic environment and confer on it an air of fancifulness have been failures.[13]

For the hardboiled school, the setting makes further demands which are fulfilled by the police station. A cross section of humanity is gathered on the premises in the course of a working day; anyone can come in and anything can happen. Auden characterizes the situation in the hardboiled school as "the Great Wrong Place," full of criminals and potential criminals.[14] If not exactly the "Great Wrong Place," the squad room brings together victim and criminal, the accused and the accusers, in a continual flow. This situation answers the requirements of the conventional formula.

Throughout the drama, but especially in the first act, Kingsley augments this slice-of-life atmosphere by interjecting brief episodes and minor characters, routine police business. The main action is interwoven with such incidents: the first-offense shoplifter who is being printed and booked, the mildly paranoiac old lady who is electronically sensitive, the yokel whose wallet has been neatly razored out of his back pocket. Against this pastiche of routine cases the detectives go methodically about their business, typing up "squeals," answering phone calls, conning the disturbed citizen, grilling the felony case. The policemen's personalities are distinctive also: Callahan, the brash wise-guy; Dakis, the bored desk man with indigestion; Brody, whose experienced roughness hides a soft heart. Routine is the order of the day, routine in the midst of violence, distress, death. The cops act as if they really have control of their world; the chaos over which they preside is for them the routine work-a-day situation. If the "falling beam" is not unusual, they have learned to step out of the way automatically. In creating this realistic surface, Kingsley uses an eye for precise detail and an accurate ear to mold the sights and sounds into an authentic police workday.

The accuracy of Kingsley's reporting, besides establishing the realistic context for the main plot development, exercises a fascination in its own right. Aristotle makes the point about the mimetic instinct in man and, whatever elaborate interpretations are legitimately developed from the mimetic principle, there is a delight in seeing the activities of one's fellows faithfully reproduced. In a scientific era when "realism" means tangible detail, Kingsley's art in reproducing the *superficies* of a police station is widely admired. Moreover, in an era of specialization, when each occupation has its own secular mystique, the inside story has a special attraction. For the man who has never seen the squad room of a police station (except on TV), the inner workings of a policeman's world are an education. Just as *Advise and Consent* depended largely on the sense of being in the inner circle of Senatorial politics, *The Desk Set* depicts the world of the private secretary, and *The Solid Gold Cadillac* depends on a knowledge of corporation structure for its humor, *Detective Story* appeals on the level of its effective portrayal of the cop's world. This appeal may distract from the main plot, but it corresponds faithfully to the proper conventional situation in detective fiction.

When Detective James McLeod steps into the squad room, he is clearly of a different stripe from the policemen around him. He is college-educated, well-dressed, efficient. His co-workers sense—and some resent—his superiority.

Callahan. I ain't no friggin barber college detective with pleats in my pants.
McLeod. (sardonically) No, you *ain't* . . . (Goes into Lieutenant's office)
Callahan. (miffed) Remind me to get that college graduate a bicycle pump for Christmas to blow up that big head of his. (O'Brien and Gallagher laugh)
O'Brien. He needling you again?
Callahan. Mm. Big needle man from sew-and-sew.[15]

McLeod is aware that his background sets him off from the other workmen in the squad room:

McLeod. Why am I wasting my life here? I could make more driving a hack. I like books, I like music, I've got a wonderful, wonderful wife—I could get a dozen jobs would give me more time to enjoy the good things of life. I should have my head examined. (DS, p. 57)

Joe Feinson, the philosophical police-buff reporter who covers the station, carries on a running debate with McLeod. Intellectually the big detective is superior to his environment. By a process of "natural selection," first and foremost, McLeod is set apart.

These characteristics, by themselves, tend to put McLeod in the "sleuth" category. The super-intelligence of the master detective immediately marks him out from his fellows, especially in contrast with "the police." The point that Callahan makes about McLeod's dressing well (Callahan himself wears a flowered sport shirt that McLeod tabs as "Pier Six") meshes with the quality of intelligence. Though McLeod would hardly qualify as a "dandy" like the detective aesthete of the English detective novel (Lord Peter Wimsey, Simon Templar), he certainly surpasses the standards set in the squad room. The anti-social aspects of McLeod's appearance and intellectual powers he holds in common with the stereotype; "haters of conventional society the dandies had been and have continued to be, along with their cousins, the sleuths." [16] But McLeod is set apart by more than his dress and his natural endowments; he is a man with a mission.

McLeod works at being a detective in order to wage war on crime. He is not "a little boy playing cops and robbers" like Callahan, or an "insurance salesman" like Brody. He is not satisfied with doing a routine job; his principles demand that he be policeman, judge and jury. Early in the first act Joe Feinson puts McLeod's attitude in perspective:

Joe. The mortal God—McLeod! Captain Ahab pursuing the great gray Leviathan! A fox with rabies bit him in the ass when he was two years old, and neither of them recovered. Don't throw water on him. He goes rabid! (DS, p. 17.)

He is confident of his ability to judge and fiercely intent on carrying out his mission. His main target in the action of the play is an abortionist named (appropriately enough) Kurt Schneider, who has been arraigned but never convicted. Schneider's lawyer insists on due process with McLeod, but the detective has his own standards:

McLeod. Counselor, I never met a criminal yet who didn't wrap himself in the Constitution from head to toe, or a hoodlum who wasn't filled to the nostrils with habeas corpus and the rights of human dignity. Did

you ever see that girl your client operated on last year—in the morgue—
on a marble slab? Wasn't much left of her, Counselor—and very little
dignity!

Sims. My client was innocent of that charge. The court acquitted him.

McLeod. He was guilty.

Sims. Are you setting yourself above the courts of the land?

McLeod. There's a higher court, Counselor.   (DS, p. 20.)

McLeod—the mortal God—feels he is entitled to speak for that
higher court. He has no great respect for due process or the judgment of the courts or the sense of responsibility in private citizens.
When the reporter defends the judiciary, McLeod replies: "Then he
[the judge] is a corrupt man himself. All lawyers are, anyway. I
say, hang all lawyers and let justice triumph." (DS, p. 58.) When
"John Q. Public" begins to yield to Brody's arguments about not
prosecuting the young man who embezzled from his employer,
McLeod insists on demanding the full extent of the law:

McLeod. This is a war, Mr. Prichett. We know it, they know it, but
you don't. We're your army. We're here to protect you. . . . You civil-
ians are too lazy or too selfish or too scared or just too indifferent to even
want to appear in court and see the charges through that you, yourselves,
bring. (DS, pp. 104–105.)

Finally, McLeod cannot accept the attitude of his fellow officers. He
battles the Lieutenant tooth and nail when there is a question of getting information from Schneider:

Lieutenant. Get what you can out of Schneider, but no roughhouse!
You know the policy of this administration.

McLeod. I don't hold with it. . . . I don't believe in coddling criminals.

Lieutenant. Who tells you to?

McLeod. You do. The whole damn system does. (DS, p. 42.)

McLeod does not identify with any segment of the police-station society. His friendship with his partner Brody and with the reporter
Feinson is conducted on his terms; he cannot respond to the rough
sentiment of the one or the cautious relativism of the other. He
wages his war for justice alone, making his own absolute judgments
as he goes along.

Independent about his ideas, the detective is also not restricted by convention in his choice of method. He does not eschew violence when aroused. When Kurt Schneider refuses to talk, McLeod swings and sends the abortionist to the hospital. He feels that Schneider has brought this punishment on himself. Though the detective does not use his gun in the course of the play, he makes no bones about his willingness to shoot if necessary. He suggests that Kurt try a run for it: "Give me the little pleasure—(touching his gun) of putting a hole in the back of your head." Schneider at first thinks McLeod is bluffing; later he is not so sure. "Go to Georgia or go to hell, but you butcher one more girl in this city, and law or no law, I'll find you and I'll put a bullet in the back of your head." (ps, p. 61.) At the denouement McLeod is himself gunned down because he leaps in to disarm the cat burglar who is holding the office at bay. If, in the detective's view, violence is useful or necessary, he is ready enough to use it.

This picture of the detective shows many similarities to the typical hardboiled "private eye" of recent fiction. Even though McLeod is a professional policeman, he acts on his own authority with a private motive. He has the requisite strict sense of justice; he is not averse to a measure of violence. Though he resembles the gentleman sleuth in his intellectual and sartorial superiority, his personal characteristics are germane to the tough private operator. Thus his isolation has a sociological significance:

New . . . is the image of crime which has ceased being a social anomaly as it had been in the old detective stories; in the new mysteries, in which a thousand fall and the hero himself must take cruel beatings before the happy end, crime seems a rather normal feature of everyday life. But organized society, the State, does not seem able to cope with it sufficiently and neither does the individual; both are not tough enough; therefore the semi-legal, semi-independent private eyes and professional toughs are needed to look out for, and lynch, the hidden forces of evil.[17]

This isolation in which the private detective must wrap himself results from his perception of the ubiquity of evil and the constant threat it poses. He acts on the assumption that society is decadent and evil and he is the one bulwark against total eclipse. McLeod has no great faith in human nature; his ability to "smell out evil" is his protection against it. Finally, if these characteristic correspondences are not conclusive, Kingsley himself explicitly links McLeod with the hardboiled hero. Joe Feinson's nickname for the hero is "Shamus" —detective story slang for "private eye."

If, as Kingsley indicates, his detective represents the abuse of police power, he is breasting the current of a popular convention. McLeod's qualities embody the characteristics of the tough-guy hero with whom the audience will tend to identify. As the conventional hero McLeod is sympathetic and appeals strongly to the audience's ideals. Kingsley himself cannot make up his mind about McLeod. He gives him a nickname which ties him into the hardboiled tradition and the two subplots which illustrate McLeod's relation to the criminal are ambiguously presented. They balance out in the scale of justice; they are by no means a demonstration of intolerance and totalitarian injustice.

The first subplot involves Arthur Kindred, charged with grand larceny, and the girl who pleads for him. In itself a routine boy-falls-in-love-with-the-wrong-sister romance, it shows McLeod holding to the letter of the law. Arthur embezzled his employer's funds to make a last-ditch attempt to win the love of Susan's sister. The boy is not a hardened criminal—as Brody (and, presumably, the audience) immediately perceives. He has a good war record and Susan pleads his case eloquently. Because the boy resembles his dead son, Brody seconds her and persuades the complainant to drop charges pending restitution of the money. McLeod will not hear of it; he holds to the letter because Arthur, whatever the reason, did steal. McLeod invokes his experience in explaining his reasons:

McLeod. When I was new on this job we brought in two boys who were caught stealing a car. They looked like babies. They cried. I let them go. Two nights later—two nights later—one of them held up a butcher in Harlem. Shot him through the head and killed him. (DS, p. 104.)

Arthur stole—and McLeod is going to see that he suffers the consequences. The other subplot deals with two burglars, Charley and Lewis, who are taken red-handed. Charley tells a good story—in fact, two or three good stories prefaced by oaths "on his mother's grave"—in maintaining his innocence. With this type, McLeod's instinct is infallible. Charley has been in jail before; he has "a sheet as long as your arm." He turns out to be a four-time loser, a vicious cat burglar, a killer. The two burglars represent the underworld, and society needs the McLeods for protection from this element. Whereas the Arthur Kindred story has the ring of melodrama and sentiment, Charley and Lewis come across as all too real.

Against McLeod's view of crime and criminals, there are the arguments of the reporter. Kingsley has said that the reporter speaks for him and has confessed that he had trouble with a preaching tone in Joe's speeches.[18] Whether the author succeeded in eliminating it is an open question. In any event, against the weight of McLeod's experience and Charley's past record and present viciousness, Joe's problems with the "epistemological question" do not carry much dramatic weight. He enjoys discussion; there is an air of dilettantism about his enthusiastic preachments.

Joe. That's what's great about it [democracy]. That's what I love. It's so confused, it's wonderful. (Crossing to McLeod) After all, Seamus, guilt and innocence!—the epistemological question! Just the knowing . . . the ability to ken. Maybe he didn't do it. Maybe she can't identify him. How do you know? (DS, pp. 57–58.)

The hero knows because he is the hero. It is his job to search out and destroy evil; the formula supports his ability to know. Joe's philosophy, in the world of the police station, seems stilted, academic, no match for suborned witnesses, fast-talking lawyers, the professional criminals. If Joe has Immanuel Kant on his side, the detective has American tradition, the empathy generated by his conformity to the mythical model.

As the figure of the hero conforms to the stereotype in essentials, the main plot follows the pattern of detective fiction. It involves a specific "mystery," the real relationship between McLeod and the abortionist and, in the wider context of the whole play, the search for, and eventual discovery of, the real criminal. The structure that ties the play together is analogous to the Aristotelean tragic pattern as exemplified in *Oedipus*. Early in the first act the lawyer introduces the specific mystery:

Sims. For over a year you personally have been making my client's life a living hell. Why?

. . . .

McLeod. (sardonically) Because I'm annoyed by criminals that get away with murder. They upset me. . . . To me your client is just another criminal.

Sims. That's your story. At considerable expense we have investigated and discovered otherwise. (McLeod turns to stare at him. Sims smiles knowingly and goes.) (DS, p. 21.)

The mystery here poises the balance between two situations; McLeod affirms his purpose and his code, "I hate criminals," and the lawyer accuses him of having a personal motive. McLeod ignores the clue as simply a fishing expedition. When the Lieutenant, the hierarch of this society, comes in, he drops the same hint to McLeod. "On Schneider—what's your poisenal angle?" (DS, p. 41.) When McLeod hits Schneider, the abortionist reveals the first real clue: "Tami Giacoppetti. She got him after me too." (DS, p. 62.) McLeod is concentrating on his purpose, bringing the abortionist to justice, and he fails to appreciate the mystery in his own relationship.

The Lieutenant, however, is determined to hunt down the facts. He confronts Sims and McLeod, and the lawyer adds one of the missing pieces to the puzzle. "Discuss it with McLeod! . . . Or his wife!" The working policeman underscores both the plot-line and his own aversion to the pulp-magazine version of the detective: "Mystery! mystery! . . . four years ago I threw my radio set outa the window. You know why: Because, goddam it, I hate mysteries." (DS, pp. 69, 71.) But, like a good detective, the Lieutenant has put two and two together. He brings in both Mrs. McLeod and Tami Giacoppetti. The mystery is solved; Mary admits that Schneider operated on her to abort Giacoppetti's child. The solution to the "specific" mystery creates the dilemma which the detective-hero must face: he hates criminals; what, then, can be his attitude toward a criminal that he loves? McLeod knew nothing about his wife's encounter with Schneider. He is faced with the facts for the first time. The simplistic world of the whodunit yields up the pattern which underlies it: the purgation of society through the discovery of the real criminal.

The notions of guilt and purgation are applied unequivocally throughout the detective novel—the murderer is guilty by virtue of his deed. No distinctions between, for instance, moral and legal guilt are applicable within the ritual structure. Up to the discovery of his wife's crime, this is McLeod's approach to guilt:

> *McLeod.* You wouldn't lie to me, would you, Arthur?
> *Arthur.* Why should I lie?
> *McLeod.* I don't know. Why should you steal? Maybe it's because you're just no damn good, hm, Arthur? The judge asks me and I'm going to throw the book at you.—Tattoo that on your arm. (DS, p. 27.)

Criminals don't have the same nervous system as other people; "they're a different species, a different breed," human garbage that the policeman sweeps up for disposal. In the convention the detective remains above evil and judges it from his superior position. He is a mortal God in his own universe. With the discovery of Mary's involvement, McLeod must face evil in his own house. The one person with whom he identified, the one society to which he belonged is also found to be corrupt. Here Kingsley departs from the conventional pattern; the play now deals with a society which includes the detective, and the problem of guilt and purgation is extended to all the personae.

McLeod's isolation is carefully qualified from the beginning of the play. When, in the first act, he talks to Mary on the phone, it is clear that his relationship with her momentarily makes a different man of him. He is warm and tender toward his angel; he is worried sick about her "psychosomatic" illness. Mary reveals that he carefully keeps his work and his home life separate. The McLeod that she knows is not the one the audience has been observing. Jim is "kind and gentle"; that is the only side of him she knows. McLeod the cop leads an isolated life; McLeod the husband appears a different man altogether. This double image represents a significant change in the character of the hardboiled hero. Conventionally, like the western hero, he is celibate. Any dealings with women are casual, non-entangling alliances and never interfere with his job. Kingsley modifies his hero thus far, juxtaposing the detective and the married man. In departing from the fictional figure, the playwright has modified the plot structure. The problem of guilt and purgation now includes the person of the detective. The action is now internal, engaging the hero's private personality. This modification of the conventional structure provides the link with the classical tragic pattern.

Thus, with the revelation of corruption in his wife, McLeod the detective and McLeod the husband come into conflict. The man who hates crime is the same man who loves a criminal. As detective, McLeod cannot accept his wife's action.

Mary. Jim, I beg you. Please understand.
McLeod. What's there to understand? . . . You got undressed before him . . . You went to bed with him . . . You carried his child awhile inside you . . . and then you killed it.
Mary. Yes. That's true.
McLeod. Everything I hate . . . even murder . . . What the hell's left to understand? (DS, p. 112.)

Mary's plea of youth and ignorance is inadmissible. This simplistic view of crime does not allow for any extenuation of guilt. As husband, however, McLeod needs his wife. Brody and Joe bring this argument to bear on his sense of isolation when Mary leaves him for the first time. Before marrying, he was dried up, lonely, cold; if he lets her go, Joe insists, he is, like the base Indian, throwing away a jewel. His own argument with Mary, when she returns to say good-bye, rests on their mutual need. She can't fall asleep unless his arms are around her; if he has to go home to an empty flat, he would blow his brains out. To this he adds the legalistic note: "Marriage is a sacrament. You don't just dissolve it like that." The attitudes of the detective and the husband do not touch, for they deal with different aspects of Mary's personality as well as with different aspects of McLeod's. The conflict of "principle" and "love" cannot be resolved on these grounds.

A complicating factor in the presentation of McLeod's dilemma is Kingsley's characterization of the wife. The reviewers have called attention to deficiencies: "Few key characters can have been more hazy than is the detective's wife as Mr. Kingsley has written her." [19] The difficulty with this characterization arises from two sources: first, Mary is the wife of a professional celibate; secondly, her counterpart in the detective-story cast of characters is conventionally a criminal type. Kingsley has to make an attractive character of a "bad" woman.

'Bad' women are those who cheat others and fool themselves, who try to escape from life. Usually they turn out to be nymphomaniacs—and here we come to a curious convention that [Raymond] Chandler shares with other writers of the tough American school. Such women are 'untouchable' even in an amoral, alcoholic world. And they are potential killers.[20]

Kingsley's heroine has the earmarks of this type. She lies to the Lieutenant; she has kept the truth from McLeod. When he confronts her with the facts and sardonically remarks, "My immaculate wife," she responds, "I never said I was." He answers, according to the convention: "You never said you weren't." (DS, p. 109.) The accusation which dissolves their marriage for good reflects the proverbial nymphomania of the bad-woman stereotype; McLeod asks her how many other men she has slept with. Mary is more than a potential killer; as McLeod sees it, she has murdered Giacoppetti's baby.[21] McLeod's view of her as detective follows the convention closely, and the justifications provided for her by the author are largely given to Joe and Brody, the humanitarians. For purposes of his message, the dianoia, Kingsley has to render her sympathetically, but again he is fighting the convention.

At the moment of reversal, Mary makes the tragic accusation. When she returns to the squad room to say goodbye, McLeod the husband is ready to forgive and forget, but the detective will not leave the husband alone. The lawyer tips the scale when he flings his wife's past into the detective's face: "Why don't you ask Mrs. McLeod if she can supply a corroborating witness?" McLeod may be able to forgive, but he can never forget:

McLeod. At an autopsy yesterday I watched the medical examiner saw off the top of a man's skull, take out the brain and hold it in his hand (he holds out his hand) like that.
Mary. Why are you telling me this?
McLeod. Because I'd give everything I own to be able to take out my brain and hold it under the faucet and wash away the dirty pictures you put there tonight. (DS, p. 140.)

Mary looked to McLeod for help and understanding, but found none. Now she turns on her husband and accuses *him* of corruption. He is a "cruel, vengeful man without a drop of ordinary human forgiveness"; he has a "rotten spot" growing in his brain. McLeod has claimed that he learned about evil from his father's cruelty to his mother; Mary points out to him: "You're everything you've always said you hated in your own father." (DS, p. 141.) Because of the rotten spot, McLeod is also capable of murder. Mary's final retort, which cuts off any further discussion, makes this point: he would take her home only to kill her "the way your father killed your mother." The wheel comes full circle; guilt is fixed on the detective. The guardian of justice and protector of innocence is discovered to be himself evil. The last criminal to come to light is the detective himself.

The detective's end dramatizes his mission, his guilt, his insight about himself. He dies under Charley's gun, attacking evil outside, and at the same time destroying the evil within himself. The four-time loser, who personifies evil by anybody's standards, has managed to steal the unwary Callahan's gun and vows to take five or six with him. McLeod jumps at him with a cry: "You evil son-of-a-bitch!" Charley shoots him down. With the bullets in his stomach, McLeod calls for Arthur's prints and tears them up.

McLeod. Give me Buster's prints. I don't know. I hope you're right, Lou. Maybe he'll come in tomorrow with a murder rap. I don't know any more. We have no case here, Lieutenant. The complainant withdrew. (DS, p. 146.)

The detective is no longer willing to judge guilt and innocence.

McLeod does not throw over his principles, but he no longer is sure that he can recognize evil. He did not recognize it in himself. He follows this admission of fallibility with his "confession." Guilt is no longer a simple concept. He confesses in the area of personal guilt: "Oh, my God, I am heartily sorry." The police-station situation makes the Act of Contrition a "confession" in both senses, and this interpretation is illustrated in the action—while one detective calls for a priest, the Lieutenant notifies the homicide squad. In this final scene the detective turns out to be, not the "perfect" hero— Sam Spade or Philip Marlowe, but a vulnerable, fallible man. When Brody tries to cheer him up by casting him with the "immortals, the indestructibles," McLeod replies, "Almost, Lou, almost." (DS, p. 146.) In this final scene the hero is human and his world the complex world of human experiences. He dies carrying out his mission, with full knowledge of his limitations and in expiation of his crime.

The strong point in Kingsley's use of the detective story conventions is also the weak point of the drama. In terms of the convention, McLeod falls because he has violated the code of the detective-hero; he became involved with society by marrying. More significantly for the drama, the use of the conventional guilt-figure in the tragic pattern creates two McLeods, the detective and the husband. Kingsley is not able to meld them into a single persona. McLeod the policeman is a consistent character; McLeod the husband never really appears. Kingsley tries to describe him through telephone calls, through Joe's concern and Brody's reminiscences, through McLeod's own dialogue. But this facet of the persona is never brought into dramatic focus. The audience is asked to take the word of others that this tender, kind, loving McLeod does exist, but it never sees this McLeod in action. To present him, Kingsley would have had to transmute the conventional detective-hero; instead, he simply tries to superimpose the husband on the stereotype.

The thesis element in *Detective Story* also poses a similar difficulty; it is responsible for what the *Time* reviewer called "hokum." [22] The rhetorical bias of the McLeod-Feinson debate, the Arthur-Susan love story, the feeble attempt to blame McLeod's intolerance on an unhappy childhood constitute the dianoia of the play; Kingsley attempts to slant it toward the police-state allegory. But the conflict which is embedded in the structure of the play is focused, not on society's difficulties with the totalitarian idealist, but on the internal struggle of the protagonist, imperfectly realized as that struggle is. McLeod is the central figure and he is a sympathetic hero; at the catastrophe he dies fighting evil, without and within himself. The rhetorical attempts to make McLeod's position an image of totalitarianism are wiped out by the intrinsic bias of the detective-hero myth and by the stature which the hero's dedication confers on him.

The tragic pattern of purgation for the individual is flawed by the two irreconciled facets of the McLeod persona, but it does manage to function, even under the welter of episodes. Structurally, the play has an obvious resemblance to *Oedipus Rex,* the classic exemplar of tragedy. Fergusson has pointed out the "murder mystery" surface of *Oedipus:*

At the literal level, the play is intelligible as a murder mystery. Oedipus takes the role of District Attorney; and when he at last convicts himself, we have a twist, a coup de thêâtre, of unparalleled excitement.

But no one who sees or reads the play can rest content with its literal coherence. Questions as to its meaning arise at once: Is Oedipus really guilty, or simply a victim of the gods, of his famous complex, of fate, of original sin? How much did he know all along? [23]

The resemblance between Kingsley's play and *Oedipus* goes deeper than surface detail. Both embody what Kenneth Burke has called "the tragic rhythm" of poiema, pathema, mathema. The hero commits himself (or is committed) to a course of action or purpose, because of that commitment he suffers, through his suffering he comes to an insight about himself. The moment of insight, the epiphany, purges the hero, releases him from the burden of his tabu-violation. McLeod has undertaken this kind of commitment, it brings him mental anguish, he discovers his own guilt. But the difference between McLeod and Oedipus pivots on the nature of the detective story formula. In the world of detective fiction, the hero is a god who is immortal, invulnerable and impeccable, a Platonic figure who must remain outside the society he protects. By definition the detective cannot be also the criminal. On the other hand, Oedipus the King is a member of the society he rules and husband to Jocasta. These three aspects of his character are part of his persona; he is at once king, citizen, husband. The same laws that operate for any member of society also operate for him. Thus, for example, the same force of character and tenacity of purpose that brought him to the throne and to his mother's bed strike him down. McLeod, on the other hand, operates on two different sets of principles; his commitment as detective is not *necessarily* related to his commitment as husband. And once he discovers his own guilt, the detective story formula breaks down completely. It provides no resources by which the detective can purge himself. Kingsley attempts to integrate the detective-hero and the husband, but the conventional pattern defeats his purpose.

Paradoxically, the naturalistic technique for which Kingsley is praised by the reviewers contributes to this failure. The police-station situation prevents him from dramatizing McLeod the husband; the moving hands of the on-stage clock demand a realistic chronological presentation that does not allow for the exploration of McLeod's past or his home life. So Kingsley is obliged to substitute exposition for dramatization—Brody and Joe and Mary talk about

McLeod the husband, but the audience never sees him in action. This is not simply a question of the dramatist's selecting an inept technique; the "naturalistic" approach confines the dramatist's presentation to the tangible, the external, the evidential. This approach suits the detective mystery because the only issue is "whodunit," and the only perspective the quasi-scientific concern with footprints under the window, the estimated time of the murder, the tell-tale open door. The dimension of human responsibility, motivation and moral guilt, with its complexity and obscurity, is not provided for within this framework.

For all these shortcomings, *Detective Story* does include a basic pattern of human experience; guilt and purgation presented through an adaptation of a popular formula. The flaws in the play are all too apparent; it does suffer from small literalness and cluttered realism. The flux of "naturalistic" episodes, the biased rhetoric, the melodramatic tone of the conclusion obscure the main movement of the play, and Kingsley's pretentious allegorizing does not help. But the figure of the hero and the hero's agon work from a conventional form to catch in a clear angle of vision one version of the ideal American and his problem. McLeod's dilemma shows the folk hero with his strengths and his weaknesses, coming face to face with an internal difficulty. The folk hero is seldom caught in such a pose; he has, in Leo Gurko's words, "seldom been projected into situations requiring anything more from him than a physical response." [24] Kingsley's failure to integrate the two facets of the hero is a failure of the imagination, an inability to transmute the crude form, but it is a failure in the right direction. The pattern of detective fiction did not provide the means for completely humanizing the hero, and Kingsley stayed too close to the pattern to discover his own means. His use of the detective-story structure and cast of characters, however, illustrates the dramatic power of the popular form and the attitudes it expresses. McLeod, the detective, pursues his purpose, learns of his guilt, dies fighting the evil in the world and the evil in himself. Though the psychological resources of his character are limited, more than a physical response has been required of him, and he responds to the best of his ability. When he goes down under Charley's gun, something like a tragic effect is achieved on the American stage.

6

Acres of Diamonds:
Death of a Salesman

The most salient quality of Arthur Miller's tragedy of the common man *Death of a Salesman* is its Americanism. This quality in the play is demonstrated by the contrasting reactions of American and English reviewers. The English took the hero at face value and found little of interest in his person or his plight:

There is almost nothing to be said for Loman who lies to himself as to others, has no creed or philosophy of life beyond that of making money by making buddies, and cannot even be faithful to his helpful and long-suffering wife.[1]

Brooks Atkinson, on the other hand, thought Willy "a good man who represents the homely, decent, kindly virtues of a middle-class society."[2] The Englishman treats Willy without regard for his American context, the New York reviewer sees him as the representative of a large segment of American society. When the literary critics measure the play against Greek and Elizabethan drama, they agree with the English evaluation; the hero seems inadequate. His lack of stature, his narrow view of reality, his obvious character defects diminish the scope of the action and the possibilities of universal application.[3] Against a large historical perspective and without the American context, the salesman is a "small man" who fails to cope with his environment. But for better or worse, Miller's hero is not simply an individual who has determined on an objective and who strives desperately to attain it; he is also representative of an American type, the Salesman, who has accepted an ideal shaped for him and pressed on him by forces in his culture. This ideal is the matrix from which Willy emerges and by which his destiny is deter-

127

mined. It is peculiarly American in origin and development—seed, flower and fruit. For Arthur Miller's salesman is a personification of the success myth; he is committed to its objectives and defined by its characteristics. *Salesman* deals with the Horatio Alger ideal, the rags-to-riches romance of the American dream.

The success myth is not concealed beneath the facade of the action; it is used consciously by the playwright in depicting the plot-situation, in drawing the hero, in arranging the events of the action. Thoughtful American reviewers and critics got the point:

Success is a requirement Americans make of life. Because it seems magical, and inexplicable, as it is to Willy, it can be considered the due of every free citizen, even those with no notable or measurable talents. . . . The citizen may justly and perhaps even logically ask—if Edison, Goodrich, and Red Grange can make it, why not me, why not Willy Loman? [4] AM DR

Willy's quest for the secret of success is central to the drama. By choosing this focus for his play, Miller is drawing on the popular mind and a popular formula from which he shapes his dramatic form.

The attitudes which the myth expresses have a long history in American culture. The success myth, as Max Weber has demonstrated, has roots in seventeenth-century bourgeois England; it came to this continent with the founding fathers and was later popularized by the efforts of Ben Franklin, its outstanding exemplar. The "land of opportunity" offered enough verification of the basic tenets of the doctrine to assure its triumph in the popular mind. Virgin land, undeveloped resources, the possibility of industrial progress, all allowed scope for enterprise and imagination. No man lacked an enterprise to turn his hand to. The successful man became the idol of the public; the road to success was pointed out from the pulpit, in the marketplace, by the family fireside. From Franklin through the nineteenth century and well into the twentieth, the success myth, and all the possible variations on it, did not lack prophets and interpreters.

The success ideology developed a basic outline in the early Colonial period and its essential shape has not changed appreciably since. The Franklin image of the hard-working, early-rising, self-disciplined, ambitious adventurer engaged the public imagination in

1758 when *Poor Richard* included Father Abraham Weatherwise's monologue on "The Way to Wealth." [5] The proverbs from the 1758 *Poor Richard* passed into the texture of the American language: "Early to bed . . . Never leave till tomorrow that which you can do today." Emerson's doctrine of self-reliance fitted neatly into this pattern; the great lecturer subscribed to the theory that the thirst for wealth and the drive to power were essential to the growth of civilization.[6] The correlation between the success ideology and the Protestant ethic has been dealt with in earlier chapters; it suffices to recall that material success was taken to be the tangible sign of God's blessing and the reward of virtue.

In the latter half of the nineteenth century the alliance between religion and business took a curious turn. Business no longer received the benediction of religion, rather religion was described in terms of business. The servant became the master in that strange cultural reversal that has been described by Will Herberg. "Organized" religion passed into the hands of the corporation; the culture began to control the religious concepts. Clergymen found no disparity between the acquisition of riches and Christianity; indeed, they were delighted to find they went hand in hand. Russell H. Conwell, a Baptist preacher and the founder of Temple University in Philadelphia, traveled over the country, preaching this gospel. His celebrated lecture *Acres of Diamonds* was delivered in large cities and at whistle-stops 5,124 times between 1870 and 1915. The central illustration in *Acres* is the story of the Arab who journeyed the world over in search of diamonds, while his successor on the farm found acres of diamonds in his own backyard. The industrious, the honest, the determined man can mine diamonds at home, in the city, wherever he is; this is Conwell's message.

The men and women sitting here, who found it difficult perhaps to buy a ticket to this lecture or gathering to-night, have within their reach "acres of diamonds," opportunities to get largely wealthy. Never in the history of the world did a poor man without capital have such an opportunity to get rich quickly and honestly as he has now in our city.[7]

Conwell is content to show that religion and business are not opposed, that religion encourages men to get rich. Ten years later Bruce Barton reduced this kind of argument to an absurdity in his life of Jesus, *The Man Nobody Knows*. The Savior, Barton proclaimed, is an epitome of success, the greatest corporate leader and the most successful advertising man the world has ever seen. He is a man of great personal magnetism, possessed of all the qualities that mark the successful executive. The wheel comes full circle when Jesus becomes a Nazarene Carnegie, and Christianity is defined in terms of United States Steel.

Today, the author whose name is most closely linked with the dream of success is Horatio Alger, another clergyman, who embodied the myth in his novels. Alger caught the quintessence of the dream and developed a formula in which to express it. The ragged urchin, bootblack or newspaper boy of humble origin capitalizes on his opportunities and, by "pluck and luck," rises to the top of the economic heap. Alger made this formula an American byword.

Like many simple formulations which nevertheless convey a heavy intellectual and emotional charge to vast numbers of people, the Alger hero represents a triumphant combination—and reduction to the lowest common denominator—of the most widely accepted concepts in nineteenth-century American society. The belief in the potential greatness of the common man, the glorification of individual effort and accomplishment, the equation of the pursuit of money with the pursuit of happiness and of business success with spiritual grace: simply to mention these concepts is to comprehend the brilliance of Alger's synthesis.[8]

Alger converted the attitude that canonized the successful businessman into a popular literary formula, the rags-to-riches romance. His heroes, often with a boost from Fortune in their background (Tom the bootblack is really the disinherited son of a successful businessman), rise to the top by seizing opportunity by the forelock, by being industrious, thrifty, devout (but not pious), common-sensical. They are likeable chaps with a ready quip and a vigorous sense of humor. They have little trouble getting employment and, once in the shop, there is no stopping them. "Ragged Dick" and "Tom the Bootblack" have that aura around them; success is natural to personalities of their stripe. In Alger as for preachers like Conwell, the key to success is not genius or gentle breeding, but "character."

At best, successful methods were merely by-products of successful character. The business man who had the right personal qualities would have little difficulty in developing the necessary managerial skills, but the possession of no amount of skill could compensate for lack of character or other essential personal traits.[9]

All success literature, of which Alger's was the fictional apotheosis, assumed that the individual could pull himself up by his bootstraps. "The Creator made man a success-machine . . . and failure is as abnormal to him as discord to harmony."[10] The Alger hero had character; luck and pluck brought him inevitably from rags to riches.

Between 1868 and 1929 Alger's books sold ten million copies, and the people who did not read the books could hardly have been able to escape the aura of the name. With the boom of the 1920s authors like Babson and Marsden and Bruce Barton kept the success doctrine before the eyes of the public. Whether they advocated success as the reward of virtue or as the result of strength or as the consequent of personality, their position was essentially the same. The secret lies inside the individual character. The emphasis can shift from one personal quality to another, but there is never any doubt where the quality is found. Moreover, if Christianity can be defined by business concepts, "virtue" can easily be reduced to "personality." The "miracles" of Jesus, according to Barton, reside in his personal magnetism. Thus, before the god Opportunity, all are equal. Those mysterious internal qualities of character—"virtue," "personality,"—become the charismatic gifts that are prayed for by the true believer and, when found, are acknowledged as the work of the Spirit. This myth, deep-seated in the American consciousness, provides the raw material for *Death of a Salesman*.

The success myth, in the hands of the playwright, becomes the model for the events of the plot, the situation and the character of the hero, but Miller uses this model in order to subvert it. His play is an anti-myth, the rags-to-riches formula in reverse so that it becomes the story of a failure in terms of success, or better, the story of the failure of the success myth. The events of the play are a mirror-image of the hero's progress. Willy Loman's history begins at the end of the line; instead of the young, determined bootblack an exhausted salesman enters, carrying, along with his sample cases, sixty years of uphill struggle. The subsequent events show him failing to overcome each obstacle, just as he has failed to achieve the phantom success he has pursued his life long. He returns from a trip without making a single sale, he braces the boss for a New York job and a salary raise (like the Alger hero) and is fired for his pains; his "boys," now well out of boyhood, make the big play for high stakes according to their father's teaching and fail. Willy finishes by facing the harsh fact that his whole life has been a lie. The triumphal ascent of the Alger hero is reversed in every particular. The rags-to-riches dream never materializes, and the salesman never escapes his rags. The race with the junkyard finds Willy an also-ran. In the collapse of the salesman, Miller attempts to illustrate the collapse of the myth.

Death of a Salesman encompasses two dimensions—the dream-world of the success myth with its merging of past triumphs, indications of glory to come, glimmering possibilities and the actual world of the small, brick-enclosed house in Brooklyn. To achieve this merger, Miller uses an expressionistic setting, a skeletonized house which symbolizes the encroachment of urban economics on the family. The "one-dimensional" roof is surrounded on all sides by a "solid vault of apartment houses." The walls of the Loman home are cut away to permit free passage to the personae in dream and reminiscence sequences. This device, along with changes in lighting, allows for a condensation of time so that the life of the family can be encompassed by the action. "An air of the dream clings to the place, a dream rising out of reality." [11] The expressionistic technique—the use of typical personae, a symbolic setting, mobility in time—follows on the mythic focus of the playwright's vision. Miller himself is conscious of the possibilities of this technique and its significance; he defines expressionism: "The stage is stripped of knick-knacks; instead it reveals symbolic *designs* which function as overt pointers toward the moral to be drawn from the action." [12] The freedom which this technique supplies allows the playwright to express the salesman's dream and his experiences in the context of the dream. The flashbacks in the course of the action can be considered hallucinatory, and the salesman can be played as mentally unbalanced, but such an interpretation takes actuality as the norm and loses sight of the mythical dimension. [13] Any attempt to decide which elements of the play are "real" and which "unreal" is as futile as trying to sort out the "historical" elements in any myth. The mythical attitude and Willy's experiences form one texture; they are the warp and woof of the salesman's world.

The typical characteristics of the Willy Loman persona establish him in the tradition of the mythical hero, or in *Salesman,* in the tradition of the anti-hero. The name is descriptive; Willy is "low man" on the economic and social totem-pole. Linda, his wife, who sees him clearly and sympathetically, calls him "a small man." He is a white-collar worker who works on salary and/or commission for a company, his economic future at the mercy of his employer. He does not show any marked intellectual capacity or training, and his wisdom, expressed in platitudes, is garnered from common-sense authorities. When he is away from home, his moral life functions according to the "traveling salesman" tradition, not excluding the clandestine affair or the blue joke. He does not, however, consider himself dissolute; according to his lights, he is honest enough. For better or worse, the salesman is intended to represent the average lower-middle-class American.

The antecedents of the salesman are also typical. For a man who resides in Brooklyn, the family background which Miller gives his hero stretches the imagination. In a sequence with Ben, Willy remembers his father, a man with a big beard who played the flute. His father, too, was a traveling salesman:

Ben. Father was a very great and very wild-hearted man. We would start in Boston, and he'd toss the whole family into the wagon and then he'd drive the team right across the country; through Ohio and Indiana, Michigan, Illinois and all the Western states. And we'd stop in the towns and sell the flutes that he'd made on the way. Great inventor, Father. With one gadget he made more than a man like you could make in a lifetime. (SALESMAN, p. 49.)

The father disappeared one day when Willy was a baby, following the Yukon gold-strike. He lived many years in Alaska, and Willy had a yearning to join him there. (SALESMAN, p. 85.) This is the stock from which Willy and his boys are sprung, American stock with a penchant for traveling and selling. This background fits an idealized model rather than any plausible or realistic family-tree.[14] As typical character, the salesman has a typical background; he envisions his origin in terms of the American experience. It is one version of the idealized experience of the race.

Willy's status in society, his family background are typical; even more of a type is Willy's identity as Salesman. He is a product of a producer-consumer society in which the go-between is a pivotal figure. Society has labeled him, and Willy has accepted the label; society has offered Willy a set of values and an objective, and Willy has committed himself to those values and that objective. In so accepting, Willy becomes THE Salesman. He cannot define himself in any other terms. So he insists in his debate with Charley that "he has a job," that he is the "New England man," even after he has been fired. His adherence to the cult of personality, of being "well liked," is a reflection of his identity; before he can sell anything and if he can sell nothing else, he must sell himself, his own personality. He has been shaped by a society that believed steadily and optimistically in the myth of success, and he has become the agent and the representative of that society.

[handwritten margin note: No Big funer no one came.]

This image of the Salesman includes the image of an older, freer America. Before the frontier closed down and the apartments closed in, before business became an impersonal, corporate endeavor, opportunity knocked incessantly. For Willy (and for the audience), the achievement possible in this earlier society is typified by Uncle Ben, the shadowy figure who appears out of nowhere, to the accompaniment of flute music, on his way to new capitalistic triumphs. Whether Ben is a projection of Willy's imagination or a real figure out of the family history is irrelevant; his function in the action does not depend on his "reality." He comes from an idealized past; he is the robber baron, the captain of industry. Ben carries with him the aura of success, and when he visits, it is only for a few minutes between expeditions. There are diamond mines in Africa, timberlands in Alaska, and mysterious appointments in Ketchikan which demand his attention. Ben's methods are illustrated in a sparring match with Biff. He is physically strong—Biff can hit him in the stomach with impunity. He is ruthless—the sparring ends abruptly when Ben suddenly trips the boy and poises the point of his umbrella over Biff's eye. "Never fight fair with a stranger, boy. You'll never get out of the jungle that way." (SALESMAN, p. 49.) This is the code of the self-made man.

Ben possesses the precious secret to success. It is summarized in his ritual chant, the formula which sums up his accomplishment: "When I was seventeen I walked into the jungle, and when I was twenty-one I walked out. And by God I was rich." (SALESMAN, p. 48.) What happened in the jungle is never explained. It is the mystery of success, the Eleusinian rite known only to initiates. Uncle Ben is the older version of the Salesman, the ruthless capitalist whose adventurous strength ripped riches from the frontier. To Willy, Uncle Ben is the palpable proof of his doctrine.

While the shadowy figure of Ben establishes the general truth that any man can succeed, Willy does not accept (or perhaps has no chance to accept) Ben's method. Ben represents the robber baron who travels out to unknown frontiers and ruthlessly carves out an empire. As Ben's method has faded with the passing of the empire builders and with the advent of the big corporations, Willy decides to rely on personality:

> It's not what you do, Ben. It's who you know and the smile on your face! It's contacts, Ben, contacts! The whole wealth of Alaska passes over the lunch table at the Commodore Hotel, and that's the wonder, the wonder of this country, that a man can end with diamonds here on the basis of being well liked. (SALESMAN, p. 86.)

This quality cannot be held in the hand like Ben's timber, but on the other hand, Ben's own formula—his inner strength and ruthlessness—is also mysterious. Willy accepts the Dale Carnegie approach to success; winning friends and influencing people become his pick and shovel to dig diamonds as industriously as Ben ever did. But Willy does not go off to Africa or Alaska, nor is his confidence in a transcendentally virtuous life. His faith in personality conceals the secret in an imponderable and makes that faith untestable by any pragmatic standard. The dream of success, in the eyes of the playwright, is the more destructive because, though indemonstrable, it has a myth-like capacity for inspiring a transcendent belief.

There are, however, certain tangible signs which characterize the personality likely to succeed. Willy discovers them in his sons. The boys are physically strong, well-built, attractive. Biff is a football hero, the captain of the high school team; Happy, if not gifted with Biff's athletic ability, has a pleasant personality and basks in Biff's reflected glory. Against this picture of the glowing athlete and the hail fellow, Bernard, the neighbor's boy, wears glasses, studies hard, and is not well liked. If physical prowess and a moderate anti-intellectualism seemed to have little to do with success, the propagators of the success ideology saw an intimate connection:

Statistics show that executives are physically stronger and larger of stature than their subordinates. For example, college presidents, as a class, are taller and heavier than the college professors. Bank presidents are physically stronger than the clerks. Railway presidents are larger and physically stronger than the employees. . . . Physical welfare is the second qualification for winning the race of making good.[15]

Biff does not have to work hard at his studies; books are not necessary for advancement. Bernard, whose scholastic efforts are the object of mild derision, supplies Biff with answers and this is only right, the homage due the personable and popular. When, in spite of Bernard's help, Biff fails in math, Willy blames the teacher. Willy shows a typical ambivalence toward education. On the one hand, attendance at college confers prestige, especially when coupled with an athletic career; on the other, education does not really make an appreciable difference in the struggle to succeed. Some self-help advocates maintained that college was actually harmful to a young man's chances. It undermined those rugged personal qualities demanded by a career by an overemphasis on the development of the mind, it fostered an interest in impractical humanistic matters, it devoured the best years of a man's life.[16] The salesman finds in his sons those qualities which point toward success. As high-school boys, they are leaders, popular with the crowd, athletic and handsome. Their present status as philandering clerk and wandering farmhand cannot erase the glory of their past potential as Willy experienced it. "A star like that, magnificent, can never really fade away." (SALESMAN, p. 68).

Willy's commitment to the success ideology directed the education of his sons. Even if success passes him by, he can still look forward to a vindication of his life in them. They have been instructed in the clichés of both the "virtue" and the "personality" school. Industry is important: whatever else can be said about Biff, he is a "hard worker." One of Willy's fondest reminiscences is the high sheen the boys kept on the red Chevvy. If Biff "gets tired" hanging around, he can paint the new ceiling in the living room. Willy's aphorisms emphasize the importance of industry and perseverance: "Never leave a job till you're finished." "The world is an oyster, but you don't crack it open on a mattress." But personality has its privileges and Willy can wink at the boys' faults in the name of personality. Biff has been a thief from his high-school days; he steals a football from the locker-room and lumber from a local construction job. Willy laughs at both thefts because they reveal the power of personality and a fearless competitiveness like Ben's. "Coach will probably congratulate you on your initiative. . . . That's because he likes you. If somebody else took the ball there'd be an uproar." (SALESMAN, p. 30.) When Charley warns Willy that the watchman will catch the boys at their thieving, Willy avers that, though he gave them hell, the boys are "a couple of fearless characters." When Charley responds that the jails are full of fearless characters, Ben adds that the Stock Exchange is also. The boys have been brought up to respect the success ideology; their success will be the salesman's vindication.

In the chronological present of the play Willy's fortunes are at low ebb. His faith in the myth is tested by harsh realities which he alternately faces and flees. He fights to hold on to his identity. This means holding on to his faith, and, in the name of faith, Willy lies constantly: about the gross sales he has made, about the reaction of businessmen to his personality, about his boys' success and importance, about his own prospects. These lies echo, not the drab reality about him, but the shining hope he has. From the observer's point of view established in the play through Charley and Linda, they are pathetic efforts to protect his identity. Willy is unfaithful to his long-suffering wife, but this infidelity is an assuagement of his loneliness on the road, a restorative to his flagging spirits, and a provision against the rebuffs of the day. When he momentarily faces reality—his inability to drive to Boston, the mounting bills and the dwindling income—he has to flee to the past and to project the future. The salesman cannot abandon the myth without reducing himself to zero. Thus he must hope.

Perpetual optimism, then, is not so much a piece of transparent self-deception as it is a necessary quality of his personality. It can be associated with the kind of wishful hoping that underlies the entire American business operation, an indefatigable spirit of the-impossible-takes-a-little-longer.

Basically this optimism represents no precise philosophical position at all, but rather a studiously cultivated sense of euphoria. It is an emotional attitude marked by a tendency to emphasize the brighter side of things. . . . It is an effusive and expansive attitude. In the business world one of its typical manifestations is the conviction that there is no assignable limit to business opportunities, that markets need not remain static but are constantly open to further development, even with territory geographically limited. It is somewhat beside the point to ask if Americans believe in this optimism. It is not a thing you believe in. It is in the air. It is felt. It has its effect, whether you elect to believe in it or not.[17]

Miller has not left this optimism hanging in the air; he weaves it into his hero's personality. Happy's diagnosis is accurate: "Dad is never so happy as when he's looking forward to something!" (SALES-MAN, p. 105.) When Willy is lost, disturbed, hanging on the ropes, he demands that this hope be fed: "The gist of it is I haven't got a story [*read:* 'lie'] left in my head, Biff. So don't give me a lecture about facts and aspects. I am not interested. Now what've you got to say?" (SALESMAN, p. 107.) Willy must have hope because it sustains him; when identity is at stake, there are matters more important than facts and aspects.

The plot structure of *Salesman* dramatizes the failure of the myth by depicting the past and present failures of the salesman. Events in the chronological present are germinations of seeds sown in the past; both present and past are inextricably bound together in Willy's consciousness:

Linda. And Willy—if it's warm Sunday we'll drive in the country. And we'll open the windshield and take lunch.
Willy. No, the windshields don't open on the new cars.
Linda. But you opened it today.
Willy. Me? I didn't. (He stops.) Now isn't that peculiar! Isn't that a remarkable—(He breaks off in amazement and fright as the flute is heard distantly.) . . . I was thinking of the Chevvy. (Slight pause.) Nineteen twenty-eight . . . when I had that red Chevvy—(Breaks off.) That funny? I coulda sworn I was driving that Chevvy today. (SALES-MAN, p. 19.)

Miller builds up a sense of fate in his drama by showing the impingement of the unalterable past upon the present. Willy's whole life has been shaped by his commitment to the success ideology, his dream based on the Alger myth; his present plight is shown to be the inevitable consequence of this commitment.

What is perhaps less frequently stressed is the bearing of the past-present relationship on the metaphysical content of tragedy. It is probably true to say that the greater proportion of the 'past' that is allowed to impinge upon, or to modify, the present, the easier it is to give the impression of a rigid or semi-rigid structure enclosing the action, and the larger the apparent content of determinism.[18]

Just as the hero's commitment comes to him as a heritage of the American past, so his sorry situation at sixty comes of his early life. Except for the deceptive expanse of time, there is no real difference in the salesman's life then and now.

The events of the first act—past and present—contrapose optimism and harsh reality. In the chronological present Willy is a tired drummer and his boys are mediocre also-rans, a clerk and a farmhand, both over thirty. Biff and Happy are lost and confused by their failure to get ahead, and Willy is at the end of his rope because he can't even drive a car any more. Willy's return home after the abortive trip is contrasted with his return in the "good old days." Then he came home to the security of his boys' adulation, bringing with him the glamor of the traveler and his own ebullient interpretation of the trip. He is proud of his boys and their potential sustains him.

Willy. Bernard can get the best marks in school, y'understand, but when he gets out in the business world, y'understand, you are going to be five times ahead of him. That's why I thank Almighty God you're both built like Adonises. Because the man who makes an appearance in the business world, the man who creates personal interest, is the man who gets ahead. Be liked and you will never want. (SALESMAN, p. 33.)

Willy "knocked 'em cold in Providence, slaughtered 'em in Boston." The patois of the rugged sportsman, of the prize ring, flavors Willy's speech and plants the image of the ideal career in his sons. It is reflected in the chronological present by Happy's wildly impractical scheme to recoup the Loman fortune. On the basis of the idea, they lay "big plans":

Happy. Wait a minute! I got an idea. I got a feasible idea. Come here, Biff, let's talk this over now, let's talk some sense here. . . . You and I,

Biff—we have a line, the Loman line. We train a couple of weeks, and put on a couple of exhibitions, see? . . . We play each other. It's a million dollars' worth of publicity. Two brothers, see? The Loman Brothers. Displays in the Royal Palms—all the hotels. And banners over the ring and the basketball court: "Loman Brothers." Baby, we could sell sporting goods!

Willy. That is a one-million-dollar idea! (SALESMAN, p. 63.)

This scheme is generated out of the heart of the myth. "Loman Brothers" has, for Willy and the boys, the ring of personality and solidarity and achievement. It would not entail entering the impersonal arena of the office; the "boys" would be "out playin' ball again." With no regular hours to cramp their freedom and no fierce outside competition, there would be "the old honor and comradeship." Sportsmanship, clean living, economic freedom would blend in a million-dollar enterprise, the ideal life crowned with financial achievement. Only the glowing pair who ran to carry their father's valises and to listen to his prideful predictions would consider such a scheme "talking sense." It is significant that Happy makes the proposal; he is Willy's double without Willy's excuse, a liar and a philanderer. The flashback sequence explains the optimism the "big plan" generates.

Willy's reminiscences also cast another shadow over the present prospect. His version of the sales trip to young Biff and Hap is contrasted with the version he gives Linda. Bills have piled up and if business "don't pick up I don't know what I'm gonna do!" Willy confesses to his wife that people laugh at him, that he is not noticed, that he talks too much and laughs too loudly so that people don't respect him. (SALESMAN, pp. 36–37.) On the road, alone and assailed with doubts, without his wife and his sons to bolster his ego, he turns to the Woman. She picked Willy out, she likes him, he makes her laugh. Willy's problems are no different in the present, except that the financial crisis looms larger and the philandering has passed over to Happy. But in the first act all difficulties, past and present, are smoothed over by a pervading optimism.

Under the spell of the dream, Biff determines to see Bill Oliver, a former employer, and ask for financial backing. Family legend has refined his theft of basketballs from the firm out of existence and converted his position from shipping clerk into salesman. This prospect raises Willy's hopes; the dream can convert the possibility into triumphant actuality. "I see great things for you kids, I think your troubles are over." Given this incentive, the salesman determines to ask for a place in New York for himself, for an office job that would take him off the road. Personality yet may carry the day.

At the outset of the second act the hopes of the evening carry over to the following morning. The boys have departed "nice and early"; "early to rise" and "the early bird" are good omens. As he considers the actual burdens of the moment, however, Willy's spirits begin to slide. His description of the consumer's fate has a symbolic reference to his own life.

> Whoever heard of a Hastings refrigerator? Once in my life I would like to own something outright before it's broken! I'm always in a race with the junkyard! I just finished paying for the car and it's on its last legs. The refrigerator consumes belts like a goddam maniac. They time those things. They time them so when you've finally paid for them, they're used up. (SALESMAN, p. 73.)

Earlier, it was made clear that Willy bought this brand because the company displayed the largest ads and, from the day of installation, the box chewed up belts. The battle of the Hastings (with Willy on the Anglo-Saxon side) was lost from the start. This discussion is a forecast of Willy's fate in the coming interview. The morning hope is somewhat revived when Linda gives him something to look forward to: the boys are going to "blow him to a big dinner." In anticipation of a victory celebration, the salesman goes off to his job-interview with renewed confidence.

The interview incidents are central to the movement of the second act. They contrast with the typical interview of the Alger formula. For the Alger hero, this is the first rung on the ladder of success. The young bootblack or newsboy immediately engages the prospective employer's attention and impresses him with his intelligence, sensible adjustment to circumstances, industry, self-confidence, and honesty. Willy and Biff fail to impress on all points. Willy's employer, some years the salesman's junior—"I named him Howard" —has not the time to listen to Willy's reminiscences. He is preoccupied with industry's newest gadget, a wire recorder. The impersonal business world no longer has any room for personality among

Personality
Lost

the machines. In a reversal of the Alger formula, the salesman's rambling convinces Howard that the company has no more use for him. He has outlived his limited usefulness, and the upshot is that Willy is summarily fired. Biff's interview is even more disastrous. He cannot even get inside the office, and far from demonstrating his honesty, he steals Oliver's fountain pen for no reason he can fathom. In terms of structure, the interview episodes, one witnessed and the other reported, are dramatizations of the failure of the myth as Willy understood it and preached it to his sons.

Their respective experiences produce different reactions in father and son. It is the pressure of past experience that is invoked to explain the difference. Willy cannot understand his defeat even when Charley, the good neighbor, spells it out for him:

When're you gonna realize that them things don't mean anything? You named him Howard, but you can't sell that. The only thing you got in this world is what you can sell. And the funny thing is that you're a salesman, and you don't know that. (SALESMAN, p. 97.)

At this late date, there is no chance that the salesman will be able to distinguish the marketable from the mythical. Moreover, he still preserves the hope of Biff's success and the prospect of the big dinner. To a man a little less the salesman than Willy, his chance meeting with Bernard, Charley's son and the high-school follower, would raise a rash of doubts. But Willy can only, in desperation, ask Bernard, who is off to try a case before the Supreme Court, about the secret of success. The lawyer does not volunteer any advice except not to worry about it. "Sometimes, Willy, it's better for a man just to walk away." (SALESMAN, p. 95.) Willy cannot walk away; he affirms his faith in his sons.

The meeting in the restaurant is an ironic reversal of the "victory" banquet. Biff's experience, as he relates it to Happy, has convinced him that his whole life has been "a ridiculous lie." He is determined to get the facts out in the open, but habit is not so easily broken. The salesman refuses to listen to "facts and aspects"; he *will* have a celebration of the glorious future. When it becomes clear that Biff will not cooperate in the lie and that Willy cannot face the truth, the Loman boys react according to the pattern. They run away from the failure their father has become and from their own failure.

They leave the old man babbling in the rest room and go off with two prostitutes. Happy is responding to his training when he denies his father before one of the floozies:

> *Letta.* Don't you want to tell your father—
> *Happy.* No, that's not my father. He's just a guy. Come on, we'll catch Biff, and, honey, we're going to paint this town. (SALESMAN, pp. 115–16.)

Happy cannot hear the cock crow; this unhappy wandering old man is not *his* father. Willy's own teaching and example flow back on his own head.

Bracketed within the restaurant sequence are two crucial past events, also the fruit of teaching and example. Biff's failure with Oliver is related to his failure in math and his flight to Boston. Relying on personality, Biff had mimicked the effeminate instructor to his face and had cut the class for football practice. In spite of Bernard's help on the exam, he lacked four points of passing, and the instructor refuses to make a concession. When the boy runs to seek his father's help, he finds the Woman in Willy's hotel room. His idol crumbles; his father is "a phoney little fake." The traveling-salesman joke becomes a traumatic experience for the boy, driving his disillusion deep and preparing him for his present insight. Biff sees the affair as a betrayal of Linda, the family and the home. The image of husband and father is broken when Willy gives the Woman "Mama's stockings." But Willy does not understand Biff's reaction; what he does on the road has no connection with his home-life. Thus all he feels is the weight of his son's disapproval. Biff has ruined his life "for spite." Willy's firing, Biff's panic at Oliver's, are linked with Biff's high-school failure and Willy's inability to cope with his boy's disillusion in the Boston hotel room.

The climactic scene in the second act is the confrontation of father and son. Because he suspects the truth, Willy is unwilling to face Biff or Linda. But this time Biff is not to be put off: "The man don't know who we are! The man is gonna know! (To Willy) We never told the truth for ten minutes in this house." Willy is no longer Salesman, no longer Father; Willy is "the man." The identity supplied by economic and familial society is stripped away and the issue is joined at rock bottom.

I am not a leader of men, Willy, and neither are you. You were never anything but a hard-working drummer who landed in the ash can like all the rest of them. I'm one dollar an hour, Willy! . . . Do you gather my meaning? I'm not bringing home any prizes any more, and you're going to stop waiting for me to bring them home. (SALESMAN, p. 132.)

But facts fall before faith and the salesman cannot admit such heresy. Willy knows who he is: "I am not a dime a dozen. I am Willy Loman, and you are Biff Loman." He simply cannot comprehend and, when Biff breaks down and sobs on his father's shoulder, Biff's emotional rapport destroys his point. There is the sudden revelation that Biff likes him; this the salesman can understand. The removal of Biff's disapproval rekindles the salesman's optimism —"that boy—that boy is going to be magnificent." In spite of all the explanations and because of the sudden emotional reunion, the myth endures. Whatever his failures on the road and in the office, Willy turns out to be "well-liked" by his alienated son.

With this realization and the resurgence of the myth, Brother Ben reappears. Ben's advice is now *ad hoc* and in the tradition of *Acres of Diamonds:* "It does take a great kind of man to crack the jungle. . . . The jungle is dark but full of diamonds. . . . One must go in to fetch a diamond out." (SALESMAN, pp. 133–134.) Ben's promise is the promise of all the self-help prophets of the nineteenth century. The salesman wanted to find his success in Brooklyn. Ben offers him his chance. There are "acres of diamonds" in his backyard. To achieve that success which thus far eluded him, Willy drives his car into the wall. In terms of the myth, his motivation is no different now than it was when he drove off to New England. His boy likes him and deserves the twenty thousand insurance money, the capital which will finally put him on the road to success. The success ideology is stronger than the reality, and he goes to his death with his goal sparkling before him.

The "success" structure in the play, as the critic immediately recognizes, is not the whole *Salesman* story. As the English critic sees Willy as a detestable little man, the American sees him as a pathetic figure who suffers deeply. The pathetic quality is produced by the playwright's emphasis on the culture that shaped the salesman's personality.[19] The pressures of economic growth in urban society created the salesman mystique and these same forces punish the unsuccessful inexorably. The 1929 crash impressed Miller greatly:

The hidden laws of fate lurked not only in the characters of people, but equally if not more imperiously in the world beyond the family parlor. Out there were the big gods, the ones whose disfavor could turn a proud and prosperous and dignified man into a frightened shell of a man whatever he thought of himself, and whatever he decided or didn't decide to do.[20]

These powers were economic crisis and political imperatives at whose mercy man found himself. The myth holds them at bay, overcomes them, puts the successful man out of their reach. As antihero, the salesman (and his family) is at their mercy. Timeinstallment buying, the enclosure of the house by apartments, the impersonal attitude of the executive illustrate these external forces. If these "hidden gods" decide to doom a generation, they can grind exceeding small. When the stock market crashed, once safe and happy millionaires left by the window. The common man does not control such a phenomenon, and the success myth does not take such catastrophes into account. Willy's faith in the myth leaves him vulnerable to the big gods.[21] No version of the success myth really equips anyone to deal with these forces.

One solution to coping with this impersonal culture is a concomitant impersonality in dealing with it. Miller dramatizes this reaction in his depiction of the good neighbors, Charley and Bernard. Charley is a successful businessman in a minor way; Bernard, the bespectacled tag-along, is a successful lawyer. Out of the goodness of his heart, Charles supports Willy and Linda by "loaning" the salesman fifty dollars a week. He drops by to play cards with Willy and generally tolerates his blustering irritability. He offers Willy a steady job. He is the lone unrelated mourner at the funeral. Out of the salesman's own mouth, the bitter truth is that Charley is the only friend he has. The good neighbor has no theory about success, no magic formula but unconcern: "My salvation is that I never took any interest in anything." (SALESMAN, p. 96.) He never preached at his son or exhibited any interest in success or money. Without preaching, Charley goes about doing good. It is not clear where all the virtue this good neighbor displays springs from. He is the good

Samaritan for whose conduct no explanation need be given. More significantly, though Charley makes no concessions to the cult of success in his actions or his manner, he knows the rules: "The only thing you got in this world is what you can sell."

Bernard is the opposite number to Biff and Happy. He, too, is a good neighbor. Though his boyhood relations with the Lomans kept him a subordinate, he holds no grudge, is still sincerely interested in Biff and respectful with Willy. Bernard has followed his father's example, if not his counsel.

> *Bernard.* Goodby, Willy, and don't worry about it. You know, "If at first you don't succeed . . ."
> *Willy.* Yes, I believe in that.
> *Bernard.* But sometimes, Willy, it's better for a man just to walk away. (SALESMAN, p. 95.)

The successful lawyer has no other word for Willy, except perhaps a footnote to the success formula; he points out that Biff never prepared himself for anything. Charley and Bernard really have no alternate faith to offer Willy. They show a distrust of the big gods and treat them gingerly. Otherwise, they are good people who sympathize with the Lomans' plight, who understand their aspirations without emulating them, who put friendship above the law. They bear witness to the vacuity of success worship, but provide no faith with which to replace it.

This is not to say that Miller suggests no alternative. On the one hand, he suggests a family solidarity centering around the wife and mother; on the other, he tentatively offers a retreat from the competitive business world to an agrarian, manual-labor society. Linda is the heart of the family. She is wise, warm, sympathetic. She knows her husband's faults and her sons' characters. For all her frank appraisals, she loves them. She is contrasted with the promiscuous sex symbolized by the Woman and the prostitutes. They operate in the world outside as part of the impersonal forces that corrupt. Happy equates his promiscuity with taking manufacturers' bribes, and Willy's Boston woman can "put him right through to the buyers." Linda holds the family together—she keeps the accounts, encourages her husband, tries to protect him from heartbreak. She becomes the personification of Family, that social unity in which the individual has a real identity.

The concepts of Father and Mother and so on were received by us unawares before the time we were conscious of ourselves as selves. In contrast, the concepts of Friend, Teacher, Employee, Boss, Colleague, Supervisor, and the many other social relations come to us long after we have gained consciousness of ourselves, and are therefore outside ourselves. They are thus in an objective rather than a subjective category. In any case what we feel is always more "real" to us than what we know, and we feel the family relationship while we only know the social one.[22]

If Willy is not totally unsympathetic (and he is not), much of the goodness in him is demonstrated in his devotion to his wife, according to his lights. Though he is often masterful and curt, he is still deeply concerned about her: "I was fired, and I'm looking for a little good news to tell your mother, because the woman has waited and the woman has suffered." (SALESMAN, p. 107.) While planting his garden, in conversation with Ben, he mutters: " 'Cause she's suffered, Ben, the woman has suffered." (SALESMAN, p. 125.) Biff is attached to his mother, and Happy's hopelessness is most graphic in his failure to be honest with, or concerned about, his family. The family's devotion to one another, even though misguided, represents a recognizable American ideal.

Linda, for all her warmth and goodness, goes along with her husband and sons in the best success-manual tradition. She tries to protect them from the forces outside and fails. The memory of her suffering and her fidelity does not keep Willy and Happy from sex or Biff from wandering. Miller's irony goes still deeper. While Linda is a mirror of goodness and the source of the family's sense of identity, she is no protection—by her silence and her support, she unwittingly cooperates with the destructive myth. Linda follows the rules laid down by the self-help advocates. She is a good home manager, she understands and encourages her husband, she keeps her house neat and is a good mother. Babson recommends a good wife as a major factor in working toward success: "A good wife and well-kept house and some healthy children are of the utmost importance in enabling one to develop the six 'I's' of success and to live the normal, wholesome, upright life." [23] Linda stays in her place, never questioning out loud her husband's objectives and doing her part to help him achieve them.

As another possible alternative to the success myth, Miller proposes a return to a non-competitive occupation in an agrarian or trade-oriented society. In the context of *Death of a Salesman* he makes this offer, not explicitly as a universal panacea, but in terms of the Lomans' problem. The good days of hope and promise in the play are connected with a warm sun and clusters of trees in the neighborhood, fresh air and gardening. The reminiscence sequences are marked by this scenic change: "The apartment houses are fading out and the entire house and surroundings become covered with leaves." (SALESMAN, p. 27.) The neighborhood once bloomed with lilac, wisteria, peonies and daffodils, but now it is "bricks and windows, windows and bricks," and over-population. Willy is a talented workman; he has practically rebuilt the house: "All the cement, the lumber, the reconstruction I put in this house! There ain't a crack to be found in it any more." (SALESMAN, p. 74.) Biff, who understands this strength in his father, has actually escaped to the West. His ambition to succeed conflicts with the satisfaction he finds on the farm:

> This farm I work on, it's spring there now, see? And they've got about fifteen new colts. There's nothing more inspiring or—beautiful than the sight of a mare and a new colt. And it's cool there now, see? Texas is cool now and it's spring. (SALESMAN, p. 22.)

Biff suspects that perhaps the Lomans have been miscast in their salesman role:

> They've laughed at Dad for years, and you know why? Because we don't belong in this nuthouse of a city! We should be mixing cement on some open plain, or—or carpenters. A carpenter is allowed to whistle! (SALESMAN, p. 61.)

So when Biff comes to realize who he is, his insight flashes out of the contrast between the office and the open sky. The things he loves in the world are "the work and the food and time to sit and smoke." And his obituary for his father is a memorial to the good days when Willy was working on the house: "There's more of him in that front stoop than in all the sales he ever made." (SALESMAN, p. 138.) Charley agrees that Willy was "a happy man with a bunch of cement." In a freer, older society, the doomed salesman might have been a happy man.

The pathos of this situation—the square peg in a round hole—is dramatized in the garden scene. After the ordeal in the office and the restaurant, Willy feels the impulse to plant as an imperative: "I've got to get some seeds, right away. . . . I don't have a thing in the ground." (SALESMAN, p. 122.) He then begins to plant his garden in the barren patch beside the house by flashlight. All the contradictions in the salesman's life come into focus. His instinct to plant, to put something that will grow in the ground, is ineffectual—he must work by artificial light, surrounded by apartment houses, in the hard-packed dirt. The seeds will not grow; Willy, who was going to mine diamonds in Brooklyn, reverts to hoeing and planting, but the urbanization of his world has already defeated him. As he plants, he talks "business" with Ben. His suicide will bring twenty thousand "on the barrelhead." This insurance money is the diamond he sees shining in the dark. (SALESMAN, p. 126.) All the forces that conspired to make—and break—Willy Loman are gathered here. His instinct to produce from the earth, the happy farmer he might have been, is frustrated by the society that has boxed him in. The dream of diamonds and his idealization of Ben have "rung up a zero"; the only way he can make his life pay off is by self-destruction.

Taken at the level of parable, the play presents the failure of the success myth by destroying the Horatio Alger image of the rags-to-riches triumph of the common man. This view of the play considers Willy as Salesman, Linda as Family, Ben as Success, and the moral of the play is the fall of the Golden Calf.[24] But Miller has not written a morality plan in *Salesman*, nor does he make the mistake of preaching. The audience says, "That's the way middle-class America lives and thinks"; it also says: "I know a man just like that." The Willy Lomans who see the play do not recognize themselves and respond to Willy's collapse with the now legendary remark: "That New England territory was no damned good!" Wrapped in the trappings of instruction is the deep personal anguish of a contemporary American that audiences can recognize.

Willy the Salesman represents all those Americans caught in the mesh of the myth and the moral pressures it generates. As a type, he is a product of social and economic forces outside himself. But in his struggle with those forces, Willy is also a suffering human being. He battles to retain his faith, is shaken by doubts about his ability to live according to his belief, humiliates himself to discover the secret that lies at its heart. His blind commitment to his ideal is whole-hearted, and if Willy the Salesman is necessarily destroyed by that commitment, the audience feels that Willy the person is worth saving.

Thus, when he goes to his death without knowing why he has lived or why he is dying, he fulfills the destiny of the type, but as an individual who has suffered, he remains unfulfilled. The Salesman can neither suffer nor be converted (he would then cease to be Salesman), but the family man—the husband and father and friend—does suffer and, by virtue of it, can change. If Willy were only an abstract set of stereotyped characteristics, a figure in a Morality play, there would be little sympathy for his plight. In the "Requiem" epilogue, the various aspects of Willy's character come in for comment. Biff's epitaph considers what Willy might have been, the happy carpenter, the outdoorsman. Charley, on the other hand, reads the apologia for the Salesman:

> Nobody dast blame this man. You don't understand: Willy was a salesman. And for the salesman, there is no rock bottom to life. He don't put a bolt to a nut, he don't tell you the law or give you medicine. He's a man way out there in the blue, riding on a smile and a shoeshine. And when they start not smiling back—that's an earthquake. And then you get yourself a couple of spots on your hat, and you're finished. Nobody dast blame this man. A salesman is got to dream, boy. It comes with the territory. (SALESMAN, p. 138.)

This speech defends Willy in the context of myth and moral, but as a justification of his uncomprehending self-destruction, it fails to consider the individual who suffered through his life and rang up a zero at the end. Linda, the long-suffering, says the last word for the husband and the father:

> Willy, dear, I can't cry. Why did you do it? I search and I search and I search, and I can't understand it, Willy. I made the last payment on the house today. Today, dear. And there'll be nobody home. . . . We're free and clear. . . . We're free. (SALESMAN, p. 139.)

Linda cannot understand the mystery as Willy could not understand it. Suffering and sacrifice, for the family, have led to the "freedom" of an empty house and the grave.

Miller, who set out to write the tragedy of the common man, is finally trapped both by the myth he is denouncing and by the dramatic form he has chosen. The salesman's version of the success myth—the cult of personality—is shown to be a tissue of false values that lead only to frustration. Miller dramatizes the problem of guilt and the reality of Willy's suffering because of his values, but, try as he may, he can neither bring Willy to an insight by which he understands his failure nor find a societal strategy that can absolve him of it. The traditional tragic pattern of action demands an epiphany, a purgation and a renewal that does not cancel the suffering of the protagonist, but that does make sense of it. Miller recognizes this demand of the form and struggles to fulfill it; in the end the myth defeats him.

At the level of dianoia, the conscious treatment of values, Miller tries to find a replacement for the success myth and fails:

This confusion [about "true" and "false" values] is abetted by the greater clarity of the rejected values which are embodied in the dream of success. The false dream is fully and vividly sketched; positive values seem rather dim and conventional.[25]

The false values, tightly woven into Willy's personality, are clearly destructive. But when Biff, the man who "knows who he is," advocates a return to the farm, it becomes clear how meager are the resources of the culture for coping with Willy's problem. The return to a pre-Alger agrarian way of life is an example of nostalgia for the garden; turning back the clock is no solution for a million city-dwelling Willy Lomans who left the farm to seek their fortunes. Charley's detachment from the myth does not supply a positive answer either. For Charley, whether he cares about it or not, *is* a success; he owns his small business and supports Willy. If the successful must protect the failures, then Willy's values are not altogether false, and the common man who cannot get along with the myth cannot get along without it either.

Society cannot absolve Willy; it can only understand and sympathize. Understanding and sympathy are not enough; Willy still goes to his "freedom" in the grave uncomprehending. At the level of dramatic action, there is no epiphany in which suffering leads to insight, that moment of revelation when the hero sees himself and his situation clearly, understands what he has lost, and finds the path to regeneration. Willy has suffered, but, because he is the Salesman, his suffering does not bring him to understanding. Miller recognizes this difficulty also and tries to circumvent it by promoting Biff to hero, by giving him the insight of which Willy was incapable. Nonetheless, it is Willy's fate that concerns us. He must go to his death hapless and deluded, but his end leaves the play without that final stage which the conventional tragic structure demands. Like the detective-hero, the salesman cannot acknowledge his mistake without also destroying his identity.

In *Death of a Salesman* Miller taps a popular formula for the structure of his drama. Although the Dale Carnegie approach, the cult of personality, is on the wane in the present generation, the drive for success is very much alive. Willy's plight, grounded in the excesses of a previous generation but fostered by attitudes still shared by the present generation, draws from the audience both recognition of the illusion and sympathy for the visionary. Willy's suffering is real and deep. America cannot accept the success myth— "Horatio Alger" is now a term of derision—but there is no real substitute for it. Because Miller has built his play around an American dream, he strikes deep into the consciousness of the audience. The contemporary American, because he cannot solve the dilemma either, becomes involved in the sufferings of Willy the person as he watches the death of Willy the Salesman.

7

The Passing of the Old South:

A Streetcar Named Desire

When superior American playwrights are under discussion, the two names most frequently linked are Arthur Miller and Tennessee Williams and the question of precedence is hotly disputed. Those critics who prefer the tightly knit, precise and objective style that characterizes Miller's work find Williams episodic and repetitious; those who see Miller's plays as mechanical and manipulated expositions praise Williams. There is an exuberance in Williams; his characters burst out in unexpected directions, his dialogue has an air of authenticity along with flashes of poetic illumination. Miller works at a condensation of effect that gives a chiseled quality to his outlines. These differences in artistry and effect are striking enough to obscure real similarities in theme and method. Both playwrights are concerned with a specific cultural milieu and both concentrate on an interpretation of that milieu for the audience. Thus, in *Death of a Salesman* Miller dramatizes the death of a myth; in his representative *A Streetcar Named Desire* Williams deals with the same theme. The death of Willy Loman represents the passing of an American dream; the confinement of Blanche DuBois is a legend about the passing of the Old South.

As their names indicate, Willy and Blanche represent types, and they express those cultural attitudes that generated the type. Just as Willy brings the values of the drummer into a now-hostile business world, so Blanche is a sensitive, romantic soul who tries to adjust to the melting-pot environment of a big city. Both dramatists explore this cultural situation; it is the relation of the type to a hostile milieu that provides the structure, the cast of characters and ultimately the action of the drama. Though the plays deal with the death of a myth, the attitudes that characterize the Salesman and the Southern Belle are far from dead; they still exert a real influence on American society. The old ideals still draw sustenance from that subterranean cavern where emotional prejudices linger. So the audience recognizes Willy and Blanche and sympathizes with their predicament. Though the individual spectator may consciously reject the attitudes of the Salesman or the Southern Belle, the response of the emotions and the imagination cannot be so easily controlled. Miller and Williams have seized on situations to which the audience responds in this ambivalent way.

The differences that arise in their treatments are not simply a matter of personal eccentricities or technical proficiency, but result from two related factors: 1) the extension of the myth they treat and 2) the relation of the playwright to the myth. The mystique of the Salesman looks first to the individual's relationship with a world outside the home. As Miller has pointed out, the attitudes of the success myth are learned in the marketplace; they are assimilated after a man has developed a set of values within the home. "Father and mother" come first and "employer, employee" much later. Though the Salesman brings these values home with him, they are not native to him. When the success myth orders a man's entire life, it produces a distortion that destroys him—this is Miller's point.

Williams, however, is dealing with a more comprehensive myth. For the Southerner the ante-bellum days represent an ideal of gracious living, an ideal that includes a code of personal honor extending into every area of his experience. Moreover, the Southern tradition is a family tradition. While the non-Southerner may identify with the frontiersman, the detective, the Horatio Alger bootblack, he cannot claim him as a blood relation. The Southerner, on the other hand, can look back on past glories that have become part of his own family history. The image of this glory, the Southern way of life, is the heritage of every Southerner from backwoods to tidewater, and he receives it as a birthright. Thus the culture with which Williams deals has greater depth and breadth than Miller's success myth; as its roots are deeper and more personal, it exercises a correspondingly greater influence on society.

The personal involvement of the playwright also exercises considerable influence on his use of the myth. Miller depicts the success myth from the outside. That is, he is able to take a detached and objective view of the Salesman even though he is unable to offer a solution to his dilemma. If Willy does not understand his problem, the playwright does. Williams, however, writes from inside the myth. Whatever his intellectual apperceptions are, he cannot detach himself from his dramatic situations. Some of his characters distinctly resemble his own immediate family, the locale of the major plays is, with two exceptions, the deep South, the plot consistently presents the confrontation of a high-strung sensitive woman and an alien environment.[1] His own background includes Tennessee ancestors and a Mississippi childhood. Williams was named Thomas Lanier after his grandfather and a Southern poet who celebrated the glories of the New South in the spirit of the Old. His early boyhood was spent almost exclusively in the company of his grandparents, his mother and his sister in the Episcopal rectory of quiet Mississippi towns. When at the age of eight he moved to St. Louis with the family, the experience was traumatic. "Neither my sister nor I could adjust to life in a Midwestern city."[2] The "big city" in the "Midwest" is a sharp contrast to the small, rural communities that framed his earliest memories, and the conflict this move provoked is the subject of his "memory" play *The Glass Menagerie*. The ideals and attitudes that Williams absorbed in his Southern childhood establish the perspective from which he wrote his plays. He is not, like Miller, writing a detached critique about an inoperable complex of attitudes that affect other people's lives; he is examining a myth which continues to influence him even as he rings its knell.

These differences in the nature of the myth and the playwright's involvement in it go far towards accounting for the different impact produced by *Salesman* and *Streetcar*. Allowing for irreducible traits of personality, the cultural pattern with which each playwright works explains what would otherwise be a vague feeling that correspondences and contrasts do exist. Both men deal with a myth; both dramatize its inadequacy. Miller's "Requiem" for Willy Loman parallels the commitment of Blanche to an asylum; the dramatic method by which these conclusions are reached is analogous, once the real differences between the subject matter and the playwright's point of view are understood. An analysis of the Southern myth and the insider's view of it should clarify Williams' attitude and his method.

One need not be a Southerner to be well acquainted with the myth; the outsider's view corresponds to and is an extension of it.

Even though they have not a proprietary commitment, Northerner and Westerner manifest the same fascination for the days "before the War" as the Southerner. All regions have been exposed to this complex of attitudes and images. Since J. P. Kennedy's *Swallow Barn* appeared in 1832, novelists have been exploiting the possibilities of the Southern tradition. The first outburst of plantation literature reached a climax in the 1850s with the novels of John Esten Cooke, a Virginian who celebrated the Cavaliers of the James River region. After the War, on the heels of Reconstruction, Thomas Nelson Page completely idealized the antebellum image of the old plantation. His books had a wide sale in the North which displayed the usual interest of the victors in the customs and culture of the vanquished. This vogue persisted into the twentieth century, most prominently in the works of Ellen Glasgow and James Branch Cabell. The latest surge of interest on the popular level was initiated by Margaret Mitchell's *Gone with the Wind,* the most inclusive and idealized fictional portrait of the Old South.

An essential reason for its popularity lies in the yet comfortably familiar theme that Miss Mitchell has chosen. "Gone with the Wind" is an encyclopedia of the plantation legend. Other novelists by the hundreds have helped to shape this legend, but each of them has presented only parts of it. Miss Mitchell repeats it as a whole, with all its episodes and characters and all its stage settings.[3]

This novel sold one million copies between June 30 and December 31, 1936, and six million copies by 1949. The reception of the movie version in the South also underscores the vitality of the myth in the popular mind.

In the event it [the movie premiere] turned into a high ritual for the reassertion of the legend of the Old South. Atlanta became a city of pilgrimage for people from the entire region. The ceremonies were accompanied by great outbursts of emotion, which bore no relationship to the actual dramatic value of a somewhat dull and thin performance. And later on, when the picture was shown in other towns of the South, attendance at the theatres took on a definite character of a patriotic act.[4]

North and South, right up to the present, the myth (and the movie) show a remarkable durability.

The general details of the plantation myth are well-known. The image of the large, white, six-columned house set amid acres of lawn and garden with a periphery of slave cabins and cotton fields provides the proper setting. The owners of the big house are aristocrats with the appropriate chivalric virtues and patrician vices. The master is autocratic, prideful, gallant; the mistress is a paragon of the domestic virtues. Son and daughter exercise a youthful license in imitating the virtues of their parents. The Negroes are devoted serfs, contented with their lot. Life on the plantation is easy and gay, a round of lawn parties, dress balls and visiting, with an occasional ride around the holdings for the master and mild direction of the house servants by the mistress. The young men and women spend their time at play and courtship. Coquetry from the lady is never mistaken for indelicacy; exuberance and high spirits among the gentlemen is always tempered with courtesy and a sense of honor. The War is a duel fought by gentlemen to preserve the old plantation and the way of life that flourishes there. Defeat may have consumed the big house and destroyed the old way of life, but it did not touch the code of honor and delicacy. So much for the popular outlines of the myth.

This popular image of the romance has been supplemented by serious writers in the novel, poetry and criticism. Though novelists like Wolfe and Faulkner do not follow the stereotype, they must still deal with the myth. Even in transcending it, these authors do not discount its impact on the Southern mind. The Nashville Fugitives, for instance, arrived at an ideal of Southern agrarianism which, if impossible to realize in the social order, could at least serve as a framework for their writings. The Old South as nostalgic image exerted an influence on the popular mind; as idea and ideal, it influenced serious Southern writers as well. The depiction of real situations perforce had to include the pressures exerted by the myth on that world.

As a Southerner writing about the South, then, Williams works with the complex of attitudes that crystallized in the myth. Foremost among these attitudes is an acute sense of time and place. The Southerner had a sense of identification with a given segment of the earth, of belonging on the ancestral estate, that the transient Northerner can only admire. As this attachment to the land became less and less a reality and the agrarian ideal came into conflict with the forces of industrialization, the Southerner became more and more aware that there was no compromise between the old modes of Southern life and "progress." [5] The sense of alienation from proper place is joined to a preoccupation with time. The inexorable march of progress and the loss of the agrarian system to urbanization and the machine is not totally explained by Yankee villainy or Southern scalawaggery; the passage of time accomplishes the defeat of the old ways. But the past is not altogether past. Gavin Stephen's remark in *Requiem for a Nun* is typical: "The past is never dead, it's not even past." Because it exists in the present, preserving the old ideals and forbidding progress, it can be destructive. Kazin puzzles over this paradox in his evaluation of Faulkner: "In the end we always seem to be reading the same story, following through the familiar formula of damnation, conscious of the same mysterious submission—extraordinarily abject—to perdition." [6] For the Southerner, the past represents a glory and a heritage; its vitality in the imagination makes adjustment to the variegated society of the present difficult. Williams, like his compatriots, attempts to cope with these contraries in his plays without, however, offering easy "solutions."

The myth, as seen by contemporary students of Southern culture, exemplifies certain specific characteristics. They maintain that the image of the past continues to exert a pressure on Southern character and that unique qualities of mind emerge. They describe these qualities as romanticism, a penchant for violence, and uneasy balance of Puritanism and hedonism.[7] Presumably, the antebellum way of life reconciled the opposing strains in these qualities; the disappearance of the old ways accentuates their opposition in the face of adjustment to a new social system. The Southern experience contains elements which, according to Cash, help account for these characteristics in the Southerner. The tendency toward unreality, toward the romantic, is reflected in the physical world he inhabited —"a sort of cosmic conspiracy against reality in favor of romance." The soft climate, the leisure available even to the backwoodsman and the yeoman farmer, the influence of the Negro kept the harsh realities of a barren countryside, fierce winters, starvation, and the austere temperament of the Anglo-Saxon at a distance. A sturdy individualism, backwoodsman independence and planter's unlimited authority melded into an inviolability of personal whim, "of which the essence was the boast voiced or not, on the part of every South-

erner, that he would knock hell out of whoever dared cross him."
Swift recourse to violence resulted from crossing him. Individualism,
violence, the tendency to romanticize formed a triple entente which
produced a natural hedonism, a variegated luxuriousness in living.
The Southerner's legendary whiskey, horses, nocturnal visits to the
slave cabins or the "Quarter," the shoot-out at the duelling oaks illustrate this characteristic. Notwithstanding, at bottom he is likely
to be a Puritan—with severe moral standards (generally applicable
to the women first), a religious enthusiasm typified by the triumph
of the evangelical sects in the South, and a strong sense of the preternatural abetted by his Celtic background and his relation with
the Negro. This stream flowed side by side with the hedonism and,
in the pre-War world, the two attitudes seldom conflicted.

His Puritanism was no mere mask put on from cold calculation, but was
as essential a part of him as his hedonism. And his combination of the
two was without conscious imposture. One might say with truth that it
proceeded from a fundamental split in his psyche, from a sort of social
schizophrenia. One may say more simply and safely that it was all part
and parcel of that naive capacity for unreality which was characteristic of
him.[8]

These qualities—so goes the myth—lived easily together on the old
plantation; in the harsh world of modern industrialism, they create
a problem for the displaced person.

This divided personality may be detected in the character traits
of key personae in the plantation tradition. The heroine of the popular romance, for example, generally has two facets: she is the fragile
virgin of heightened sensibilities, modest, graceful, delicate; she is
the vivacious adventuress who flirts and dares and teases: Melanie
Hamilton and Scarlett O'Hara of *Gone with the Wind*. But the ideal
figure of the romance is a combination of these types, "a crystal-
lization of all legends of fair women."[9] She is young, in her teens,
lavishly costumed, the image of youth and splendor. In a sense, her
age allows for the contrary qualities she displays, but, as Gaines
points out:

There is a hint of deeper psychological charm in the heroine of this fascinating age, a hint that expresses itself even in the contradictions. This
bundle of complexes is excitingly inconsistent; she is both impulsive and

reserved; frivolous even inconsiderate, but charitable; frank, yet co-
quettish—no trait of character is more frequently employed; heartless as
the lady of chivalry, tender as Cordelia.[10]

Cut loose from a protective society or manifested in a mature
woman, these contrasting traits of character lose some of their
attractiveness and take on a neurotic tinge.

The hero of the Southern romance often displays an equally
ambivalent set of characteristics. The dynamism of a Rhett Butler is
counterpoised by a neurasthenic Ashley Wilkes who typifies a long
tradition of nervous, sensitive gentlemen—Augustine St. Clare to
Quentin Compson. Their refinement has a feminine shading which
can be combined, as in Faulkner's Quentin, with a reckless violence.
Though Ashley can ride off to fight with Yankees without losing a
delicate sensibility, there is a division in the soul of the hero that
cannot be composed outside the tradition. This dichotomy did not
escape the vigilant observer: "Now and then a perceptive Southerner even noted that the traits of the Hothead and the Hamlet were
expressions of the same fundamental failure of character." [11] In the
romance both hero and heroine function well enough in their own
world; once outside that context—in Faulkner's world or Wolfe's—
they appear crippled or doomed.

As might be expected, this curious tendency to schizophrenia
leaves its mark on the style of the serious author who works inside
the tradition. Perhaps its most enigmatic expression is the peculiar
combination of the comic and the pathetic that has been singled out
as characteristic of Southern writing. There is a strain of exaggeration, of Southwest humor, running through Faulkner's novels; there
is an air of lush overripeness in Wolfe's work that verges on the
comic. This strain is tightly interwoven with the pathetic and the
tragic. The critic who is unable to fathom this quality can easily put
it down as an artistic flaw:

Even if it be admitted that Faulkner's effort has been to express the inex-
pressible, to write the history of the unconscious, to convey some final
and terrifying conception of a South that seems always to exist below
water, the impression one always carries away from his novels is of some
fantastic exertion of will, of that exaggeration which springs from a need
to raise everything in Yoknapatawpha County, Mississippi, to its tenth
(or its hundredth) power because there is not sufficient belief, or power,

or ease in his conception of Yoknapatawpha County, or the South, or human existence in general.[12]

Whatever the source of this combination of comic and tragic, this tendency to enlarge and to dramatize larger-than-life, it is a feature of Southern writing which produces a resemblance between the author and his characters. The writer, too, has a divided psyche and recognizes it; he cannot take the myth altogether seriously; on the other hand, he cannot dismiss it as so much magnolia and moonshine. He agonizes over the situation and laughs at the futility of this agonizing; he cannot avoid the one or indulge the other. The impractical and "unreal" love of the past is a psychological reality that the author must face, and he cannot face it without mixed emotion.

Tennessee Williams writes his plays out of the matrix of this tradition. He not only uses the plantation myth as an artistic point of departure, as Miller uses the success myth, the attitudes which shape his drama derive from his background, his education and his temperament. The Deep South setting of the plays situates the action in his own cultural milieu, his characters are Southerners, the action involves a clash between the Old and the New. A consideration of the autobiographical elements in the dramas, therefore, necessarily includes a consideration of the common cultural elements. Whereas *The Glass Menagerie* is unabashedly autobiographical and contains considerable private revelation, *A Streetcar Named Desire* moves more deliberately into the mainstream of Southern experience.

Williams begins by situating *Streetcar* in an old section of New Orleans, a city with a cosmopolitan air, but with an Old South tradition. The section of the city is poor, but not slum-poor: "It has a raffish charm. The houses are mostly white frame, weathered grey, with rickety outside stairs and galleries and quaintly ornamented gables." [13] The aura around this setting is vaguely decadent, suggesting that the old attitudes, like the houses, have faded. Expository sections in the opening scenes contribute to this impression by suggesting the same fading and merging in the social milieu. The neighborhood is mixed, white, black and brown; Eunice, the upstairs tenant, converses with a colored woman and one of Stanley's poker companions is a Mexican. References to the bar around the corner, the bowling alley and Fritz's garage complete the lower-middle-class atmosphere. This setting makes up the actual dimension, the world in which Stanley Kowalski is at home.

When Blanche comes on the scene, another dimension enters with her, the world of the old plantation. She arrives from the ancestral territory of the DuBois, the rural community of Laurel, Mississippi. She brings memories of the family home, now lost to the inevitable march of time, to death and taxes. Though there is no lengthy description of the plantation, it has substance for everyone in the play. Stanley refers to it as "the country place," the "plantation," "the place with the columns." (STREETCAR, pp. 34, 37, 129.) Blanche recalls the land sold by her forebearers, the graveyard on the property, the lawn that stretched in front of the house. The image of the big, white, columned house, nowhere explicit in the dialogue, the acres of land, the round of entertainments, teas, cocktails and luncheons, all the glories of antebellum living, are contrasted with the crowded flat in the run-down section of the city; Blanche calls attention to this contrast at every opportunity.

> *Blanche.* What are you doing in a place like this?
> *Stella.* Now, Blanche—
> *Blanche.* Oh, I'm not going to be hypocritical. I'm going to be honestly critical about it! Never, never, never in my worst dreams could I picture —Only Poe! Only Mr. Edgar Allen Poe—could do it justice! Out there I suppose is the ghoul-haunted woodland of Weir. (STREETCAR, p. 17.)

The name of the city subdivision, the name of the plantation and the town emphasize this contrast in a rather heavy-handed symbolism. The plantation was called "Belle Reve"; Blanche DuBois—"white woods"—lived near Laurel; the apartment is located in the "Elysian Fields," which, with a fine double-edged irony, looks like a horror to Blanche. She rode to the home of Stanley and Stella on a streetcar named Desire and another named Cemeteries, passing from the land of the living through the graveyard to the "happy islands." The temporal dimension of the action, then, includes the past, the "beautiful dream," and the present, a period of decadence for Blanche, of happiness for those who need not remember the past like Stella or who have no past to remember like Stanley. The spatial dimension extends from the two-room flat to the old plantation. This is the world of *Streetcar*, time past in time present and the spacious plantation superimposed on the stifling city apartment.

Into the settled environment of the Elysian Fields Blanche comes as an outsider, a foreign element from another time and place. She is the Southern heroine, faded around the edges but still very recognizable.

She is daintily dressed in a white suit with a fluffy bodice, necklace and earrings of pearl, white gloves and hat, looking as if she were arriving at a summer tea or cocktail party in the garden district. She is about five years older than Stella. Her delicate beauty must avoid a strong light. (STREETCAR, p. 11.)

This impression of soft fabric and light airiness has the ring of authenticity about it; Mary Chesnut has a description of the "perfect beauty" in Charleston before the war: "She is as beautiful as flesh and blood ought to be, and she is always exquisitely dressed. Today it was soft mull muslin, all fluffy and fluted and covered with Valenciennes lace." [14] The lavish costumes of the belle are part of the tradition and Blanche carries this kind of wardrobe with her.

Stanley. Look at these feathers and furs that she came here to preen herself in! What's this here? A solid-gold dress, I believe! And this one! What is these here? Fox-pieces! (He blows on them.) Genuine fox fur-pieces, a half a mile long! . . . Bushy snow-white ones, no less! . . . Pearls! Ropes of them! . . . Bracelets of solid gold, too. . . . And diamonds! A crown for an empress! (STREETCAR, pp. 36–7.)

Though the jewelry, as Stella points out to her husband, is glass, and the fox furs inexpensive summer-wear, Blanche dresses up to the role of the plantation belle.

Blanche's personality also measures up to the image. She exhibits the idiosyncracies of the Southern heroine in profusion, adding to the schizoid impression by her frantic attempts to hold on to her youth. She plays the refined delicate lady and the flirtatious adventuress, both in a state of electrically nervous tension. She worries about her privacy in the two-room flat, she is fastidious about her person—hot baths and fresh perfume lift her spirits immeasurably—she has the proper intellectual veneer, quoting poetry with appreciation. With Mitch, the prospective suitor, she maintains her "old fashioned" morals. In the face of finances she is the helpless, fuzzy-headed female; the plantation slipped through her fingers to become a pile of papers placed in the "big, capable" hands of Stanley

Kowalski. The other side of the coin shows Blanche the coquette, promising excitement and love-play, the woman who can and does take the initiative. She plays this game with Stanley.

> *Blanche.* I'm going to ask a favor of you in a moment. . . . Some buttons in back! You may enter.
>
> ·
>
> *Stanley.* I can't do nothing with them.
> *Blanche.* You men with your big clumsy fingers. May I have a drag on your cig? (STREETCAR, p. 39.)

At one point in their discussion, Blanche playfully sprays Stanley with her perfume atomizer. This kind of fencing is out of Stanley's province; Blanche is playing with fire. His reaction does not show the proper gentlemanly restraint: "If I didn't know that you was my wife's sister I'd get ideas about you." She uses the same approach more successfully on Mitch who has some glimmering of an idea about how the game is played. He comes carrying a bouquet of roses. Blanche helps the embryonic gentleman over the rough spots: "Look who's coming! My Rosenkavalier! Bow to me first . . . now present them. *Ahhh—Merciii!*" (STREETCAR, p. 95.) In one brief, revealing scene Blanche drops her assumed coyness, but significantly the penchant for romance remains. A seventeen-year-old newsboy enters to collect for the paper, and Blanche holds him.

> *Blanche.* Young man! (He turns. She takes a large, gossamer scarf from the trunk and drapes it about her shoulders.) Young man! Young, young, young man! Has anyone ever told you that you look like a young Prince out of the Arabian nights? (The Young Man laughs uncomfortably and stands like a bashful kid. Blanche speaks softly to him.) Well, you do, honey lamb! Come here. I want to kiss you, just once, softly and sweetly on your mouth! (Without waiting for him to accept, she crosses quickly and presses her lips to his.) Now run along, now, quickly! It would be nice to keep you, but I've got to be good—and keep my hands off children. (STREETCAR, p. 96.)

Blanche combines in her personality the qualities of the Southern heroine and, no matter what disillusioning or degrading experiences she has undergone, she never relaxes in her role of Southern belle.

Periodically even Blanche recognizes that the belle depends on the society around her for protection, on the understanding of the gentlemen who idolize her, and on her youth. When the play opens, Blanche has already lost the plantation and her youth. She has to battle to keep control, for the schizophrenia latent in the traditional type has begun to rise to the surface. So she holds onto her ideal, the "beautiful dream." She conceals her wrinkles by shading the naked bulbs with paper lanterns, and her drinking by insisting that she rarely touches it, and her isolation by recalling the Shep Huntleighs to whom she can appeal whenever disaster brushes too close. All this deception is justified by the romance to which she adheres, by her faith in the fundamental rightness of the old order.

Mitch. You lied to me, Blanche.
Blanche. Don't say I lied to you.
Mitch. Lies, lies, inside and out, all lies.
Blanche. Never inside, I didn't lie in my heart. (STREETCAR, p. 137.)

Blanche has to lie to hold onto the truth she lives by—the truth of the myth. But she has outlived its protection and the myth itself betrays her. Mitch was her last hope of security and that hope is broken by the code of the Southern gentleman. When Mitch discovers that Blanche had turned to promiscuity as an escape from her troubles, he refuses to marry her because she is "not clean enough to bring in the house with my mother." (STREETCAR, p. 139.) He cannot understand that Blanche tried to capture her youth again with the young soldiers on the lawn, that flirtation led to trouble for the aging belle. So he tries his luck and Blanche holds to her standards—even with all hope gone, she will not "put out" for Mitch. When he touches her, she screams "Fire!" [15] In her own mind Blanche never lets go of the myth so that finally, after the rape, she withdraws completely into her plantation world. The heroine cannot exist out of her element.

Stanley and, by association, Stella form a society of the actual, the present, in complete opposition to Blanche's world of romance. From Blanche's point of view, Stanley is a "foreigner," a man who knows no tradition. He and his friends are "heterogeneous types," Polacks. Blanche lumps all such outsiders together:

Stella. Stanley is Polish, you know.
Blanche. Oh, yes. They're something like Irish, aren't they?
Stella. Well—
Blanche. Only not so—highbrow? (They both laugh again in the same way [uncomfortably].) (STREETCAR, p. 21.)

Stanley sees himself in a different light; he is no Polack. Moreover, though people from Poland are Poles, not Polacks, Stanley is "a one hundred percent American, born and raised in the greatest country on earth and proud as hell of if, so don't ever call me a Polack." (STREETCAR, p. 126.) There is no schizoid tendency in Stanley's personality; he knows his place in the world and holds it confidently. He is quick to protect his rights at home and abroad. He questions Blanche about the loss of the country place because he shares a right in his wife's property and doesn't like being swindled. When his wife calls attention to his manners and his language at the dinner table, he begins throwing china because every man is a king in his own home. He does not believe in gallantry: "I once went out with a doll who said to me, 'I am the glamorous type, I am the glamorous type!' I said, 'So what?' . . . That shut her up like a clam." (STREETCAR, pp. 41–2.) Stanley's self-possession is no more evident than in his attitude toward sex—he is powerful and attractive, he knows it, he enjoys it without any scruple. Stanley inhabits a secure world in which he is king.

Stella emerged from the plantation cocoon to adopt Stanley's way of life. Her husband dominates her completely; though she loves Blanche and remembers the old customs, his touch compensates for any sense of loss. Being somewhat unimaginative, Stella has made the transition easily. She can now read comic books, go down to the tavern and the bowling alley, swap experiences with Eunice, and clean up the flat after the poker parties with no sense of degradation. Though this image may seem a far cry from the old plantation, there is one aspect in which Stella resembles the stock persona of the plantation mistress. The mistress is traditionally submissive to her husband; as lord and master, he carries on his own affairs while the wife occupies herself with domestic matters. Thus, once the round of balls and parties is over, the Southern woman is expected to retire to domestic affairs and leave larger issues to the men. The fact is that Stella has adjusted to her husband's way of life, and this adjustment corresponds with Southern tradition about the wife's place in society. Thus the rebellion against Stanley that Blanche instigates never really materializes. Though Stella loses her delicacy and purity, she does not miss them. Williams' implication that her sexual rapport largely accounts for her adjustment raises a question that requires consideration later on. In any event, her sexual dependence reflects the dominance that Southern tradition ideally proposes of master over mistress.

Mitch the awkward suitor fits the pattern of the Southern gentleman *manqué*. He is attracted by Blanche's unique qualities; though he is not quite equipped to understand her, he is sympathetic and respectful. When Blanche accuses Stanley of bad manners, Mitch replies: "I don't see how anybody could be rude to you." He is willing to take her evaluation of the situation and to abide by her rules: "Just give me a slap whenever I step out of bounds." (STREETCAR, p. 103.) In Mitch's character, though he sees himself as the self-sufficient male, there are traces of Ashley Wilkes. His mother dominates him, he worries over her, and this makes him a pathetic figure among the poker players.

Mitch. I gotta sick mother. She don't go to sleep until I come in at night.
Stanley. Then why don't you stay home with her?
Mitch. She says go out, so I go, but I don't enjoy it. All the while I keep wondering how she is.

. . . .

Mitch. You are all married. But I'll be alone when she goes.—I'm going to the bathroom.
Stanley. Hurry back and we'll fix you a sugar-tit.

(STREETCAR, pp. 49–50.)

There is a suitable touch of romance in Mitch's past—he carries a watch inscribed with a quotation from Elizabeth Barrett Browning that commemorates the death of his first love—"a very strange girl, very sweet." Because Blanche's gentility strikes a chord in him, he is able to talk about his mother and about the inscription. Because he is confused, he can get along in the Kowalski world; his gaucherie provides a protective shield under which he can carry on a private commerce with his ideals. His dependence on his mother and his vague appreciation of the Southern ideal make him vulnerable.

So, as the closest approximation to Shep Huntleigh she can find, Blanche looks to Mitch for security in Stanley's world. It is ironic that the code of the gentleman that Mitch understands so imperfectly and that first attracted him to Blanche is instrumental in destroying their relationship. Mitch completes the cast of characters by filling the role of the Southern gentleman; he too is caught between two worlds.

This colorful and richly drawn set of dramatis personae tend to overpower the events of the play; the flow of words and images so illumine the personalities that they gloss over the events. Williams' dialogue is laced with exclamations and repetitions that achieve a verse effect without making the persona a mouthpiece for the author. Also, incidents give the impression of belonging to specific personae; for instance, the outbursts of violence—the fight in the kitchen, smashing the china, the rape—are Stanley's moments; verbal fencing and nervous conversations belong to Blanche; Stella and Mitch move alternately in the auras of Stanley and Blanche. No given action stands out as sharply as the actors. Nonetheless, beneath the flow of the dialogue and the color of the personalities, there is a plot structure which deserves some attention. As we have come to expect, the action makes its own statement that goes deeper than any assertions in the dialogue (or any statements about the dialogue and characterization) to establish the meaning of the play. On the level of the plantation tradition, the adaptation of stereotypes indicates one analogue for the events. The plot resembles the Civil War romance and uses that basic pattern of events—the invasion of an established society by an alien force which is determined to overthrow its way of life. In an ironic reversal of the romance, it is the Old South that invades the lower-middle-class American society. The structure, then, may be summarized: the arrival of the invader, a marshalling of forces and enlisting of allies, a reconnaissance of the enemy, the climactic conflict, and the defeat of the invader. (The Southern romance manages to combine historical defeat with a moral triumph—the superiority of Southern ideals or the conquest of the Northern hero by the Southern belle.) Blanche invades Stanley's domain armed with a traditional sensibility and culture. She attempts to win Stella's support and half-succeeds; she launches a desperate campaign to win Mitch. Stanley fights back by checking into the loss of the plantation, by uncovering Blanche's recent past and the scandals in Laurel. Blanche probes Stanley's defenses with flattery and a flirting manner; Stanley is ruffled by her superiority and reconnoitres till he discovers the chink in her armor. The final conflict occurs in the bedroom where Stanley arrays himself in his virility and "rapes" Blanche. Blanche herself is partially responsible for the triumph of force and material resources over sensibility and ideals. The structure recapitulates the sequence of events in the Civil War romance, but the playwright has adapted it to his own purposes.

It is ironic that the battle is fought this time on Stanley's ground, giving him an advantage that doubly insures Blanche's defeat. This reversal, making the Old South the invader, has a twofold effect. The image of the myth conjured up by the pattern insures a sympathy with the Southern cause. The antebellum way of life that Blanche represents exerts its wonted fascination. Moreover, Stanley's reactions reflect the standard charges leveled against the Yankee army in the romance: destruction of property, looting and rape. Stanley smashes dishes, rummages through Blanche's trunk and finally rapes her. These actions swing the sympathies of the audience to the Southern belle. On the other hand, the structure makes a different comment because Blanche is cast in the role of invader. As far as Stanley's world is concerned, she is the outsider, the disruptive influence. By realigning the pattern in this way, the impact of the romance analogue is transmuted into an emotional and conceptual ambiguity.

This mutation in the romance structure suggests a pattern that requires further comment. The *Gone with the Wind* stereotype produces certain clear resonances that the playwright uses, but once he varies that pattern, then another more universal structure appears. This other analogue has not gone unnoticed. Mary McCarthy, in her review of *Streetcar*, waspishly suggests that Williams should really have written "a wonderful little comic epic, The Struggle for the Bathroom." [16] By viewing the plot as a variation on the visiting mother-in-law motif, she finds an opportunity to satirize Williams' too obvious symbolism and his rhetorical flourishes, and she reduces the play to a tempest in a bathtub. In spite of a tendency to use the review as a showcase for her devastating wit, McCarthy puts her finger on an underlying comic pattern. The unwelcome guest, as we have seen in the discussion of *The Cocktail Party*, has a comic function that can be traced back to the alazon of Aristophanic comedy.

> The unwelcome intruders who so often thrust themselves upon the hero . . . arrive after the victory of the Agon is already won. The scene of sacrifice, cooking or feasting has no sooner begun than an oracle monger, a poet, or an informer presents himself to interrupt the proceedings or to claim a part of the good things. The Impostors are always pitted against the hero who draws out their absurdities with mocking irony.[17]

Blanche's entrance and her subsequent treatment by Stanley fits the pattern of the Impostor, as Cornford describes it. The real agon is over when Blanche enters—that is, the outcome is a foregone conclusion. Because the South has been defeated, the issue is never in doubt. In the world of the Kowalskis, Blanche is an impostor; she is not the lady she pretends to be. She imposes herself upon the home life of Stanley and Stella without any right to share in their love-feast, she is mocked and derided by the hero, she is finally routed by the disclosure of her pretense. Moreover, her character as antagonist is related to the character of the impostor; as Cornford points out, the same traits distinguish both:

> (1) he [the antagonist] disturbs and outrages the rites which no profane eye should see; (2) he vaunts his insolent authority in boasts, whose vanity the power of the god will expose; (3) he is set at nought, beaten, blinded, torn to pieces, cast out.[18]

Blanche's actions again reflect this type. She makes an issue of the curtains that separate her sleeping quarters from the married couple's, she disrupts the ritual of the poker game (Mitch observes: "Poker should not be played in a house with women"), she criticizes Stanley's manners at the dinner table. Her boasting lies about her life in Laurel, about her rich suitors, and her superior attitudes toward the environment and Stanley's background are exposed by Stanley and lead to her destruction. Blanche meets the fate proper to the Impostor and the Antagonist.

If Aristophanic satire seems a far cry from Broadway and the Old South, it is helpful to recall that, among modern playwrights, Chekhov uses this pattern in *The Cherry Orchard* and that Chekhov is one of the major influences on Williams.[19] The main plot of *The Cherry Orchard* is an adaptation of the intruder motif. The freed serf Lophakin imposes himself on the aristocratic Ranevskys and, although he ends up with possession of the family estate, he is never accepted into the aristocracy. Rather than capitulate to the nouveau riche, the family packs and leaves the premises with the echo of axes in the distance. Stanislavski saw fit to interpret the play as the tragic passing of an era with the deserted servant Firs as a symbol of the old regime, but Chekhov himself thought of it as a comedy.[20] In using the intruder motif, Williams followed Chekhov and selected a model with a traditional meaning.

The combination of these two patterns, the Civil War romance and the comic, produce a tension in the play. The intruder is conventionally an unsympathetic character, and the comic structure leads to a celebration of the virtues and the triumph of the established society. But Blanche is not only intruder; she is also the heroine of the romance. Moreover, she establishes some right to consideration, at least from Stella.

Blanche. I, I, *I* took the blows in my face and my body! All of those deaths! The long parade to the graveyard! . . . You came home in time for the funerals, Stella! And funerals are pretty compared to deaths. . . . Yes, accuse me! Sit there and stare at me, thinking I let the place go! *I* let the place go! Where were *you!* In bed with your Polack! (STREETCAR, pp. 25–6.)

The history of her unhappy marriage to a young homosexual who committed suicide supports her right to understanding and sympathy; her drinking and her promiscuity are efforts to escape from these memories and to hold on to her youth. At the conclusion of the play, when she is forced to withdraw completely into the unreal plantation world, the emphasis falls on her pitiable situation. Rough, impersonal handling by the hatchet-faced matron from the institution terrifies her; she is rescued by a gallant doctor who understands. In this scene she is no longer an Impostor, but a lady with a right to chivalric treatment. But only *after* her defeat, her complete collapse, does she escape the role of intruder and impostor. Because Blanche is simultaneously heroine and intruder, she arouses both sympathy and revulsion in the audience. This double role, along with the modification of the plantation myth in combination with the intruder pattern, is responsible for the apparent confusion at the heart of the play.

The interpretation of Blanche's role with relation to the meaning of the play has given rise to dissension among the critics. The director of the Broadway production, Elia Kazan, saw the significance of the intruder motif and was disturbed by it:

He's [Stanley has] got things the way he wants them around there and he does *not* want them upset by a phony, corrupt, sick, destructive woman. *This makes Stanley right.* Are we going into the era of Stanley? He may be practical and right . . . but where the hell does it leave us? [21]

On the other hand, Joseph Wood Krutch opts for the Southern heroine who has the proper instincts, is on the side of civilization and refinement, while the world of Stella and her husband is a barbarism.[22] Stanley has his advocates—not excluding the playwright —and his position is not without merit. He has the earmarks of the D. H. Lawrence hero in contact with the realities. There is not a nervous bone in his body, and his virility affords a haven for himself and for his partner.[23] While they are choosing up sides, the critics do not overlook Stella. Her vacillation between Blanche and Stanley is symbolic—she is drawn to her sister's point of view, but only the security of her marriage saves her from Blanche's fate.[24] Perhaps closer to the bone, the critic can find a more remorseless influence lurking behind the scenes; time is the real villain, the time that has relentlessly moved the Old South out of range.[25] The point is that each one of these positions is tenable, it simply depends which aspect of the drama the critic considers, which level of meaning or structure he decides is most significant, whether the plantation legend or the established society is preferable. The ironic juxtapositions in the treatment of character and especially in the use of the structure make it clear that the playwright himself could not decide.

This ambivalence results from the playwright's position relative to the myth. Williams writes from inside and, because he is caught up in the tensions of the myth, he has no resources by which to resolve them. Thus the romanticism that is characteristic of the Southern temperament—and Blanche's outstanding trait—is also a problem for the playwright. The conflict between Puritanism and hedonism and that penchant for violence which the cultural historian attributes to the Southern character are attributable to the author as well as to his play. Williams himself cannot escape the excesses of the syndrome he is investigating; they crop out at every level. Unlike Miller, Williams' detachment is very imperfect and his artistry reflects the dilemma he is trying to explain.

A tendency to exaggerate affects every facet of the drama. In his characterization Williams cannot leave well enough alone. He wants to impress on the audience that Blanche has had tragic experiences in her past life. So he piles horror on horror—her homosexual husband, his suicide, the deaths in the family, the loss of Belle Reve, her dismissal for promiscuity—and brings them up to date with a rape by her sister's husband. Stella has succumbed to Stanley's masculinity. Well and good. But she has succumbed so completely that she now reads comic books in bed like a "narcotized Eastern idol." On his first meeting with Blanche, Stanley "gets comfortable" by taking off his shirt: this carries the "rough stud" image to an extreme. The symbolism in the play also occasionally gets out of hand. Williams cannot resist underlining the implications of the title:

Blanche. What you are talking about is brutal desire—just—Desire!—the name of the rattle-trap street-car that bangs through the Quarter, up one old narrow street and down another . . .
Stella. Haven't you ever ridden on that street-car?
Blanche. It brought me here. (STREETCAR, p. 79.)

The cadence that gives Blanche's dialogue its piquancy sometimes spills over into Stanley's speeches. When he is grunting out monosyllabic replies, he is flat-toned, direct and believable. But in longer sequences his speech takes on an imaginative quality:

Stanley. Our supply-man down at the plant has been going through Laurel for years and he knows all about her and everybody else in the town of Laurel knows all about her. She is as famous in Laurel as if she was President of the United States, only she is not respected by any party! (STREETCAR, p. 113.)

Williams tends to carry a good thing too far and, by overstepping the bounds, begins to resemble his heroine.

Along with this tendency to exaggerate, there is a liberal sprinkling of violence throughout the play that functions as a counterpoint to Southern gentility. The cultured code of the planter receives a rough shaking-up from Stanley. The wild fight in the kitchen is immediately preceded by a scene in which Mitch and Blanche waltz about the room to a Viennese air. The romantic absorption of Mitch and Blanche is broken by an oath; Stanley snatches the radio and tosses it out the window. Then he takes on the whole kitchen in a wild brawl. When Stella runs upstairs to escape by spending the night with a neighbor, Stanley stands out on the street bellowing. When Blanche and Stella badger him about his table manners, he clears the table by smashing cup and saucer on the floor. In the climactic bedroom scene Stanley is able to match Blanche move for move. When the disillusioned Mitch tried to fumble at her, Blanche routed him by screaming "Fire!" Such refinement will not work with Stanley—Blanche smashes a bottle and threatens him with broken glass.

> *Stanley.* What did you do that for?
> *Blanche.* So I could twist the broken end in your face!
> *Stanley.* I bet you would do that!
>
> . . . .
>
> *Stanley.* Oh! So you want some rough-house! All right, let's have some rough house! (STREETCAR, p. 151.)

The helpless Southern belle turns tiger when she is threatened, but she is overcome as much by Stanley's sexuality (and the "hot trumpet" from the Four Deuces) as by his violence. Violence permeates the atmosphere—it is not simply attached to one or another character. Stanley senses it in Blanche when he describes her as a wildcat, a school of sharks, a tiger. Stella confesses her excitement when, on their wedding night, Stanley smashed all the light-bulbs in the flat with the heel of her slipper. This penchant for violence, then, can be attributed to the playwright; it is another facet of a tradition that exalts sensitivity and refinement.

The clash between the Puritan view of sex and hedonism is related to this violence. In *Streetcar* sex is oversimplified and exaggerated—the playwright is of two minds about it. Between Stanley and Stella sex is too simple and vital; with Blanche (and what remains of Blanche in Stella) it is too destructive. Husband and wife drown their differences in the physical act; after their squabble they come together moaning "like two animals," and Stanley makes her forget the plantation and her old life by "getting those colored lights going." His virility, underscored at every turn, constitutes a large portion of his superiority. To attribute this kind of power to pure sex bespeaks a fascination in the face of a mystery that has its horrific side. Stella has lost all sense of dignity and much of her sensitivity; sex has helped to destroy Blanche. The Puritan awe of its power mingles with an exaggerated sense of that same power. One critic thinks that the ambiguity in *Streetcar* results from Williams' inability to decide for sex or against it; would that the matter were so clear-cut.[26] In order to have any positive opinion about it at all, Williams has to detach it from any moral or traditional context, i.e., from the myth; when he tries to consider it within the myth, he finds it fascinating and destructive. In the Civil War romance this opposition can be sublimated or at least ignored, but on emerging into the cold light of Stanley's world, it creates an insoluble dilemma.

These tensions in *Streetcar* are then expressions of the Southern mind, an artistic representation of the Southern character. One last point remains to be explained—a kind of organic unity that melds these opposing elements together. The ironic use of the comic structure that underlies the plantation myth functions as a bond of union. By calling on a comic structure, Williams indicates that he is aware of his own excesses. The resonances that this structural pattern calls up are reminiscent of, for example, Faulkner's wry humor-mixed-with-pathos. Perhaps, at bottom, the comic is the only defense that the Southerner has against his own temperamental orientations to romance and violence and an unbalance about sex. As long as he can wryly contemplate his own seriousness, a precarious compromise can be worked out. For while the tradition remains operative, these characteristics continue to form the Southern mind. The recognition that the Kowalskis are in the ascendant demands that the tradition, the myth with its preoccupation with the past, be treated half-humorously—for good or ill, the treatment can be only *half*-humorous. Williams' ironic reversals, especially his use of the intruder motif with its comic structure, are a self-protection against the powerful attraction of the myth and a dramatization of the conflict that goes on in the mind of the Southerner.

To say, then, that *Streetcar* is a "confused" play is to acknowledge the tensions at work in it; to say *why* it is confused is to describe the way these tensions are dramatized. No amount of analysis will "solve" the dilemma in the play; there is no middle road (that the playwright can find) between Blanche and Stanley. The unity that the play does possess, however, comes from its attempt to deal with the whole picture, the quandary of the Southerner, without extenuating, or minimizing, or offering facile solutions. Williams has called his plays personal therapy, but his fantasies are not, like the man who cannot stomach apple pie, purely personal. Blanche's dilemma, and Williams', is that of the Southerner, who has lost a culture and a way of life and who is caught between two worlds, one gone with the wind, the other barely worth having.

The Long Shadow of the Law:
The Crucible

Among popular forms perennially in favor on Broadway and in the television ratings, the courtroom drama ranks with the leaders. Numerous television series have used the format, from simple whodunits like *Perry Mason,* in which the trial is a device for discovering the criminal, to *The Defenders,* which used the courtroom drama to present controversial issues in legal principle and in practice. Recent Broadway seasons have featured a wide spectrum: *Billy Budd, The Caine Mutiny Court Martial, Witness for the Prosecution, The Andersonville Trial, Twelve Angry Men.* This format has inherent qualities that attract the playwright of any age: a clear division between protagonist and antagonist, gradual revelation of the facts, application of facts to principles, suspense leading to the climax of a verdict. Though the formula has never been neglected (*Oresteia, Measure for Measure, Volpone, St. Joan*), it is most favored in democracies, where the Law is venerated and the Court the principle instrument of justice. Beneath the trial formula and the trappings of the Law, there is a complex of attitudes that includes veneration for these institutions. The courtroom has become the sanctuary of modern secularized society and the trial the only true ritual it has left.

The development of these attitudes toward the Law and its ritual began early in American history. Our society from its beginnings had a respect for, and confidence in, the Law. Tom Paine, in *Common Sense,* voiced an ideal which, though it has been variously interpreted, has retained its fascination for the American mind:

But where say some is the King of America? I'll tell you Friend he reigns above; and doth not make havoc of mankind like the Royal Brute of Great Britain. Yet that we may not appear to be defective even in earthy honors, let a day be solemnly set apart for the proclaiming of the Charter; let it be brought forth placed on the Divine Law, the Word of God; let a crown be placed thereon, by which the World may know, that so far as we approve of monarchy, that in America THE LAW IS KING.

For the contemporary bureaucrat as for the revolutionary patriot, "government under the Law" expresses the democratic ideal: equal rights for all, protection both for the individual in his legitimate endeavors and for society from the depredations of unprincipled individuals, justice meted out with an impersonal, unprejudiced hand according to ordinance. In the Law, so the democrat holds, all opposites are reconciled; the individual and the community, freedom and regimentation, the rule of principle and the rule of men. As the King is the principle of order in a monarchy, so the Law is considered the source of order in a democracy.

In America more obviously than elsewhere, there has been a tendency to regard the Law as the embodiment of "moral law" and "natural law," as well as a *corpus juris* inherited from legal tradition. The nineteenth-century concept of "fundamental law" was made up of these two and was looked on as absolute and immutable.[1] This attitude, foreshadowed in Paine's juxtaposition of Bible and Charter, received concrete expression in the dominance of church and courthouse in the nineteenth-century village and town. When the influence of the church declined, the Law necessarily exerted a greater influence than ever. The corpus of the common law and the system by which it is administered has acquired an aura of permanence and infallibility. On these elements, according to the American creed, rests the security of the citizen and the stability of his way of life.

Belief in this idea has engendered a veneration also for the courts and the lawyers who practice in them. Every culture has some sort of spiritual government that is entrusted with the ideals of that culture. In America the Courts are at once the receptacle and the guardian of those ideals. "Our spiritual government today centers in the judicial system. Here is the bulwark of all the older symbols and theories both legal and economic. Here is the stage on which the ideals of society are given concrete reality." [2] This attitude is most manifest when the courts come under attack.

Americans alone of Western people made constitutionalism a religion and the judiciary a religious order and surrounded both with an aura of piety. They made the Constitution supreme law, and placed responsibility for the functioning of the federal system on the courts. The Supreme Court, in time, became the most nearly sacrosanct of American institutions.[3]

The dignity and inviolability accorded the Supreme Court is shared by the whole judicial system. The judge, *ex officio,* holds a position of influence and respect, and in his own courtroom, he is absolute master. The legal profession, while not so exalted, shares some of this distinction with the judiciary. Reverence for the Court and respect for the lawyer is a reflection of an abiding belief in justice and equality administered under the Law.

One of the most persistent attitudes embodied in the myth of the Law is the notion of a "fair trial." "The notion that every man however lowly is entitled to a fair trial and an impartial hearing is regarded as the cornerstone of civilized government." [4] The Law is seen as watching over legal procedures and guaranteeing impartiality by "due process." The general outlines of the procedure are: a preliminary hearing; an indictment which discloses to the accused the nature of the offense; a trial in which evidence is presented fully and an opportunity given to the accused to introduce and respond to all relevant issues; an appellate review of both the law and the evidence; a permanent written record of the entire proceedings.[5] The "fair trial" aspect of our view of the Law provides for the protection of the individual from "mob rule" and tyranny.

Another attitude, generally and vaguely opposed to the ideal of fair trial, is the sacredness of law enforcement. As the Law protects the individual from injustice, it also secures the rights of society against the criminal. This aspect of the myth emphasizes the absolute nature of the principles involved and demands that principles be applied to the facts impersonally, beyond purely personal discretion. If laws are not enforced, and disrespect for the law allowed to flourish, then chaos results.

If we look at the two attitudes expressed by the myth, in theory they seem to involve a number of contradictions: the individual in the democracy must be free, yet the rules laid down by society constrain him; a permanent unyielding code must be enforced without respect to persons, yet justice can never ignore persons; the majority must rule, yet minorities are entitled to their rights. When these theories are applied to criminal law, the same type of contradiction appears:

An attorney should not take cases the winning of which imperils the forces of law and order; every criminal, however, is entitled to a defense; criminal lawyers, however, should not resort to mere technicalities; nevertheless, they should do everything legally possible for their clients.[6]

These contradictions, if spelled out and adverted to, would paralyze the legal system; they can subsist together only because they are resolved in practice. In the American system, the trial reconciles these attitudes in a ritual action. It is a genuine ritual—a communal, sacrosanct ceremony that expresses the beliefs of the community and, within the limits of the myth, provides for the purgation of the individual and order in the society.

The trial ritual—the structure of the action and the actors involved—dramatizes both the fair-trial and the law-enforcement aspects of the myth. It is an investigation of innocence and guilt in terms of an application of facts and motives to principles. There is a clear declaration of the issues, a marshalling of forces into opposing camps, a verdict in which justice is done. The opposing camps—prosecution and defense—represent, broadly speaking, the two extremes; the prosecution maintaining the rights of society and the defense the rights of the individual. The judge represents the absolute nature of the law and arbitrates the application of facts to principles. In its verdict, the jury resolves the opposition between these two forces under the direction of the judge. As peers who can evaluate the motives and actions of the accused and as citizens who respect the law, the members of this body represent both the individual and society. Thus they can weigh the case and make an objective judgment. Ideally, the verdict has the status of absolute truth that encompasses all the attitudes of society. Dramatically, it is the epiphany that resolves the agon.

The ceremonial nature of this action is underscored by the circumstances that surround it and by the formalized treatment it is given. Even the criminal taken red-handed is not considered guilty until the jury is in and the verdict rendered. The protocol of the court-room—the baliff's cry, the judge's robes, the formal language—are all part of the ritual atmosphere. The set procedure, with its rubrical consistency, also emphasizes the ceremonial structure. These details declare that the trial is a ritual in which (ideally) justice is done and in which the contradictions in the democratic system are reconciled.

One of the most instructive attempts by a contemporary playwright to make use of the trial ritual and the attitudes that surround it is Arthur Miller's *The Crucible*. Plays like *The Caine Mutiny Court Martial* use the formula in a straightforward way to vindicate the hero's actions or, at least, his motives; in such plays the trial is a convenient dramatic device for presenting the action. The probity of the court is taken for granted; due process is the means by which the defense can insure justice for the individual. Miller's play not only uses the formula as a dramatic framing device, but also raises the question about the value of the trial itself as an instrument of justice. At the heart of *The Crucible* is the relation of the individual to the Law, and the author's probing into this area makes the play a significant work. Miller has described the playwright's art in terms of the Law: "In one sense a play is a species of jurisprudence, and some part of it must take the advocate's role, something else must act in defense, and the entirety must engage the Law." [7] Whether or not this analogy holds true for his other efforts is a moot point; in *The Crucible* he consciously uses history and the trial formula to investigate the American attitude toward the Law.

Miller's play is based on actual records of a seventeenth-century incident in colonial Salem, but it has clear parallels with contemporary events. Attempts to write historical drama for the modern theatre have not been notably successful; perhaps they have never been except when the past is dealt with in terms of the present. Maxwell Anderson failed in spite of his Shakespearean style, and his *Elizabeth the Queen* and *Mary of Scotland*, while they tap a remote sense of Anglo-Saxon pride, today seem almost as dated as Boker's *Francesca da Rimini*. Conversely, currently popular history plays—*Man for All Seasons, Luther, Becket*—make the story a vehicle for modern themes: the folly of depending on the common man or the purity of the law, religion as a psychophysical phenomenon, the inevitability of a cultural clash even when individuals are personally engaged. For the dramatist, history serves as a glass in which the audience sees its own image.

The Crucible opened on Broadway January 22, 1953, at the height of the furor stirred up by the accusations of Senator Joe McCarthy. In February of 1950 McCarthy had addressed the Ohio County Women's Republican Club in Wheeling, West Virginia. In his speech, as the Wheeling *Intelligencer* reported it, he claimed to have "in his hand" a list of two-hundred-and-five known Communists in the State Department. With this broadside the panic was on. The "threat of Communism from within" became a serious consideration in national politics and in the attitudes of Americans; McCarthy became a rallying point for conservatives the country over. By 1953 investigations of this charge (and the variants which McCarthy later added) were being undertaken on a nation-wide scale. The Senator used his Congressional privilege to investigate people in public life, and everyone who had had any connection with the Party felt the pressure of public opinion and a sense of insecurity about their position and their public image. Miller's own record in this regard was not unblemished and the matter became a personal threat.

It was the fact that a political, objective, knowledgeable campaign from the far Right was capable of creating not only a terror but a new subjective reality, a veritable mystique which was gradually assuming even a holy resonance. The wonder of it all struck me that so practical and picayune a cause, carried forward by such manifestly ridiculous men, should be capable of paralyzing thought itself, and worse, causing to billow up such persuasive clouds of "mysterious" feelings within people.[8]

He was deeply disturbed as he watched men who had known him well for years pass him by "without a word" because of this terror "knowingly planned and consciously engineered." McCarthyism was in the air and it had all the qualities—for those personally affected —of the witch-hunt. Miller consciously draws the parallel; his plays are efforts to deal with what was "in the air." "They are one man's way of saying to his fellow men, 'This is what you see every day, or think or feel; now I will show you what you really know but have not had the time or the disinterestedness, or the insight, or the information to understand consciously.'"[9] Once the Communist issue settled into the background, the playwright could protest that the real inner meaning of the play is not simply an attack on McCarthyism, but a treatment of the perennial conflict between individual conscience and civil society—"the handing over of conscience to another and the realization that with conscience goes the person, the soul immortal, and the 'Name.' " [10] In any event, there is a parallel between what happened in Salem under the Puritan theocracy and what happened in Washington under the aegis of anti-Communism, and this parallel has its impact on Miller's treatment of the historical record. In a broader perspective, the myth of the Law and the ritual of the trial shape the structure of the play and help determine its ultimate dramatic meaning.

If the reign of Law is central to the American democratic ideal and if the "fair trial" is the ritual which insures its inviolability, the worst of all perversions in this area is a "bad" law enforced by a "corrupt" court. It is quite clear that, in the real order of things, any particular law is judged not by an absolute standard, but by one relative to a public consensus, and that this consensus can change. Thus, for instance, the trial of Joan of Arc seems a blatant miscarriage of justice, not because the judges failed to adhere to due process or to apply the letter of the law, but because a heresy law itself no longer compels any agreement from society at large. Prosecutions for heresy no longer fit into popular notions about the area of legal inquiry. Therefore, Joan's trial, by standards of due process "so eminently fair," has long appeared to be a travesty of justice.[11] Because the last appeal in a democratic system is to the courts and because the Law is the bulwark of social order, any vision of corruption in the judiciary, any use of the law against the tenor of the popular mind, becomes the occasion for a general outcry. So, after the fact, the Sacco-Vanzetti case and the McCarthy investigations can be dubbed witch-hunts, whether due process was observed or not. This corruption is always laid at the door of particular individuals or a particular community because it cannot be attributed to the idea of the Law itself. Miller, in *The Crucible,* deals with the perversion of the Law in the township of Salem and, by extension, with a persistent threat to any democratic system.

In the light of this belief—that corruption is of the individual—it is worth noting that Miller found his inspiration for the play in a bit of personal information embedded in the trial records:

I had known of the Salem witch-hunt for many years before "McCarthy-ism" had arrived. . . . I doubt I should even have tempted agony by actually writing a play upon the subject had I not come upon a single fact. It was that Abigail Williams, the prime mover of the Salem hysteria, so far as the hysterical children were concerned, had a short time earlier been the house servant of the Proctors, and now was crying out Elizabeth Proctor as a witch, but more—it was clear from the record that with entirely uncharacteristic fastidiousness she was refusing to include John Proctor, Elizabeth's husband, in her accusations, despite the urging of the prosecutors.[12]

Though the major issue in the play deals with the individual and society and with judicial corruption, Miller found his dramatic motivation in a domestic triangle. There is no question of the law as such being at fault; it is the motivations of individuals that are to provide an understanding of the hysteria that created and prolonged the witch-hunt. Within the structure of the trial formula Miller investigates these motivations and the actions which flow from them in relation to the guilt or innocence of individuals and of the community.

The trial formula, when it is not simply a framing device for a detective-story plot, is an investigation of innocence and guilt in terms of an application of facts and motives to principles. In order that guilt or innocence be proven, the individual declared responsible for evil or exonerated of it, the ritual provides for a clear definition of the issues, and a marshalling of forces into opposing camps. The resulting agon is presided over by judge and/or jury representing the impartiality of the principles (which are not always included in any particular law or set of laws) from which justice emanates.

The dramatic uses of this formula can be various. In the melodramatic treatment, the hero is falsely accused and vindicated by the verdict with the onus falling on a clearly defined group of villains or on a single vicious individual. More complex versions of the pattern depend on a less definite division of responsibility. For instance, the hero can be declared legally guilty according to a "bad" law or by a corrupt court, thus throwing the real guilt on the community that supports the law or fails to impeach the court. The implied result is the purgation of society for whose renewed sense of justice the hero is responsible. A third version declares the hero really guilty under a good law, thus revealing a hitherto unacknowledged guilt to him (and to the audience). When the protagonist as individual or type stands convicted in the light of genuine principles, the trial pattern assumes a tragic orientation. So, even though the trial is essentially a purification ritual, its dramatic effect varies according to the distribution of guilt and innocence. *The Crucible*, even though it does indict the community, includes a complicating variant because the protagonist, besides answering a formal charge, must satisfy his own conscience about his innocence.

The structure of events, then, involves two investigations, two indictments, and two verdicts. Proctor is arraigned by the court for witchcraft; Proctor weighs the guilt of his infidelity to his wife. These two issues are carefully interwoven by the playwright, for Proctor's guilty relationship with Abigail Williams provides him with the evidence to prove the official testimony of Abby and the girls fraudulent. Thus the investigation of the witchcraft charge involves his confessing to adultery. These two issues, both of which involve Proctor's guilt, interrelate to determine the meaning of the play. What is ultimately at stake is the relation of the individual to a society governed by men under the Law. Whatever Miller intended to do in his play, *The Crucible* makes a statement about this relationship.

In one of his headnotes Miller makes a claim for his historical accuracy in depicting the events of the witch trials. The play is situated in the appropriate historical context of time and place. Salem of 1692 is depicted as an isolated community, self-contained by the surrounding forest; its spiritual government and the secular arm are in the hands of Puritan divines and the law is the law of the covenanter; the dialogue has a suitable seventeenth-century flavor. The action runs chronologically within the setting so that the realistic progression fits with the logic of the trial formula and the historical event. But the playwright adds to this perspective another dimension—a consciousness of the significance of these events to a present-day democracy. The "good people" in the cast of characters have attitudes which reflect contemporary ideals rather than the historical Puritan outlook. Thus the playwright does not mechanically reproduce the 1692 situation and exploit it for its inherent dramatic values; rather through the attitudes of the protagonist, his allies among the villagers and one of the inquisitors, he includes a perspective relevant to the audience. Miller himself was aware of this broader dimension. He explains that his realism does not imply an attempt at slice-of-life drama; he felt that the expressionism of *Death of a Salesman* would be unnecessary:

I had found a kind of self-awareness in the bloody book of Salem and had thought that since the natural realistic surface of that society was one already immersed in the questions of meaning and the relations of men to God, to write a realistic play of that world was already to write in a style beyond contemporary realism.[13]

Perhaps this self-awareness is better attributed to the playwright than to the trial records; in any event, there is a dimension in the play which anticipates the modern attitude toward the Salem incident, whether history includes it or not.[14]

As a defendant in the courtroom and protagonist in the drama John Proctor is very recognizable. He is a farmer, a man of substance in the community without being a land-grabber like the malicious Thomas Putnam. Though he lives outside the ambit of the village, he acts as a respected member of the community. In his dealings with others, neighbors and servants, he is straightforward, honest and somewhat unpolished. When he comes looking for his delinquent servant girl, there will be no nonsense: "I'll show you a great doin' on your arse one of these days. Now get you home; my wife is waitin' with your work!"[15] This rugged individualism also informs his attitude toward religion—positive, undogmatic with more than a touch of scepticism on the witchcraft issue.

Putnam. I do not think I saw you at Sabbath meeting since the snow flew.
Proctor. I have trouble enough without I come five mile to hear him preach only hellfire and bloody damnation. Take it to heart, Mr. Parris. There are many others who stay away from church these days because you hardly ever mention God any more. (CRUCIBLE, p. 245.)

He cannot brook the idea of the minister who should be a servant to the parish making himself the authority: "I do not like the smell of this 'authority.'" Neither is he a sombre or a solemn man; he has that quality which distinguishes a line of American heroes, a love of nature and the outdoors. His first scene with Elizabeth dwells on fertility and the beauties of nature.

Proctor. This farm's a continent when you go foot by foot droppin' seeds in it.

Elizabeth. (coming with the cider) It must be.

Proctor. (drinks a long draught; then, putting the glass down) You ought to bring some flowers in the house.

Elizabeth. Oh, I forgot! I will tomorrow.

Proctor. It's winter in here yet. On Sunday let you come with me, and we'll walk the farm together; I never see such a load of flowers on the earth. . . . Lilacs has a purple smell. Lilac is a smell of nightfall, I think. Massachusetts is a beauty in the spring. (CRUCIBLE, p. 262.)

This quality—the touch of the poet, the appreciation of nature— relates to Proctor's predicament with Abby. The girl has gauged his temper, he is no "cold man." She tempted him and, being a man of strong passions, he fell. By the time the play opens, the nagging of conscience has produced a resolve not to touch her again. The affair, as far as Proctor is concerned, is over and done with; he has confessed to his wife and honestly is trying to make it up to her. In short, Miller's protagonist is no Puritan, no hypocrite; he has the democratic virtues (and vices) that render him recognizable to the audience.

With Proctor are associated the "good people" of the village. Giles Corey, the homespun old curmudgeon who battles for his rights in court, Rebecca Nurse, the sainted lady of the village with a wide reputation for charity, are also caught in the web of the law, the one because he injudiciously wanted to know what his wife was reading in her books, the other because she could not save Goody Putnam's children. Corey manifests the same kind of individualism as Proctor; he will not accept the tyranny of his neighbors or the injustice of the court. Rebecca Nurse also shows a blessed scepticism by suggesting perhaps the malice of the villagers, rather than the practice of witchcraft, is responsible for the evil that is abroad. During the course of the action one of the prosecutors, Mr. Hale, is converted in a dramatic acknowledgement of Proctor's position. These personae reflect the protagonist's qualities and so are related to him in the course of the action.

The opposition is concentrated in Abigail Williams who bridges the official investigation and Proctor's personal struggle. The "evil" in the play focuses on Abigail as fountainhead, even though she is not its most chilling expression. It is not her actions that condemn her: dancing in the woods by modern standards is no crime, her desire for John Proctor is rendered quite understandable, her uncle's superciliousness is riding for a fall. Rather, it is the means she uses to pursue her ends. She is willing to sacrifice the community and everyone in it, to subvert the function of the Law, in order to gain her objectives. Her wickedness, then, amounts to a shrewd use of the hypocrisy, greed and spite that thrive in her neighbors under the pretext of seeing justice done. Her power arises from her ability to convert her psychic energies and the willful pursuit of her own objectives into a genuine visionary hysteria. At bottom Abby knows that her prophetic fit is self-induced, that the witchcraft she denounces is non-existent; but once the fit is on her, she can produce a convincing performance and induce the same kind of hysteria in the children. Her real diabolism is her misuse of the sacrosanct office of witness to gain her own ends.

With her are associated the "bad people" of Salem, those who are shown to be greedy and spiteful like the Putnams, those who are envious of power and status like Parris and Cheever. When witchcraft is murmured in the streets, the concealed feelings and grudges come to the surface. Thus the sterile Putnams cry out on Giles Corey for his land and Rebecca Nurse for her good name and her large brood. Parris sees an opportunity to put down the rebellious "faction" (Proctor and Corey) in the parish which refuses him ownership of his house and golden candlesticks for his altar. They can invoke the letter of the law, the witchcraft ordinance, for their own purposes. Conventional belief supports the mischief they do in the name of tradition. Their evil, like Abigail's, is a misuse of law and the court, institutions which everyone must respect as the source of order in the community. This evil, if execrable, is intelligible, for it looks to personal gain and satisfaction of the ego.

Between the Proctor faction and the bad people is the official judiciary, the judges and members of the court. The court represents the force of the Law, impersonal and impartial, which reconciles letter and spirit, law enforcement and individual rights. An attitude of reverence for the Law permeates the play. Mr. Hale comes armed with its authority, "allied to the best minds of Europe—kings, philosophers, scientists, and ecclesiasts of all churches." His armful of tomes, he pompously declares, are weighted with authority. Here are principles with the certainty of law to test by:

Hale. Now let me instruct you. We cannot look to superstition in this. The Devil is precise; the marks of his presence are definite as stone, and I must tell you all that I shall not proceed unless you are prepared to believe me if I should find no bruise of hell upon her. (CRUCIBLE, p. 252.)

Hale proceeds with his investigation calmly, impersonally, sounding his warning about going beyond the facts, and relying on his authoritative books. When the official inquiry opens, the court possesses the same sense of solemnity and definitiveness. Elizabeth calls it "a proper court, four judges sent out of Boston, weighty magistrates of the General Court." When Proctor threatens to rip the Governor's warrant, Cheever, the clerk of the court, warns him not to touch it. Constable Herrick's nine men must arrest Elizabeth—it is so ordered by the court. (CRUCIBLE, p. 281.) When, in the third act, Judge Danforth is introduced, he is wrapped in the dignity of his office and knowledge of the law. After a disturbance in the courtroom and an outcry by Giles Corey, he interrogates the old man:

Danforth. Who is this man?

. . . .

Giles. My name is Corey, sir, Giles Corey. I have six hundred acres, and timber in addition. It is my wife you be condemning now.
Danforth. And how do you imagine to help her cause with such contemptuous riot? Now be gone. Your old age alone keeps you out of jail for this.
Giles. They be tellin' lies about my wife, sir, I—
Danforth. Do you take it upon yourself to determine what this court shall believe and what it shall set aside?
Giles. Your Excellency, we mean no disrespect for—
Danforth. Disrespect, indeed! This is disruption, Mister. This is the highest court of the supreme government of this division.

(CRUCIBLE, p. 287.)

Even the rough old yeoman is impressed with Danforth and has no doubts about his being a good judge. On this point the record shows, and Miller acknowledges, that due process is Danforth's middle name. Even in the face of Proctor who ripped his warrant and damned the court, the judge is prepared to "hear the evidence." Whatever motives they might have, the men-at-law conduct their cases with a fine show of impartiality. In the end Danforth and Hale are shown to have been on different sides of the fence; Danforth is joined to Abigail and the forces of evil and Hale becomes an advocate of the individual with Proctor. But this fourth-act epiphany derives its full significance only in contrast to the image of dignity and impartiality that the judges and the lawyers demonstrate in the first three acts.

Though she is one of the accused and John Proctor's wife, Elizabeth, in the early scenes, shares this dramatic function of the judiciary because she rules on Proctor's personal guilt with regard to his infidelity. Proctor makes this function clear:

Proctor. I cannot speak but I am doubted, every moment judged for lies, as though I come into a court when I come into this house!

Elizabeth. John, you are not open with me. You saw her in a crowd, you said. Now you—

Proctor. No more! I should have roared you down when first you told me your suspicion. But I wilted, and, like a Christian, I confessed. Confessed! Some dream I had must have mistaken you for God that day. But you're not, you're not, and let you remember it! Let you look sometimes for the goodness in me, and judge me not.

Elizabeth. I do not judge you. The magistrate sits in your heart that judges you. I never thought you but a good man, John—(with a smile)— only somewhat bewildered.

Proctor. (laughing bitterly) Oh, Elizabeth, your justice would freeze beer! (CRUCIBLE, p. 265.)

The wife is a mirror of the magistrate; she is unemotional, impersonal about the relationship. She stands in much the same position with regard to John and Abigail as Danforth does to the witches and the community. This is another link between the two plot-lines. The "cold wife" cannot arrive at a fair decision about her husband because she relies on the "evidence" and the letter of the law.

The opposing camps are finally drawn up according to their attitude toward the Law. The protagonist and his allies, whether or not they believe in the existence of witchcraft, do not believe in the rigid enforcement of this law in Salem. They see that, literally, the letter killeth. The antagonists, whether believers or not, stand by the rigid enforcement of the letter for their own purposes. The judiciary, bound by the Law to do justice, is charged with deciding between these two camps.

By choosing the witchcraft law and by giving his protagonist modern attitudes, Miller puts audience judgment and sympathy beyond all doubt. Today's audience cannot take the possibility of witchcraft seriously; the implication for us is that no enlightened citizen of any age would be able to take it seriously. When some of the citizens of a community see a law as outmoded, that is, when a significant minority take a contrary stance, any rigid enforcement of such a law must be considered unjust and undemocratic. (Consider the civil rights issues of the recent past.) The audience can reasonably anticipate that the trial, as a ritual that reconciles differences and vindicates the right, will justify the position of Proctor and his allies.

The events that precede the trial dramatize at once a fear that reason may not prevail and a confidence that the Court will acknowledge the right. In spite of the hysteria of the children, the malevolence of townsfolk like the Putnams and the self-interest of Pastor Parris, Hale is convinced that the innocent have nothing to fear. The orderly course of official inquiry by an impartial investigator should guarantee the outcome, but it is clear that Hale cannot control the forces at work. Though we want to share his confidence in the legal process, the indictments, based on Abby's evidence, raise serious doubts about the outcome of the trial.

In the trial itself Miller carefully compounds faith in the ritual as the instrument of justice with the fear that it cannot cope with the irrational forces at work in Salem. The solemnity of the Court and Danforth's attention to due process accords with the sense of confidence in the ritual. The Judge follows its prescriptions faithfully, he works calmly and impersonally with the government at his side. "This is the highest court of the supreme government of this province," he thunders at Giles Corey, "do you know it?" (CRUCIBLE, p. 287.) When Giles wishes to present evidence in his wife's defense, Danforth insists on form: "Let him submit his evidence in proper affidavit. You certainly are aware of our procedure here, Mr. Hale." (CRUCIBLE, p. 287.) When John Proctor protests that the children have been lying and that the Putnams are guilty of collusion, Danforth replies that he has found their evidence convincing:

You know, Mr. Proctor, that the entire contention of the state in these trials is that the voice of Heaven is speaking through the children? . . .

I tell you straight, Mister, I have seen marvels in this court. I have seen people choked before my eyes by spirits; I have seen them stuck with pins and slashed by daggers. I have until this moment not the slightest reason to suspect that the children may be deceiving me. (CRUCIBLE, pp. 289, 291.)

With this warning Danforth hears Proctor's evidence. He is too good a lawyer to act arbitrarily. When Cheever cries out that Proctor plows on Sunday and Hale breaks in to protest that a man cannot be judged on such evidence, Danforth replies: "I judge nothing." Hale then pleads for a lawyer to plead Proctor's case, and Danforth replies, logically enough, that since witchcraft is an invisible crime, only the witch and the victim know the facts and that there is nothing left for a lawyer to bring out. Proctor's case is built on Mary Warren's confession, and Danforth properly charges the children to consider the seriousness of their position:

Now, children, this is a court of law. The law, based upon the Bible, writ by Almighty God, forbid the practice of witchcraft, and describe death as the penalty thereof. But likewise, children, the law and the Bible damn all bearers of false witness. (Slight pause.) Now then. It does not escape me that this deposition may well be devised to blind us; it may well be that Mary Warren has been conquered by Satan, who send her here to distract our sacred purpose. If so, her neck will break for it. But if she speak true, I bid you now drop your guile and confess your pretense, for a quick confession will go easier with you. (CRUCIBLE, p. 299.)

The rhetoric of this charge to the witnesses may lean toward raising doubts about the advisability of retraction, but its burden is fair enough. Danforth applies the rules of procedure scrupulously, yet the tide is running against Proctor and the good people. The ritual is seen to be no guarantee that justice will be done as it becomes painfully clear that the Court, with the blessing of the Law, is going —as Giles Corey cried out earlier—*to hang all these people.*

There is a factor missing from Danforth's administration of the law; Miller dramatizes one aspect of this missing ingredient in the actions and attitudes of Mr. Hale. When he first appears on the scene to conduct his inquiry, Hale uses the conventional tests that he finds in his books. John Proctor is suspect when he is able to recite only nine of the Commandments; his wife has to prompt the tenth: "Adultery, John." From his experience in Salem the minister

learns to see beyond logic and authority and assess the human motives necessary to balance the scales of justice. In the courtroom
John Proctor finally has to play his trump card and accuse Abby of
lechery; his wife Elizabeth alone can support his allegation.
Though Proctor testifies that he has never known his wife to lie,
rather than expose her husband to infamy she speaks "nothing of
lechery." (CRUCIBLE, p. 307.) Danforth has his answer; Proctor has
perjured himself. But Hale speaks out for intuition against the legal
process:

> *Hale.* Excellency, it is a natural lie to tell; I beg you, stop now before
> another is condemned! I may shut my conscience no more—private ven-
> geance is working through this testimony! From the beginning this man
> [Proctor] has struck me as true. . . . (Pointing at Abigail) This girl has
> always struck me false. (CRUCIBLE, p. 307.)

Though the minister has no law to back up his intuition, he is willing to make it a conscience matter. As Proctor has used "common
sense" to object to the witchcraft investigations, Hale invokes his
feelings to support Proctor's accusations against Abigail. But the
Law as due process has no room for intuition. Danforth refuses to
add this in; Hale's intuition and Proctor's common sense are not
evidence. Because the Judge refuses to admit this human factor, the
good people have no recourse.

The other aspect of the human factor for which the Law makes
no provision is emotion. Due process provides no tool for coping
with the kind of hysteria that the children's shrieking generates.
Emotional reactions have a real impact on the Court (and the audience), yet this impact cannot be included in the record. "The witness cried out" or "(confusion in the courtroom)" is no substitute
for the atmosphere of mystery and/or conviction that results from
the emotional outburst. From the beginning of the investigations
Abigail has been able to turn this weapon against logic and common
sense. Whenever her probity is called into question, she transmutes
the dry, question-and-answer proceedings into enthusiastic pulsings.
In his preliminary investigation, Hale is searching for the truth
about the dancing in the forest and begins to close in:

> *Abigail.* I want to open myself! (They turn to her, startled. She is en-
> raptured, as though in a pearly light.) I want the light of God, I want the
> sweet love of Jesus! I danced for the Devil; I saw him; I wrote in his

book; I want to go back to Jesus; I kiss his hand. I saw Sarah Good with the Devil! I saw Goody Osburn with the Devil! I saw Bridget Bishop with the Devil! (CRUCIBLE, p. 259.)

Neither Hale's authoritative books nor his fledgling intuition are proof against this kind of outburst. Here Abby discovers a power that can be summoned up at will against her enemies.

The source of this emotional power, as is evident from the imagery, lies in Abby's sexual experience. Her outbursts are orgiastic, full of latent sexuality. It is this energy that cannot be weighed in the balance, that initially paralyzes Hale and terrifies the onlookers. Abby's experience with Proctor, hidden from the town, is channeled into her vision, producing a real hysteria in herself and the rest of the children. She introduced them to this mystery in the forest—the naked dancing—and so established a covenant of secret guilt and desire that supports their conspiracy in court. At this point John Proctor's "private sin" has implications for the community.

This emotional outburst has as much to do with Proctor's downfall as Elizabeth's lie. At the crisis of the trial, when Mary Warren's testimony threatens her, Abby calls up this hysteria. Danforth has turned his questioning on her: "Is it possible, child, that the spirits you have seen are illusion only, some deception that may cross your mind when—" (CRUCIBLE, p. 303.) Abby calls up a "cold wind" and all the girls shiver. She sees a yellow bird on the rafters—Mary Warren's spirit tempted from her by John Proctor's diabolism. Threatened by the same fate she has helped thrust on others, Mary Warren breaks and cries out against Proctor. Again this hysteria has a complement of sexual overtones. The yellow bird with claws and spreading wings recalls Tituba's flying to Barbados and the sexual freedom of the forest; the serving girl responds by describing Proctor's tempting in sexual images: "He wake me every night, his eyes were like coals, and his fingers claw my neck, and I sign, I sign . . ." (CRUCIBLE, p. 310.) Though Abby is shamming and the children recognize it, the emotions that fly about the courtroom are very real, the more so because they tap that forbidden well-spring, sexuality, which the Puritan community cannot (or will not) recognize for what it is.

This emotional factor in the case is not accounted for by the rules. It is irrational, a-logical, but very real. Once the witchcraft scare has spread through town, it becomes the channel by which fear, greed, sexual repressions, irresponsibility can be sublimated into "evidence." The Law can help create a scapegoat on which the secret sins of the community can be visited. Judge and jury must ferret out the secret source of such emotion and expose it to view. This is asking a great deal of the judiciary; yet if the trial is to work at all, it works because judge and jury manage to have proper intuitions about human values in a case. So the conditions by which the Law is an effective tool of justice include an ability to perceive, through a maze of technicalities, the whole issue and to deal with it in a humane fashion. The "evil" in Danforth and in Abigail is their lack of this humanity.

Because the Law cannot cope with emotion and its irrational springs and because the ritual cannot substitute for a lack of intuition (wilful or not), the verdict goes against John Proctor and his allies, the order of things is reversed, justice is not done and the Law itself becomes the instrument of perversion.

In the trial, Miller has dramatized the deficiencies of the Law in the hands of an evil court interpreting a bad law. In the fourth act he attempts to frame a solution to this problem. He reintroduces Danforth and Hale, representatives, respectively, of the letter and of the humane view of the Law. Danforth visits the jail to find Parris overwrought because of Abby's treachery and Hale defiantly working to persuade the prisoners to confess. It becomes perfectly clear to the Judge that the girls' testimony was fraudulent, if he had not known this all along. But the hanging verdicts are now on record; twelve have been hanged for the crime of witchcraft, and pardon for the rest would necessarily be a confession of error on the part of the court. Rebellion is stirring in a neighboring town and chaos threatens the theocracy that Danforth represents. So the decision must be upheld and the law enforced.

Danforth. Now hear me, and beguile yourselves no more. I will not receive a single plea for pardon or postponement. Them that will not confess will hang. . . . Postponement now speaks a floundering on my part; reprieve or pardon must cast doubt upon the guilt of them that died till now. While I speak God's law, I will not crack its voice with whimpering. If retaliation is your fear, know this—I should hang ten thousand that dared to rise against the law. (CRUCIBLE, p. 318.)

Danforth makes explicit here an attitude which underlies his role during the trial sequence. Though misapplied, the principle of law enforcement is recognized as valid by the audience.

As we have seen above, law enforcement is part of the American attitude toward the Law; it must be upheld or anarchy follows. It is just as important to the American ideal as the fair trial. When the individual takes upon himself the prerogative of deciding which law may be obeyed and which disregarded, the community feels that the bulwark of order has been breached. Thus the icy wind that blows when Danforth speaks is not the chill of his malevolence and inhumanity only, as some critics claim and as Miller himself seems to think.[16] Danforth appeals to a principle that the audience recognizes as plausible. Otherwise, he would pose no real threat. In spite of the fact that his own personal motives include the preservation of his own position in power, and thus are evil, he is defending an attitude that Americans recognize as necessary. Thus the tension in the action includes a tension that exists within the myth itself; the opposition between respect for the Law as such—even a bad law—and a respect for the right of the individual to dissent.

Miller finally tries to reconcile these polarities by turning attention to John Proctor. Proctor is no Puritan and no hypocrite; he has, as pointed out above, all those qualities that make a man acceptable to modern society, including a sense of isolation in his guilt. His private sin which, through Abby, contributed to the conviction of the innocent remains unabsolved. His wife, in their final confrontation before the execution, confesses that his guilt is also hers: "It needs a cold wife to prompt lechery." (CRUCIBLE, p. 323.) But Proctor, who has set himself outside the law, cannot accept martyrdom; he is not fit to die with Rebecca Nurse in the odor of sanctity. There is no final assurance that he is worthy, either in his sacrificial defense of the innocent before the court or in Elizabeth's assumption of responsibility for his sin.

Elizabeth. You take my sins upon you, John—
Proctor. (in agony) No, I take my own, my own!

. . . .
Elizabeth. Do what you will. But let none be your judge. There be no higher judge under Heaven than Proctor is! (CRUCIBLE, p. 323.)

The ultimate verdict of the play, then, is to be Proctor's decision about his own state of soul.

To clarify this situation dramatically, Miller has his hero hesitate before the prospect of dying for his beliefs. Mr. Hale, who has failed to move Danforth from his purpose, has been urging the condemned to confess because "Life is God's most precious gift; no principle, however glorious, may justify the taking of it." (CRUCIBLE, p. 320.) Though Proctor confesses in Hale's terms: "I want to live," a natural fear of death is not his only motive, it is rather a continuing sense of guilt and unworthiness. Elizabeth has to remind him that he is his own judge now; he cannot find justification or condemnation except in his own conscience.

John Proctor does find justification within; his "motive" lies in the discovery that Danforth intends to publish his confession. He will neither implicate others in his "crime" of witchcraft, nor allow Danforth to use his name to justify their deaths. When he discovers that he cannot concur in their legal lie, he is able to absolve himself and so die for his convictions:

> *Hale.* Man, you will hang. You cannot!
> *Proctor.* I can. Now there's your first marvel, that I can. You have your magic now, for now I think I see some shred of goodness in John Proctor. Not enough to weave a banner with, but white enough to keep it from the dogs. (CRUCIBLE, p. 328.)

When Proctor goes to execution, personal honor triumphs over the deficiencies of the Law and the conspiracy of malicious clique and corrupt court.

This epiphany satisfies the exigencies of the structure; Proctor goes to his death purged of guilt and seeing meaning in his sacrifice. But his triumph is an individual victory only; it does not touch the radical oppositions dramatized in the play. In fact, it only adds another dimension to them. The legal system in America, because it is the font of order and justice, has acquired a sacral aura. Progressively it has been dealing, not only with crime, but also with moral guilt. Because, in the popular mind, the verdict of the court is also a moral judgment, we tend to operate on the assumption that the Law, institution and ritual, can one day become a *perfect* instrument of justice, that is, it can become an instrument of absolution as well as acquittal.[17] So in contemporary criminal law, the issue is not confined to the fact of commission, but is equally engaged with the motive. Psychiatric observation is increasingly admissible as evidence. Thus the Law reaches out toward those hitherto private areas, dealt with in the past by pastor or priest, to create a strategy that will deal with the communitarian forgiveness of guilt. (Whether or not we can ever hope to achieve this objective is not at issue here.) Miller, in *The Crucible,* dramatizes the tensions that make the trial a questionable instrument of justice and the contradiction that lurks at the center of our myth of the Law. He tries to resolve these polarities by insisting that only the individual can be an adequate judge of his own private actions. The hero, all his sins upon him, must cope with the spectre of guilt alone. The audience is left with the suspicion that self-absolution begs the question; the old adage applies: no man is a good judge in his own case.

In stereotype, dramatic use of the trial pattern depends on the public's faith that this ritual infallibly reconciles contraries, *solvuntur ambulando.* When it is used as a framework in conventional drama, for instance, the verdict of the court resolves all differences between individual and society and makes evident the innocence or guilt of the individual and his society. The logical progression of the ritual gives the verdict the appearance of absolute truth (or as close an approximation as man can reasonably expect). In plays like *The Caine Mutiny Court Martial* or *Saint Joan,* the trial reveals the truth even when the verdict is one-sided. The audience, whose posture is that of the jury, can detect prejudice in the judge, or a vicious prosecutor, or an inept defense counsel. The dramatist can see to it that they do. So this ritual, at least on the stage, ordinarily does what a ritual should do, that is, guarantee the desired result.

The Crucible, however, uses the trial pattern, not as a framework, but to explore the attitudes that underlie the ritual itself. The formal symmetry of orderly investigation, indictment, presentation of evidence and verdict is broken by hysterical outbursts; the support that due process, in the hands of an humane and unbiased judiciary, provides the truth is undermined by the inhumanity of Danforth. The man who is caught between the grinding stones of a corrupt court and an evil law may save himself in the end by becoming his own judge and jury, but the dramatic fact in *The Crucible* is the grinding. The ritual fails, and the hero is isolated with his guilt.

In his epilogue, Miller tries to insist that sacrifices like Proctor's eventually do have a relationship to the whole community:

In solemn meeting, the congregation rescinded the excommunications— this in March 1712. But they did so upon orders of the government. The jury, however, wrote a statement praying forgiveness for all who had suffered. . . . To all intents and purposes, the power of the theocracy in Massachusetts was broken. (CRUCIBLE, p. 330.)

This comment may allay the playwright's scruples, but it is not part of the dramatic experience. The play makes its own statement by conveying, with a sense of urgency, the opposition between two American ideals: the need for Law and law enforcement and the right of the minority to dissent. In dramatizing this tension, it also calls attention to the need for a ritual that can deal with communal and individual guilt. In the absence of such a ritual John Proctor's triumph is finally a mystery, unaccommodated man holding, for personal reasons, to a personal vision. The black-gowned shadow of Danforth is not blotted out by the rising sun and Proctor's sacrifice.

A Green Corner of the Universe:

Our Town

Our Town has a theatrical quality that distinguishes it from the plays we have been dealing with. Wilder uses no scenery and no act-curtain. The play begins with an announcement by the Stage Manager that is calculated to draw attention to the bare stage and to insist on the audience's consciousness of its role as spectator. No realistic props are used, the Stage Manager steps into the action from time to time and reads bit parts, lapses of time and flashbacks are announced and commented on. Moreover, there is no "hero" in the conventional sense, no central figure on whose decision the plot pivots. In fact, there is very little plot. The play presents the daily life of a small town over some seventeen years. The dramatis personae are not memorable; they have no qualities that carry them beyond the soap-opera stereotype. According to the canons of the "well-made play" or even of modern expressionism, *Our Town* is a pretentious, sentimental collection of clichés. Yet the play was well received on Broadway in 1938 and continues to hold a fascination for American audiences. Brooks Atkinson gave this tribute to its impact:

By stripping the play of everything that is not essential, Mr. Wilder has given it a profound, strange, unworldly significance. There is less a portrait of a town than the sublimation of the commonplace; and in contrast with the universe that swims around it, it is brimming over with compassion. Grover's Corners is a green corner of the universe.[1]

The untraditional devices, the presentational, non-realistic mode have received considerable attention, but their over-all significance needs further investigation. For *Our Town* approaches pure ritual in method and illustrates, in a unique way, the power of the myth in modern drama.

In the plays dealt with thus far, the mythical element has not been absent. The playwrights have used the myth as substructure and have filled out the pattern with specific incidents and individual personae. By elaborating the structure with "realistic" character motivations and concrete incidents, they fixed the action in time and space to give it the appearance of reality. This "realistic" treatment, to a greater or less degree as the play approaches "slice-of-life" naturalism, conceals the mythical structure and makes it serve the life-like details. The play is then once removed from the myth, and each author can find his own way of realizing it. This "realistic" dramatic mode may be described in classical terms as the involution of the universal (myth) in the particular. Its method involves: 1) adding a locale and a temporal dimension, 2) giving the characters precise motivations, 3) filling out the categories of the pattern with concrete episodes that are causally related to the motivations. To the pattern of the myth the playwright gives a local habitation and a name. This is the most common mode of "imitation" in modern Western drama.

It is possible to deal with the myth more directly, to express a complex of attitudes in a non-realistic mode. This kind of drama will necessarily have strongly ritual characteristics. It is commonly accepted that myth and rite are expressions of the interpretations that a community puts upon archetypal experiences like birth, maturity, death or purgation, and initiation. As myth is the verbal expression of these interpretations, ritual is their interpretation in action. Because it is an interpretation of the archetypal, the ritual has characteristics that set it off from other actions whether actual or imitative. It takes place in a universalized space and time, that is, it does not happen "here" or "there," but at the center of the universe, in a space that includes all space; it happens in a "present" that includes all time. The actors in the ritual are not so much individuals as types: priest, chorus, victim. The action of the ceremony can be reduced to categories: separation, testing, communion, for instance, in initiation rites. These categories do not have any logical sequence nor is motivation expressed; one event follows the other because the archetype has it so. The playwright, then, can employ these ritual techniques without displacement if he chooses.[2] This ritual, non-realistic technique tries to express the complex of attitudes that comprise the myth in its own terms, that is, as ideal interpretations of experience by the community. *Our Town* is a play that uses this technique, that expresses an American myth—the ideal of equality, democracy and meaningful daily life for the common man that emanates from a specifically American complex of attitudes—in a ritual mode.

The ideal with which Wilder is working is the rural community, the vision of small town life, a kindly, middle-class, democratic existence. As distant an observer as de Tocqueville pointed to the New England township as the highest political form evolved by the Americans. "The township of New England," he wrote, "is so constituted as to excite the warmest human affections, without arousing the ambitious passions of the heart of man." Institutional freedom was honored by an unconscious ritual observance, and all extremes of class and wealth were leveled off into a golden mean. This image of the ideal community is little different from the image presented at the turn of the century by novelists like Booth Tarkington and Dorothy Canfield Fisher, and summarized by Vernon Parrington:

(1) A land of economic well-being, uncursed by poverty and unspoiled by wealth; (2) A land of "folksiness"—the village a great family in its neighborliness, friendliness, sympathy; (3) Primarily middle-class, and therefore characteristically American, wholesome and human in spite of its prosaic shortcomings; (4) The home of American democracy, dominated by the spirit of equality, where men are measured by their native qualities.[3]

To adapt this image to drama Wilder found it necessary only to add the religion of the folk—a mild Protestantism that is integrated into the life of the town, an undogmatic faith that does not prescribe or proscribe, but meshes with the democratic aspirations of the people. The characteristics that de Tocqueville described in the 1830s and that Parrington enumerates a century later are exemplified point for point in Grover's Corners. The play gives dramatic shape to this vision of the ideal American community.

All the details in *Our Town* are typical of this ideal. The village lies in a valley at the foot of "our mountain." Main Street splits the town; its grocery and drug store are the focus of social life. There is the public school and the high school and a wide variety of churches: Congregational, Presbyterian, Methodist, Unitarian, Baptist "down in the holla' by the river," and Catholic "over beyond the tracks." [4] The houses all have backyards and there is only light horse-and-buggy traffic on Main Street. Outlying farms add to the rural flavor. The people who live in Grover's Corners are, according to the editor of the town paper, "lower middle class: sprinkling of professional men." The political statistics and the form of government reflect a staunch conservatism within the democratic process: "eighty-six percent Republicans, six percent Democrats, four percent Socialists; rest indifferent." (OUR TOWN, p. 29.) The town is run by a board of selectmen and all males vote at twenty-one. But economic status, politics and religion are not divisive factors; easy commerce between classes is taken for granted. Social and economic problems are handled on an individual level: "The citizens do all they can to help those who cannot help themselves and those that can they leave alone." (OUR TOWN, p. 39.) The milkman and the constable and the newsboy each makes his own contribution to the running of the town —as do doctor and editor. Each is respected as an individual; each delivers his product to the neighbors with a sense of accomplishment in a spirit of friendly largess. There is no race-problem, no employer-employee agitation, no keeping up with the Joneses. Grover's Corners is a society conscious of its community, whose members are basically good.

Even the shortcomings of the town and its citizens are typical and generally simply provide an occasion for greater good. The town's life is rather dull—"Very ordinary town, if you ask me. Little better behaved than most. Probably a lot duller." (OUR TOWN, p. 29.) Yet dullness does not discourage the young people, for they generally settle down there; in fact, serenity might be a fair synonym. The choirmaster's drinking offers the ladies an opportunity for innocent gossip and everyone a chance to exercise charity. The minister keeps him on at his work and even suicide does not excommunicate him. When a boy forgets to chop the week's wood supply, his father gives him a little talk, the essence of tact and common sense, leaving the boy thoroughly abashed and eager to redeem himself. The admitted lack of "culture" in the town is balanced by interest in, and attention to, nature—listening to birdsong and watching the sun rise over the mountain. These defects are the other side of the coin of

American virtues: simplicity, regularity, compassion and kindliness.

The basic unit of society in Grover's Corners is the family. The community is constituted by families living together, working in tandem, intermarrying with neighbor's son or daughter. The play pivots around the lives of two typical families, the Webbs and the Gibbses. Each has two children, a boy and a girl. The identity of the adults is established primarily by their parenthood—they are Mother and Father, and their lives are focused here. They exercise a wise supervision over the children and their deep affection has a matter-of-fact gloss. Mrs. Webb and Mrs. Gibbs make good breakfasts, string beans, get the children off to school. Choir practice at the Congregational Church and mild gossip afterwards provides them a social outlet sufficient for Grover's Corners. They have little ambitions of their own—to see the ocean, to visit "Paris, France, where people don't talk English and don't even want to," but they are not really disturbed by their stability. (OUR TOWN, pp. 25–6.) Mr. Webb and Dr. Gibbs, professional men in the small-town manner, share their concern for their family with a concern for the town. The doctor knows his patients and sacrifices for all of them—he goes out on night calls in Polish town, then attends to Mrs. Wentworth's stomach trouble. When advisable, he enlists the aid of the neighbors in dealing with his boy; the constable checks on George's smoking. The editor picks up news items from the milkman and the constable and tries to keep mistakes in the paper at a minimum.

Son and daughter accept the world of their parents, and their own interrelationships are typical. George Gibbs' little sister Rebecca annoys her big brother with her presence and her questions; he tolerates her. When George prepares for his wedding, his little sister retires to her room and cries. George and Emily get along as athletic hero and the-girl-next-door should. They take one another for granted till that moment when they realize how they feel about each other. George typifies the red-blooded, good-hearted American boy; Emily is everybody's version of the girl next door. George respects his parents even though he sometimes forgets to chop wood for his mother, he is not very good at his studies, he captains the baseball team; he is honest, shy about showing emotion, devoted to his family. Emily is a good student, reasonably attractive, helpful to her mother, earnest with George. When they decide to marry, they are willing to settle down on a farm near town and make a life that will mirror their parents'. Like the town itself, there is nothing unusual about the personae except their consistent typicality.

Thus far the ingredients of Wilder's play resemble those of a thoroughly sentimental, idealized potboiler after the manner of Tarkington or Fisher. This is the American that Meredith Nicholson eulogized in *The Valley of Democracy*, that Sinclair Lewis satirized in *Main Street*, that H. L. Mencken stigmatized as the "booboisie." If Wilder had chosen to depict Grover's Corners "realistically," his play would have the same dated, tired quality that brands the small-town novel of the 20s. As it is, *Our Town* resembles no real town on hill or in valley; it corresponds to an ideal whose model exists potentially in the attitudes of every American. The theoretical expression of this ideal may take shape something like this:

The individual feels himself to be a part of a social unity and harmony, which is regarded as the embodiment of universal and objective ideals and as a reflection of an ultimate harmony in nature. He finds emotional security and fulfillment, not through the assertion of his will against the natural and social environment, but through participation in the processes of nature and in the collective enterprise of society. Yet in subordinating himself to the social order, he does not deify it or endow it with absolute and final authority. . . . The synthesis of individual will and social discipline, without which there can be no high civilization, is to be found not in intellectual formulas, but in the sentiment of patriotism, in moral and religious idealism, and (as Whitman declared) in "the manly love of comrades." [5]

Living in "our town" includes a social unity and harmony with nature, the fulfillment of the individual within the community. It inculcates patriotism and moral principles and friendly social interchange. To be born into this community is to be born into the warm bosom of a family, to grow up there is to be nurtured by wise and affectionate parents and neighbors. To marry there means deepening the bonds of friendship into a closer tie and starting a new family that is the image of the one left behind. To die there means resting quietly among people you know and love. Though this image is ideal, the play escapes sentiment and cliché because of its mode of presentation. The ritual method makes all the difference.

Wilder is not unaware of the implications of his presentational technique. When he writes about the play and about playwrighting, the terms "myth," "fable," and "ritual" recur frequently. He is concerned with patterns, with the universals that the theatre can present:

The theatre longs to represent the symbols of things, not the things themselves. All the lies it tells—the lie that this lady is Caesar's wife; the lie that people can go through life talking blank verse; the lie that that man has just killed that man—all those lies enhance the one truth that is there—the truth that dictated the story, the myth.[6]

In "Some Thoughts on Playwriting" he indicates that his concept of myth and story goes beyond the details of narrative; myth, fable, story are patterns that address themselves to the "group mind."

It rests on the fact that (1) the pretense, the fiction, on stage would fall to pieces and absurdity without the support accorded to it by a crowd, and (2) the excitement induced by pretending a fragment of life is such that it partakes of ritual and festival, and requires a throng.[7]

In statements like these, Wilder echoes the findings of the Cambridge anthropologists and anticipates some of the critical theories of Northrop Frye. Wilder acknowledges that the "truth" with which the dramatist works is an expression of that complex of attitudes which exists in the mind of the community. The myth that he presents in *Our Town* falls into that category that Frye calls "apocalyptic"—myth operating at the top level of human desire.

In terms of narrative, myth is the imitation of actions near or at the conceivable limits of desire. The gods enjoy beautiful women, fight one another with prodigious strength, comfort and assist man, or else watch his miseries from the height of their immortal freedom. The fact that myth operates at the top level of human desire does not mean it necessarily presents its world as attained or attainable by human beings. . . . The world of mythical imagery is usually represented by the conception of heaven or Paradise in religion, and it is apocalyptic, . . . a world of total metaphor, in which everything is potentially identical with everything else, as though it were all inside a single infinite body.[8]

Our Town deals with the apocalyptic aspect in the American complex of attitudes—the vision of the ideal life, the aspirations of the community at their highest pitch. To represent this ideal plausibly, in a realistic context, would destroy its ideality; whether or not the apocalyptic is attainable in the practical order is irrelevant to the myth. The truth which Wilder is dealing with is the truth of the vision as apocalypse, as ideal; thus his mode of presentation is attuned to the vision.

There is a significant difference between Wilder's approach and Frye's. The critic considers myth exactly as Gilbert Murray considers it in his study on Euripides—as a structural principle of the work which prescinds from the belief of the playwright and the audience. Wilder, however, assumes that the complex of attitudes shared by author and auditor provide a bridge of communication, that the recognition of the group-mind produces a community spirit, a ritual, a festival. The vital audience attitudes toward basic human experiences—life and death, innocence and maturity, insight and wisdom—are presented so that the audience recognizes its own ideal. It follows that the audience participates in the drama and that the dramatist can recognize the presence of the audience without violating any "realistic" convention. Thus the universe of the ritual drama, the universe of *Our Town*, includes the audience.

Relevant to incorporating the audience into the play is Wilder's concept of the action of the play taking place in a perpetual present.[9] If the audience is a participant, then audience time and play time are identical, not in the "realistic" sense that one minute of time on stage equals one minute of audience time, but in the sense that both times become one "moment" of experience. The apocalyptic, the ideal, is not subject to the vagaries of temporal duration. Ritual drama creates its own present which annuls duration, a "now" that encompasses and so transcends time's continuum. "I have set," Wilder remarks about *Our Town*, "the village against the largest dimensions of time and place."[10] Actually, he has done more; he has included the action in a single, infinite mind so that all time is contemporaneous. Ritual time allows vast stretches of history to be concentrated in a moment. The action, then, takes place in its own universal situation—"a life of a village against the life of the stars."

The Platonic overtones of these positions are obvious; they are corroborated by Platonic doctrines in Wilder's short plays and novels.[11] He also appeals to the philosopher in "Some Thoughts on Playwriting" for support of his views:

It is no accident that when Plato arrived at the height of his argument and attempted to convey a theory of knowledge and a theory of man's nature, he passed over into story telling, in the myths of the Cave and the Charioteer.[12]

Actually, it is possible to consider the mythical elements in Plato not as the culmination of the theorizing, but as its matrix. The Ideas are a rationalization of the primitive tendency to refer reality to that which "imitates" the primal action of the gods or the demi-divine ancestor. The "really real" (*to ontos ōn*) exists in the "other world" beyond time, space and change—the permanent world of the archetype and the myth. Looked at from this point of view, the Platonic system is a formulation in philosophic terms of the mythopoeic primitive mind.

This primitive ontology has a Platonic structure; and in that case Plato could be regarded as the outstanding philosopher of a "primitive Mentality," that is, as the thinker who succeeded in giving philosophical currency to the modes of life and behaviour of archaic humanity.[13]

In aesthetic terms, this version of Platonism explains the necessity of Wilder's theatrical techniques. The "truth" after which he searches is the ideal in the group-mind, and his method is to reproduce this truth in its own ritual and archetypal terms. Thus, given the Platonic Weltanschauung, Wilder's play is more "realistic" than the more conventional realistic drama.[14]

Wilder's use of presentational devices illuminates a fact generally overlooked about so-called "realistic" drama: "realism" itself is a tissue of conventions, a mode of presentation (or better, representation) just as arbitrary as those of ritual drama. The realistic play depends on the conventions of chronological time, delimited place, motivational consistency in well-defined personae, cause and effect in the order of events. In short, the "realism" consists in an accurate phenomenalistic representation for the senses and in logical consistency for the mind. The ritual play, on the other hand, depends on the consistency of the action with the attitudes of the group-mind, and its conventions are those of the rite and the archetype. Thus all time is one time and space is universal; the action occurs in an immutable "now" and in a universal "everywhere." The action is structured according to fundamental experiences—the rhythm of the seasons, the progress of the day, universal human categories. The motivations of the personae are not explored; they tend to be types rather than individuals. It is even possible for one persona to assume different identities; changes of identity cannot violate verisimilitude when everything is potentially identified with everything else. Cause and effect then cannot flow from personal motivations; events occur because they are part of a larger structure—the cycle of nature or of growth or of knowledge. Wilder's presentational method, therefore, consists of a set of conventions which dramatizes the apocalyptic vision, the ideal. One of the most important devices for achieving this effect is that of the stage manager.

The Stage Manager in *Our Town* combines in a single persona functions which are related to the mythical use of time and space, the identification of actor and audience, the existence of the world of the play within a single "body" or mind. In the first instance, the State Manager functions as regisseur; he has complete control over the world of the play. The drama begins when he announces, from a bare stage, the title and author and names of the principal actors. He describes the geography of the town, thus creating Grover's Corners with his words. He opens and closes the episodes by calling the actors on and thanking them when the scene is finished. He provides the "motivation" for the scenes simply by asserting his role. His control of the action on stage is absolute. He comments, choruslike, on the action. His commentary is omniscient and wide-lensed, though his manner suggests the cracker-barrel philosopher. The range of knowledge displayed is much broader than might be expected from any authentic country sage, and the local-color touch disguises, without altogether displacing, the god-figure. At the beginning of Act II, for example, he notes significant changes that have occurred in the three-year interval between acts. Heat and cold have cracked the mountain and spring rains have washed down the dirt; babies not born in Act I are beginning to talk and some adults have moved over the brink of old age. (OUR TOWN, p. 56.) The touches of whimsy and the folksy manner are worthy of the country stores and the hot-stove leagues of rural America, but the function which the Stage Manager exercises here is not simply narrator. He can manipulate time at will, he can move the action along, when necessary, he can metamorphose into other personae and step into the action, retaining, however, his general identity as supervisor. In the courtship scene, he plays the drugstore proprietor and in the wedding the minister. While retaining his identity as regisseur and commentator, he can momentarily assume a persona. That he does retain his basic role is clear from his commentary as minister in which both roles are combined. This mobility melds episode with comment and produces an on-stage continuum that is symbolized by his multiple functions.

He has an equally intimate relation to the audience, for, besides being an "actor," he is also the ideal spectator. His point of view is a heightened version of the spectators' in that he is conscious of the universal aspects of the action. As superior to the actors, he manages the action, so as superior spectator, he can elaborate the meanings of the episodes. He acknowledges their presence directly throughout and controls them as he does the actors—excusing them at the intermissions and dismissing them at the conclusion. By acknowledging their presence, by assimilating their point of view, by controlling their universe, the Stage Manager establishes an identity with the audience. Thus he occupies both worlds, links the audience to the stage and unites them in a single dimension.

In both relationships—to actors and audience—the Stage Manager resembles the coryphaeus of Greek drama, the leader of the chorus. In the development of Attic tragedy this role underwent considerable mutations; Wilder's technique manages to incorporate both early and late functions in his regisseur. The chorus-leader emerged from the group to "answer the chorus"; once detached from the *thiasos,* the crowd of worshippers, he became the principal actor, the impersonator.[15] But with the development of impersonation and the rise of mythologizing realism, the chorus and their leader ceased to preside over the action and became "a body of lyrical attendants, 'ideal spectators.' "[16] Wilder's coryphaeus incorporates both functions and in a superior way. It is this superiority that emphasizes the ritual mode.

Greek plays invariably begin with a prologue, and it is now well recognized that this prologue developed out of a more primitive ritual formula (prorrhēsis) which served originally, like the Sanskrit *nandi,* not to introduce the characters but to inaugurate the religious ceremonies at which the play was performed. Moreover, the single speaker into whose mouth the prologue is placed in the Canaanite text answers exactly to the Sanskrit sūtradhāra and the Greek chorēgos, i.e., the priestly "presenter" of the sacred pantomime.[17]

The leader of the chorus—commentator, actor, representative of the community—can be traced back to the priest regisseur of the ritual action. This hieratic aspect of the Stage Manager encompasses his other functions; he presents the ritual to the audience while at the same time representing the audience in the ritual. He is the bridge between the group-mind and the action.

As the "presenter" he creates the "now" in which the ritual action occurs. His control of time does not merely imply that he can stop and start the action; he can also define the universe in which the action takes place. We have remarked that the ritual as ritual does not take place in an historical duration or in a specific locale; it is an escape into atemporality.

All the rites and all the behaviour patterns [of the primitive] . . . would be comprised in the following statement: "If we pay no attention to it, time does not exist; furthermore, where it becomes perceptible—because of man's 'sins,' i.e., when man departs from the archetype and falls into duration—time can be annulled." Basically, if viewed in its proper perspective, the life of archaic man (a life reduced to a repetition of archetypal acts, that is, to categories and not to events, to the unceasing rehearsal of the same primordial myths), although it takes place in time, does not bear the burden of time, does not record time's irreversibility: in other words, completely ignores what is especially characteristic and decisive in a consciousness of time.[18]

The first step in establishing this atemporal "now" is taken through the identification of Stage Manager and audience. His "time" is also audience time; so he can compress past, present and future, Grover's Corners time. In his opening monologue he remarks that William Jennings Bryan made a speech in Grover's Corners and adds, in the same breath, that in five years the first automobile will come along Main Street. (OUR TOWN, p. 6.) When Dr. Gibbs appears on his way home, the interlocutor can remark that Dr. Gibbs died in 1930, that the new hospital is named after him and that his wife died long before him. None of this negates the "now" of the action because the audience sees Dr. Gibbs walking down the "street" and so the

Grover's Corners dimension is coextensive with the audience "now."

To this comparatively brief span which is contracted into a "moment" are juxtaposed long stretches of history, in either direction. Right now (audience time) they are building a new bank in Grover's Corners and in the cornerstone a copy of the play will be enclosed so that future generations will know more about "our town" than the flat historical facts like the Treaty of Versailles and the Lindbergh flight. He then remarks on civilizations past: Greece, Rome and Babylon; all that is known of them is the names of kings, wheat and slave contracts. "Yet every night all those families sat down to supper . . . and the smoke went up the chimney—same as here." (OUR TOWN, p. 40.) Between Babylon and "the people a thousand years from now" is inserted the "history" of the town itself. The earliest graves in the cemetery are dated 1670–1680 and the names on the headstones are the same as the families living here now, Grovers and Cartwrights and Gibbses and Herseys. Also buried on the hill are veterans of the Revolution and the Civil War. These ancestors are present at the wedding of George and Emily—"millions of them." They too are included in the "now" of the play. Thus the small segments of time bounding the episodes—May 7, 1901; July 7, 1904; February 11, 1899—are situated in this vast continuum which stretches in either direction from "now." And because this continuum is made available to the group-mind, it is encompassed in the "now."

Though in his opening monologue the Stage Manager locates "our town"—latitude 42 degrees 40 minutes; longitude 70 degrees 37 minutes—his precision is unnecessary, for Grover's Corners is much more centrally located than that. In the middle of the first act he calls on the professor from the state university to describe the geological situation of Grover's Corners. With proprietorial pride he points out that the town lies on Pleistocene granite with a more recent shelf of Devonian basalt two or three million years old. The foundations of the houses in "our town" are anchored in ancient granite; there is nothing temporary or unstable about them. But even this situation is not the entire truth about the location; Rebecca, in the most commented-on speech of the play, completes this dimension. She recounts the extraordinary mailing address on a letter to Jane Crofut, Crofut Farm. To the customary information was added planet, solar system, universe and finally the Mind of God. (OUR TOWN, p. 54.) Based on bed-rock, surrounded by the stars which rise over "our mountain" and criss-cross over the cemetery, the town is also seated in the omnispatial, omnitemporal "now" and "everywhere" of the eternal mind.

Thus Grover's Corners sits on the foundations of the earth, surrounded by the ages; the townsfolk dwell with Indians, pilgrims, boys in blue. From this center the universe stretches out to the stars, and the whole is encompassed in the mind of God. The bare stage, the lack of act-curtain and realistic props, symbolize this universe—the stage stretches up into the darkness of the "fly" and off into the wings and out to the back of the house. No box sets or valances or tormentors bind the audience's imagination to time or place. The focus of this universe is the town itself so that, for the time of the play, Grover's Corners becomes the center of the universe, an *axis mundi*. This reflects the attitude of the primitive toward his city and his region.

What we wish to emphasize is the fact that the world which surrounds us, civilized by the hand of man, is accorded no validity [by the primitive] beyond that which is due to the extraterrestrial prototype that served as its model. Man constructs according to an archetype. Not only do his city or his temple have celestial models; the same is true of the entire region that he inhabits.[19]

Because the town is situated in the "Mind of God," it clearly corresponds to the celestial model; it *is* that model realized for the ritual. If this explanation seems too Platonic for any credibility, we must remind ourselves that the characteristics of the archetype as it exists potentially in the group-mind, in the attitudes of the audience, are identical with the celestial model: changeless, enduring, a place where opposites are reconciled into perfect harmony.

Apropos of the situation as *axis mundi*, Wilder uses a topographical feature which has immemorial symbolic overtones. "Our mountain" dominates the region from the beginning of the play. The Stage Manager says: "The sky is beginning to show some streaks of light over in the East there, behind our mount'in," and tells us that the cemetery lies up there. (OUR TOWN, p. 10.) At the beginning of Act III he situates the cemetery on a windy hilltop, open to the sky, to sun, moon and stars, not far from Mount Monadnock. The cemetery on the mountain, the "high place" of the old religions, is an important part of Grover's Corners. (OUR TOWN, p. 99.) That part of the community which has passed on wait quietly among the mountain laurel and lilacs. For the primitive mind every city and palace is a replica of the sacred mountain: the archetectonic symbolism of the Center may be formulated as follows:

1. The Sacred Mountain—where heaven and earth meet—is situated at the center of the world.
2. Every temple or palace—and by extension, every sacred city or royal residence—is a Sacred Mountain, thus becoming a Center.
3. Being an *axis mundi,* the sacred city . . . is regarded as a meeting point of heaven, earth and hell.[20]

Of course, Wilder does not depend on the collective unconscious to establish his "Center"; he carefully constitutes it with the detail discussed above. But his devices correspond to the immemorial ritualistic situation almost point for point.

The basic structure of the action of *Our Town* is the progression of universal human experience—birth and growth, marriage, death. These events are unique in the life of the individual. They form the basic pattern for every life. Thus the pattern is both linear (for the individual) and cyclical (for the community). The structure combines both these aspects. For George and Emily the maturing process, the wedding, the funeral occur but once; for the community life is a round of such events. Related to the cyclical pattern is the rhythm of the seasons and the hours. And ultimately the cyclical pattern in the life of the individual (i.e., "harmony with nature") is revealed against the linear movement as of the utmost significance. A chart might help visualize some of these interrelations (parentheses indicate flashback):

Morning	*Stage Manager*	*Night*
ACT I	ACT II	ACT III
Daily Life	Marriage	Death
Spring	Summer	Summer—Winter
May 7, 1901	July 7, 1904	1913—Feb. 11, 1899
Sunshine	Rain—Sun	Rain—Snow
Morning	Morning	Afternoon
Afternoon	(Afternoon—Evening)	(Morning)
Night	Afternoon	Night

The archetypal implications of the seasons and of nature have been pointed out in detail by Northrop Frye. Spring is the season of comedy, of birth and rebirth, of the reinstitution of society; summer is the season of romance, the quest of the hero, his adventures and final triumph; winter is the season of irony, that mode of literature in which the characters exhibit a power of action inferior to that of the poet or the audience. Act I celebrates the familial society and its abundant life in the sunshine; Act II, with the recent fertilizing rain drenching the grass, deals with the noon of adventure and discovery and the wedding which crowns the adventure; Act III combines the mythos of summer and winter by revealing, in flashback, the contrast between the dead Emily and the unperceptive family.[21] Within the context of this pattern the typical details of the episodes take on a larger significance.

The triad of episodes in the first act emphasizes the routine of family life. The first episode, morning, begins with the deliveries of the milkman, the paperboy, and the doctor with the constable overseeing the town's affairs. Then breakfast in the Gibbs household, the mother preparing the morning coffee (which becomes a ritual repeated as part of the morning routine in Acts II and III) and breakfast for the children who bolt their food and rush off to school. After breakfast the mother feeds the chickens, strings beans and gossips with the next-door neighbor. The afternoon episode shows the children coming home from school, George concerned with baseball and Emily with her forensic accomplishments. The daughter helps her mother with the beans and herself to conversation which concludes with the common adolescent complaint: "Oh Mama, you're no help at all." (OUR TOWN, p. 38.) The evening episode shows the father reading, the mother returning from choir practice and street-corner gossip, the children at their homework and their star-gazing. Unremarked by the townsfolk the cycle of life also goes on: the doctor delivers a pair of twins, Mrs. Gibbs and Mrs. Webb speculate on the maturing of George and Emily, Emily worries about her attractiveness, the constable on his evening round wonders to the editor how Simon Stimson is "goin' to end." The rhythm of the town's life is attuned to the rhythm of the day. The ordinary life in Grover's Corners moves along like clockwork.

The same triadic structure is noticeable in the second act, but the emphasis shifts from the routine activity to the unique event. It is George and Emily's wedding day. The central episode in the act, the courtship flashback, is the most private and unique action in the play, and the structure builds up to and away from this moment. But, even within the context of this unique event, Wilder emphasizes the universal and the typical. The State Manager's comments which introduce both the act and the wedding episode insist on the pattern, the communal nature of the experience. New babies have been born; people who thought themselves young have noticed the signs of age. And before the wedding he notes: "People were made to live two-by-two." (OUR TOWN, p. 88.)

The first episode—the morning of the wedding—begins in the routine way, with breakfast and coffee and the groom coming downstairs. Against the self-conscious nonchalance that covers his nervousness, his awareness of the momentous step he is taking, is ranged the reminiscence of the parents and the parents-in-law who recall *their* wedding mornings. When the Stage Manager introduces the flashback, he insists that the audience supply the universality by thinking back to the days of their youth and the experience of first love. George and Emily then reenact, at the Stage Manager's bidding, the moments in which they discover that they were meant for each other. At Mr. Morgan's soda fountain the boy and girl make their decision, that personal, once-in-a-lifetime decision for which there are as many analogues as members of the audience. This involution of the universal in the particular is completed by the presence of the Stage Manager in the scene—as Mr. Morgan. The third episode in this act—the wedding—is a slow movement away from uniqueness. George and Emily are both caught in a moment of panic before going to the altar. Suddenly George feels that he is being pushed into manhood, that he is being forced to "grow old." He does not want to step out from the crowd, to stop being just "a fella." This revelation is made to his mother—her admonition that he is now a man, free of his mother's aura of influence, brings him to his senses. She emancipates him and he accepts. Emily turns to her father; she too wants to stay as she is, "her father's girl." The fear of the unknown, of the new status the marriage commitment brings about, is typical enough, and Emily's fears are quieted, not by her father, but by her husband. All she wants is someone to love her; George takes her in his arms and promises that he will try. After this symbolic cleaving to one another, George and Emily lose their individuality and become "bride and groom." The Stage Manager's voice is heard reading the formula of the vows and Mrs. Soames, as typical spectator (and, undoubtedly, as audience representative), sheds a sentimental tear over the bridal couple and their lovely wedding. (OUR TOWN, p. 95.) The Stage Manager's comment (as the minister) completes the consideration of the wedding from the standpoint of the community—as part of the universal pattern. "M. . . . marries N. . . . millions of them. . . . Once in a thousand times it's interesting." (OUR TOWN, p. 96.) *This* wedding is interesting because it is ideal; that is, it represents the union which binds society together in happiness. When the bride and groom run joyously up the aisle through the audience, this ideal is realized for its members.

The third act deals with separation and death. Structurally, Wilder, as he himself has pointed out, uses Dante's *Purgatorio* as a model. The reference is significant because the seven-tiered mountain of the *Commedia* and the mountain above Grover's Corners are both the place of epiphany. Here occurs "the symbolic presentation of the point at which the undisplaced apocalyptic world and the cyclical world of nature come into alignment," where the pilgrim gradually recovers his lost innocence and casts off original sin.[22] Here Emily discovers how ideal life in "our town" really is. In the central episode of this act—Emily's return to an ordinary, routine day—the cyclical pattern is shown to be meaningful, itself part of the apocalyptic world. From her vantage-point on the mountain, the *axis mundi* where heaven and earth meet, she realizes how unique the routine really is.

While Wilder employs the Dantean model and the archetypal mountain-top, the vision he is working with remains specifically American, and so he has to deal with a difficult experience. In American culture there is no satisfactory communal ritual for coping with death, as books like Jessica Mitford's have pointed out. It is interesting to note that Wilder does not use the word "death" at all in this act, and he uses the expression "the dead" only once. He has to create an image of death consonant with the group-mind which recoils from its finality. He solves this problem simply enough: really, "the dead" have not died at all; they have just "passed on."

The cemetery is still part of Grover's Corners; here the dead sit quietly "without stiffness." When they do speak, Wilder directs, their tone is to be matter-of-fact, without sentimentality and, above

all, without lugubriousness. (OUR TOWN, p. 107.) They remain part
of the community, their placid condition reflects the invocation "rest
in peace," they are waiting for something. They have "passed on"
up the hill—this remove is not far and it is only psychologically
definitive; they slowly forget about their past lives. Elsewhere
Wilder has formulated this view of death:

All this prepares us for the statement that Americans never die; they are
killed or they go away, but they are not dead. This is in great contrast, of
course, to the Europeans who "wait for" their death, prepare, foresee, be-
wail or accept their death. This . . . is obviously related to other elements of the American religion, that all you have is in every moment of
your consciousness (and that you like all you have) and so self-contained
is every moment of consciousness that there is nothing left over for expectation or memory. The American, then, who has lost that moment of
consciousness is not that European thing called "dead" so fraught with immemorial connotations—he is gone away.[23]

The first episode dramatizes this view; the undertaker meets Sam
Craig, an old resident of Grover's Corners who has been away for
years. They comment on the "sad journey" they are taking, and the
visitor wanders among the gravestones, trying vainly to recall the
people buried there. It is not so strange that the dead gradually forget the living; like Sam Craig from Buffalo, they too have "been
away."

The arrival of Emily into this company creates a contrast which
sets the tone for the flashback episode of her return to life. She
comes, a little dazed, but very much more alive than those ranged
on the chairs. There is news to tell them all—what is going on in
town—but the dead are not interested. Emily has not yet had time
to forget, and Mother Gibbs' advice about resting and being patient
is premature. All watch the funeral in the rain without emotion,
then settle back into a patient calm. But Emily is not ready for this
yet; she feels that she can return to life and determines to do so—
on an "unimportant" day, her twelfth birthday. This flashback is at
the center of the final act and is the climax of the play.

The pattern of this "routine" day follows exactly that of the first
episodes in Acts I and II. The milkman, the paperboy, the constable
make their morning rounds, talk about the weather—it is a cold
winter day, Mr. Webb is coming home from a trip upstate, Mrs.
Webb is getting breakfast and the children are dressing and coming

downstairs. The homely details are the same—if Emily's bow "were a snake, it would bite" her. The birthday gifts are passed out at the breakfast table and discussed matter-of-factly by the mother and the father calls for his "birthday girl." Into this routine Emily brings a consciousness of past and future that resembles the Stage Manager-audience point of view. Her consciousness reinforces the perspective and sets into sharp focus the universal aspects of the situation—the unity of the society, love and protection by the parents for the children, of children for parent—each living the good life in the bosom of the family. The *un*consciousness of Emily's mother and father contributes to this dimension in that they do not foresee or understand. Thus for them this "moment" is part of a duration which flows on, not a "now" whose full implications are "too beautiful to bear." For Emily, the Stage Manager, the audience, this "routine" day, set against the background both of full human experience and of the *axis mundi* dimension, is an escape from time and meaninglessness into the ideal. The values inherent in the experience of ordinary everyday living in "our town" are illuminated for the moment by the ideal.

This epiphany of the significance of the ordinary cannot endure long. The linear view of time is not altogether absent even from this point of view. The scene creates a nostalgia which, in another context, would be sentimental. Emily goes back to her home from her place in the cemetery and from her present situation into a world of childhood just emerging into adolescence, to February 11, 1899—the "good old days" of the last century. The tendency to idealize the past is strong in the American; it is characteristic of him to relegate the ideal to the past, to the period from which he has just emerged. This nostalgia brings tears to the eyes—even though the individual is conscious that the good old days are a fiction of his imagination. The vision of them—which Wilder has created—nonetheless exercises a fascination. The ideal remains an ideal for all its impossibility of fulfillment.

This moment cannot last and so Emily must return to her grave. All the pathos of the backward glance is gathered into her farewell speech:

Goodby, goodby, world. Goodby, Grover's Corners . . . Mama and Papa. Goodby to clocks ticking . . . and Mama's sunflowers. And food and coffee. And newly-ironed dresses and hot baths . . . and sleeping and waking up. Oh, earth you're too wonderful for anybody to realize you. (OUR TOWN, p. 124.)

Without the perspective given by the ritual dimension, this speech would be unbearably sentimental. But because of that dimension, its impact is heightened. The linear progression of the movement reasserts itself at this point—Emily cannot go back permanently; once past, the moment cannot be recalled. At this point it becomes clear that Wilder's message and moral do not really answer the structure:

Emily. Do any human beings ever realize life while they live it?— every, every minute?
Stage Manager. No. (Pause) The saints and poets—they do some. (OUR TOWN, p. 125.)

The implication here is that, if the individual tried hard enough, perhaps he could join that company; in any event, "realizing life" is the only possible escape from time, and that escape is possible only to the few and is at best temporary.

In the end the playwright does hold out a hope that has permanence. It is not dogmatic or unequivocal, but it takes the curse off the picture of death. The dead, according to the Stage Manager, are waiting for something important, for a purification in which the earthly part of their being burns away and the eternal part emerges. (OUR TOWN, p. 102.) There is the possibility, then, of another remove to a permanent condition—nothing quite as definite as the Resurrection, but something transcendent. This final change is related to and symbolized by the stars. Though the dead lose interest in the earth, they are fascinated by the stars (just as the children were in the first act). The stars function here as a symbol of that "eternal part" that is to emerge ungrained; they preside over the conclusion of the play. When the Stage Manager dismisses the audience to rest—the image of the rest to which Emily retires, death's second self—he remarks on the stars "just chalk . . . or fire doing their old, old crisscross journeys in the sky." (OUR TOWN, p. 128.) This imagery recalls the classical connotations of the heavenly bodies and their fire in Western culture:

The imagery of light and fire surrounding the angels in the Bible, the tongues of flame descending at Pentecost, and the coal of fire applied to the mouth of Isaiah by the seraph, associates fire with a spiritual or angelic world midway between the human and the divine. . . . In short, heaven in the sense of sky, containing the fiery bodies of sun, moon, and stars, is usually identified with, or thought of as passage to, the heaven of the apocalyptic world.[24]

The stars shine over Grover's Corners at morning and through the night binding together the hope of the dead and the endeavors of the living in an eternal dimension.

The culmination of the play's structure, then, is an apotheosis of the ordinary, the routine aspects of daily life. As the democratic elements in the myth make the common man the hero of this society, the playwright makes the common man's experience central to his drama. He attributes an absolute value to this experience—the value which is acquired by correspondence with the apocalyptic vision, the ideal. Thornton Wilder's brother, Amos, describes modern society in terms which the playwright would approve:

In contemporary society large numbers of men live without roots and without the natural ties that are essential for psychological health. The organic bonds with nature and the community are broken, and the primordial institution of the family is attainted.[25]

The ritual of *Our Town* reestablishes these ties and removes the stain from family life. If it fails to mend all the fences, it fails because of a defect in the vision itself. In spite of every effort to put daily experience in an eternal present, the perspective that makes daily life meaningful is a nostalgic backward glance. The irony of the last act lies in the fact that Emily understands from the grave. The people who are living the experience cannot understand it: "They don't understand, do they?" The small town is a thing of the past— at least, the rural community like Grover's Corners exists only in memory. Wilder himself implies as much by situating the scene of Emily's return in winter and in the final year of a dying century. Thus the only approach to its perfections is nostalgia and the primary emotion which contemplation engenders is a wistful pathos. The linear movement of time is not really overcome because the attitudes that undergird the rite do not include a real rebirth.

The myths of the primitive community do not bind their members in time this way. The cyclical view that they embody is more amenable to renewal and escape.

From the standpoint of a primitive community, Life is not so much a progression from cradle to grave as a series of leases annually or periodically renewed, and best exemplified in the revolution of the seasons. . . . A regular program of activities is established which performed periodically under communal sanction will furnish the necessary replenishment of life and vitality.[26]

The Dionysian ritual that provides a basic pattern for Greek drama concludes, it will be remembered, with the god reborn and a wedding. Death is a phase in this rite, but only as a preparation for rebirth. The archetypal analogues of the renewal of the year, the daily birth and death of the sun, the progress to wisdom through suffering, are invoked to illustrate and demonstrate the validity of this vision. In a sense, on her return, Emily is reborn, but she cannot remain with those who have not been born again. The descent of the hero to the underworld, which Campbell describes, always culminates with his return to the mundane world, carrying back with him some boon to men.[27] His rebirth includes the ability to communicate with the world and to the world the wisdom he has acquired. From her perspective on the other side of the grave, Emily tries to communicate her sense of communion to her mother. She sees her family together now and fragmented by separation in the future; she is at once a little girl in the warmth of the family circle and a woman dead in childbirth. (OUR TOWN, p. 123.) Her mother cannot really look at her nor appreciate the moment of communion because she does not share Emily's consciousness; there is no criterion in the experience itself that renders it immediately meaningful. Only when it lies in the past, can it be fully appreciated.

For all this, it is not fair to consider Wilder either an "allegorist" or a "representer of civilized human life everywhere in all ages." [28] Fergusson sees the playwright as a didactic dramatist platonically preaching a "faint religious humanism" and scores him for writing soap-opera dialogue and drawing cliché characters. In Fergusson's rather inexact recollection of the play (he refers to "cherry phosphates" and Emily's return on her *fourteenth* birthday) the aphorisms stick fast and the details of the action go glimmering. A theory constructed from some of the statements in the play is not to be equated with the ritual action; speculating on the doctrine that "one should live life every, every moment" is not quite the same as undergoing the immediate histrionic experience. Fergusson, who has presented brilliant ritual analyses of other dramas, for example, *Oedipus* and *Hamlet,* seems to be denying the same privilege to the modern playwright that he extends to Sophocles and Shakespeare. Actually, it is more likely that Fergusson finds the American attitudes in *Our Town* somewhat unpalatable in the cold light of the morning after. Burbank, on the other hand, ignores the specifically American quality of the myth. Wilder does not portray "the eternal and universal residing in the collective 'human mind' "; he is dealing with the collective American mind, or, if this seems too provincial, with the modern Western mind as realized in the American. If one reduces the meaning of the play to a capsule, that the essential failure is a failure to love every moment, and presumes that this statement is a universal, he becomes fair game for the cultural anthropologist. The ultimate "meaning" of the play is its expression of an American ideal in a ritual mode.

The effectiveness of *Our Town* and its ability to wear well is the result of its faithful correspondence to the ideal in the group-mind. If the audience does blubber when Emily goes back up the hill to her grave, it is because they recognize a "truth" and mourn its transitoriness. The wells of emotion that are tapped here lie deeper than the critical apparatus of the conscious mind; they disappear into that region where cultural aspirations are formed and mature. The logical faculty can demonstrate how many are the contradictions that such a vision contains, and the critical faculty can perform numerous post-mortems, but the ritual mode defies such operations. The American ideal as a strategy for encompassing basic human experiences may well be found wanting; nonetheless it is the American ideal.

Wilder's ability to discover the content of this ideal and to present it in its proper setting is the strongest feature of the play. Had he tried to project this content in a realistic mode, much of the impact would have been lost.[29] At this point, the mode of presentation and the content mesh inextricably together. Because *Our Town* is a dramatization of the ideal, it is a compendium of the motifs that run through modern American drama. These include: the tendency to glamorize the past, the identification of the good life with closeness to nature and rural life, the equation of democracy and social harmony, the centrality of the common man as hero, spatial remove as a solution to the problems and difficulties of every-day life, a tendency to view existence as a linear progression to oblivion. Wilder's own addition to this list—the "faint religious humanism" —cannot really be separated from the other items; what he canonizes here is that indefatigable American optimism. But Wilder, through the ritualistic mode of presentation, has rendered the ideal in its own terms—out of time and space, against a universal background, in terms of archetypal actions and the rhythm of basic experiences. Reason may rebel and logic squirm, but the ritual mode has its way. Whether or not one agrees with these attitudes, with the American ideal, Wilder's presentation of them makes as clear a statement as the stars that crisscross over Grover's Corners.

Fun and Games in Suburbia:
Who's Afraid of Virginia Woolf?

The placid citizenry of Grover's Corners and the sophisticated suburbanites of New Carthage in Edward Albee's *Who's Afraid of Virginia Woolf?* are light-years apart. Social harmony, closeness to nature and love within the family circle, except as nostalgic ideals, are not apparently operative in a large segment of the affluent American society of the 1960s. Racial strife, brush wars abroad, the rise of the cosmopolis and the decentralization of family life (talk of togetherness is symptomatic) are the facts that fly in the face of these ideals. Awareness of a deep uneasiness is inescapable, and misgivings about "the American way of life" churn below the surface of the group-mind. Given this uneasiness, the ideals that shape and sustain our societal institutions can become conventional defenses against the truth; we can avoid confronting problems by the standard procedure of repeating slogans and affirming faith. Edward Albee lays open the center of this uneasiness by dealing with "our town" of the 1960s—the American family in suburbia. His treatment is a satiric indictment, sometimes savage, of American manners and mores and the cultural assumptions that shape them. Ideals that Wilder exalts as milk and honey in the Promised Land Albee attacks as the leaven of the Pharisees.

The essential problem that is covered over by manners and mores, as Albee sees it, is the break-down of real communion between individuals. "We neither love nor hurt because we do not try to reach each other," says the protagonist of *The Zoo Story*. Observing social amenities and accepting a stereotyped role make it possible for people to converse without communicating, to live together while remaining strangers. Because Albee feels strongly the alienation of the individual in the midst of a group-oriented society, his work has an affinity with the continental playwrights of the Absurd; because he feels that social conventions have become defense mechanisms that contribute substantially to this alienation, his method is that of the satirist.

Though the playwright of the Absurd is also satirist, Albee does not belong to the tribe of Beckett, Ionesco and Genet. The satirical spirit holds the foibles of society up to ridicule in order to restore a balance; the Absurdist goes farther:

Behind the satirical exposure of the absurdity of inauthentic ways of life, the Theatre of the Absurd is facing up to a deeper layer of absurdity— the absurdity of the human condition itself in a world where the decline of religious belief has deprived man of certainties. When it is no longer possible to accept simple and complete systems of values and revelations of divine purpose, life must be faced in its ultimate, stark reality.[1]

Thus, Absurd drama brings modern man face to face with the Void and explores this moment of confrontation dramatically—what grips the mind, what images occur to the visionary, what emotions arise at this moment. This confrontation is the subject matter of Absurd drama and the individual's reaction to it is the form. Albee does not go this far; *Virginia Woolf* does not insist on the ultimate meaning-lessness of existence and of the struggle to communicate. Whether man *can* communicate or whether communication is ultimately worth-while Albee does not decide; he does attack the manners and attitudes of society that keep man from communication. Once the artificial barriers are down, then we can see whether or not there is a hope of community. Albee uses the satirist's ax to demolish these barriers.

"Satire," says Northrop Frye, "is militant irony: its moral norms are relatively clear, and its assumed standards against which the grotesque and the absurd are measured." [2] At first glance, it would seem that Albee has no "moral norm" against which to measure American society. He attacks its most cherished assumptions—that the marriage bond is a source of communion, that the business fail-ure is a weakling, that fertility is a blessing—without offering any systematic replacements for these attitudes. He is no Swift who can point to reason and experience as a norm when he exposes the fool and lashes the knave; Albee's *reductio ad absurdum* does not balance abuse against a proper use of objective norms of behavior. Nonetheless, he does invoke, implicitly, a "moral norm"—*Virginia Woolf* demands that the spectator recognize that societal standards can become defenses that the individual uses to avoid the pain of facing reality. The title is a riddle whose answer enunciates this norm. The threat that is "Virginia Woolf" is the world of fantasy that the attitudes of society can support.

The satirical thrust of the play is indicated by the ironic way in which Albee constructs his façade—setting, dialogue, character-types —to represent a recognizable segment of the American scene. George and Martha live in the small New England town of New Carthage. Their "wonderful old house" suggests the renovated middle-class home with tiled bathroom, door-chimes and a portable bar. There is a comfortable supply of liquor on hand. This atmosphere is lifted to a level of sophistication by the intellectual aura of a college milieu, and invested with more than a suggestion of decadence by the name of the town. "New Carthage" is an ironic comment on the usual comparison (itself not altogether favorable) of American and Roman civilizations. *Carthago delenda est;* the "Romans" of New Carthage are in the process of destroying themselves from within. The enemies leveling the town are its occupants.

The situation of the play—a married couple entertaining another couple—resembles that of a Noel Coward drawing-room comedy, a house party in miniature. The two couples drink together and carry on a conversation in what would be Noel Coward fashion were it not for the language. The elements typical of the situation are submerged by the shock of the dialogue which is very atypical—at least for the stage. The language is not the polished, veiled innuendo that might be expected from this social class (or in the drawing-room comedy), nor do the characters thrust and parry with rapier-like repartee. The weapons here are finger-nails. George and Martha, from the beginning of the play, "tear at one another's vitals" like truck-drivers. The opening expletive sets the tone: "Je*sus.*" Host and hostess do not moderate their language for the sake of the guests; Nick's attempt at polite small-talk is cut off quickly by George's sarcasm and Honey is "monkey-nipples" and "angel-tits" to George, a comparative stranger. By having his characters talk like teamsters, Albee satirizes a social institution which allows strangers to talk brightly together without revealing their real feelings. This house party is *different;* it begins on the level that Eliot's *Cocktail Party* reaches painfully by small-talk indirection. In *Virginia Woolf* Albee begins one layer down by making explicit the conflicts that standards of politeness conceal.[3] Thus the contrast between the accepted norm and the real situation is implicit while, at the same time, the playwright points to a blight in the relationships among the characters that is more than social. As George points out: "When one gets down to bone, there is always the marrow." The marrow is what Albee is after.

The cultural attitudes that come under fire in *Virginia Woolf* cut across the spectrum of American culture: the success myth, the image of American manhood and womanhood, the institution of marriage itself. These attitudes are defined in the games that are played (which we will investigate as such later) by host, hostess and guests. Their relationships involve certain assumptions on which the action of the play makes an ironic comment.

The marital relationship of George and Martha is qualified, in the first instance, by George's failure to advance in his profession. He is *"in* the History department," but he is *"not* the History department." Even marrying the boss's daughter, the classic climax of the Horatio Alger success-story, is no help to him. "Bogged down," he grows old without hope of preferment. The fact that he cannot compete successfully in academia makes it clear that he could not succeed anywhere. He is, under a façade of wry detachment, the antithesis of the go-ahead charmer that the success myth praises. Martha taunts him with his failure and his intellectuality:

He'd [George'd] be . . . no good . . . at trustees' dinners, fund raising. He didn't have any . . . personality, you know what I mean? Which was disappointing to Daddy, as you can imagine. So, here I am, stuck with this flop. . . .
George. (Turning around) . . . don't go on, Martha. . . .
Martha. . . . this BOG in the History Department. . . .
George. . . . don't, Martha, don't. . . .
Martha. . . . who's married to the President's daughter, who's expected to *be* somebody, some bookworm, somebody who's so damn . . . contemplative, he can't make anything out of himself, somebody without the *guts* to make anybody proud of him.[4]

Failing at his job, George cannot come up to standard as husband. The conventional image demands that the husband be breadwinner, the dominant figure in the household, a practical man of affairs. He is a flop and Martha cannot respect him. She controls the activities of the household; George does not know that she has invited guests; he does not assert his rights when she sets out to seduce Nick. Nick's appraisal, though more cautious, is the same as Martha's: "You ineffectual sons of bitches . . . You're the worst." (vw, p. 111.) George does not meet the minimum standards for a husband set by society. Albee has made sure that George cannot hide behind the mask of achievement. When his worth as a person emerges in the action, it will be clear that it is not dependent on his achievement of status either in the business world or at home.

The character of Martha, as counterpart to George, is an unpleasant parody of the independent and aggressive American female. Her vulgarity, which George underscores at every turn, offsets qualities that the stereotype holds up for admiration. She cultivates the appearance of fertility in spite of her age, she exercises independence in satisfying herself by dominating her environment. If she lacks spiritual refinement, if she dominates her husband, this is not the way she wanted it.

Martha. My arm has gotten tired whipping you.
George. (Stares at her in disbelief) You're mad.
Martha. For twenty-three years!
George. You're deluded . . . Martha, you're deluded.
Martha. IT'S NOT WHAT I'VE WANTED! (vw, p. 153.)

The judgment of society sits lightly on such a woman because she is only reacting to the abdication of responsibility by her husband. Nonetheless, Albee makes the stereotype repulsive, softening it only by the note of frustration that marks Martha's braying.

Nick and Honey function as contrasts to George and Martha. Nick is the dominant male headed for success, bright, young and aggressive without being too crass (at least at the outset) about it. He has a consuming self-interest and a driving ambition which he masks by a cool deference. His sexual attractiveness makes him a foil for Martha and provides the material for "Hump the Hostess."

Honey is the defenseless female, the weaker partner. She is slim-hipped and infertile, given to hysterical pregnancies, no match for the figure Martha cuts. Nick and Martha, then, represent in outline two stereotypes in American culture. Each will suffer, in the course of action, a transformation that amounts to an ironic commentary on a "realistic" societal standard of judgment. The games these people play will strip away the masks and expose both bone and marrow.

Though the traditional Western view of the institution of marriage, rooted in Judaeo-Christian values, is not universally accepted in practice, Americans still pay lip-service to an ideal of married stability and communion. The recent flurry of concern about "togetherness" both reflected a sense of loss of values and also paid tribute to the ideal. In *Virginia Woolf* marriage is a matter of expediency. It is the occasion for a vivid antagonism, a highway to success and an opportunity for sexual "fun and games." Martha married George because she was infatuated and because she and her father saw in him a successor to the presidential chair. "I actually fell for him. And the match seemed . . . practical, too. You know Daddy was looking for someone to . . . take over when he was ready to . . . retire." (vw, p. 82.) Nick married Honey because her father was rich and he wanted to avoid a scandal. Now marriage provides Nick and Martha with opportunities for adultery. This is the rule, not the exception, in New Carthage. George remarks that "musical beds is the faculty sport around here." (vw, p. 34.) This activity is more than just "fun and games"; it is also the way to promotion. "The way to a man's heart is through his wife's belly." (vw, p. 113.) The "serious" aspects of the marriage commitment are not fidelity and communion but expediency and "the games people play." The playwright accentuates the satirical contrast between the accepted ideal and the George-Martha relationship by making the really serious business of the play go on in the context of "fun and games."

In order to make this contrast vivid, Albee draws on another American attitude. By and large, the American public takes games very seriously. Dedication to bridge, to golf, to following football and baseball teams is part of the cultural heritage; "being a good sport" is a social virtue. This attitude is the more significant since, in a fragmented culture that has no agreed-upon values, the game creates a severely limited world, tightly organized with absolute rules and values. It generates a miniature culture that exists outside the context of satisfaction of immediate wants and appetites.[5] It constitutes a community, a society, that works together voluntarily according to the order prescribed by the rules. In fact, the distinction between game-experience and life-experience does not lie in the playfulness of one and the seriousness of the other, but rather in the absoluteness and disinterestedness of game-values opposed to the relativity and self-interest of life-values. In *Virginia Woolf* only the game supplies a value-system that is meaningful. The rules provide a context for an expression of the personality when they are observed and, even more significantly, when they are broken. These people who cannot love can constitute a play-world of vicious games in which they reach one another by hurting.

The antagonistic spirit that informs this game-world is established from the outset of the play. Even on the level of "ordinary" conversation between husband and wife there are small contests of knowledge and wit: what is the name of the Bette Davis movie? who's afraid of Virginia Woolf? and of alcoholic capacity: "Martha, I gave you that prize years ago. . . ." (vw, p. 16.) When the guests arrive, Nick senses this antagonism and tries to stay aloof from it, to play the neutral guest. George immediately sets about alienating him by not allowing small-talk.

Nick. (Indicating the abstract painting) Who . . . who did the . . . ?
Martha. That? Oh, that's by. . . .
George. . . . some Greek with a mustache Martha attacked one night in . . .
Honey. (To save the situation) Oh, ho, ho, ho, Ho.
Nick. It's got a . . . a . . .
George. A quiet intensity?
Nick. Well, no . . . a . . .
George. Oh. (Pause) Well, then, a certain noisy relaxed quality, maybe? (vw, pp. 21–2.)

These antagonisms will fluctuate somewhat. George and Nick, left alone while the ladies go upstairs, confide in one another. These confidences involving the past turn out to be less trustworthy than the revelations of the games.

The content of the games allows the partners to strike at each other by revealing the nature of their private lives. George's failure to achieve distinction in the History department and his abortive attempt at novel-writing are the bases for "Humiliate the Host." (vw, p. 38.) Nick's opportunistic marriage to Honey and her hysterical pregnancy allows George to retaliate in "Get the Guests." (vw, pp. 93, 103.) Martha's attraction to Nick, her attachment to her successful father and her desire for revenge in the face of George's indifference to her infidelity provide the ingredients for "Hump the Hostess." (vw, pp. 9, 15, 53, 55.) Martha's revelation to Nick and Honey that she and George have a son is the foundation for "Bringing Up Baby." Each game results in an excursion into the private world of the individual, a probe that is calculated to hurt the antagonist while justifying the actions of the prober. The innocuous partygame is thereby turned into a means of attack and defense; it creates a miniature culture with rules, conventions and a valuesystem. The rules are subject to change without notice, it is true, but the antagonist can always turn about and create a new game in response to the challenge.

The games move into the area of the private experiences of the past when "Humiliate the Host" moves from a discussion of George's academic failure (a public fact) to his failure as a novelist. This latter sniping makes use of a private fact that George has covertly revealed to Nick, "bergin" as a mispronunciation of "bourbon." It allows the guests a glimpse of George's past. Up to this point he has been able to score points by ridiculing Nick's specialty and Martha's vulgarity, now he feels his identity at stake. He tries to call a halt: "THE GAME IS OVER!" (vw, p. 136.) Martha refuses to stop and makes it clear that the incidents of the novel are, at least for the purposes of the game, autobiographical.

This breach of confidence establishes a new set of rules which George promulgates for "Get the Guests." "This is my game! You played yours . . . you people. This is my game!" (vw, p. 142.) He then uses Nick's confidential statements to construct an allegory that slashes to the bone of Nick and Honey's marriage. As George was hurt by Martha's betrayal of him before the guests, so he adroitly adapts her technique to get revenge on the company. In selfdefense, he cuts Nick down to size in front of Martha. "Blondie and his frau out of the plain states came." Honey is literally sickened by the recital and flees to the bathroom; George and Martha add up the score in the interval.

Martha. You make me sick.

George. It's perfectly all right for you . . . I mean, you can make your own rules . . . you can go around like a hopped-up Arab, slashing away at everything in sight, scarring up half the world if you want to. But somebody else try it . . . no sir! (vw, pp. 151–2.)

Martha then accuses George of masochism—"My arm has gotten tired whipping you." George's countercharge is in the same vein: "You're sick." The real antagonists are now squared off—Martha will play the game suggested earlier by George, "Hump the Hostess." (vw, p. 139.) He accepts the challenge: "You try it and I'll beat you at your own game." (vw, p. 158.) Martha's "own game" involves changing the rules at whim in order to strike home more surely; it is now a struggle to the finish.

"Hump the Hostess" develops to a stand-off in which the game degenerates from a test of wit and invention, however cruel, to destructive action. Huizinga remarks that "the predominance of the antagonistic principle does lead to decadence in the long run" because the real feelings that are aroused cannot be easily controlled by the rules.[6] While Martha leads Nick on, George sits in the corner reading a book. Among the standard ground-rules for "Hump the Hostess" is a possessive attitude on the part of the husband, based on proprietal rights if nothing else. Instead, George assumes the intellectual's pose of unconcern so that Martha cannot claim a victory. The spectator knows, however, that he has been stung: after Martha goes upstairs with Nick, he "stands still . . . then, quickly, he gathers all the fury he has been containing within himself . . . he shakes . . . he looks at the book in his hand and, with a cry that is part growl, he hurls it at the chimes." (vw, p. 174.) In the chiming of the doorbell and in his conversation with Honey on child-bearing, he discovers the ultimate weapon with which to "get" Martha: the "murder" of their son. The final game will be "Bringing Up Baby."

George's references to their "son" have contained a note of warning from the beginning of the play. It is clear that "the kid" is a hole-card that George would rather not play.

George. Just don't start in on the bit, that's all.
Martha. The bit? The bit? What kind of language is that? What are you talking about?

. . . .

George. Just don't start in on the bit about the kid, that's all.

(VW, p. 18.)

Martha does "start in" quite early in the games and "Hump the Hostess" tips the balance; George will murder the child. Martha is soothed into telling the story of their son to Nick and Honey who have now been reduced to spectators. The antagonism that characterized the earlier games is heightened by a head-on collision, Martha claiming that she protected and perfected their son, George claiming the opposite. He then delivers the *coup de grâce;* their son is dead. A dazed Honey corroborates the statement; George "ate" the telegram that contained the announcement. Martha is shattered and defenseless:

Martha. You're not going to get away with this.
George. (With disgust) YOU KNOW THE RULES, MARTHA, FOR CHRIST'S SAKE, YOU KNOW THE RULES!
Martha. No!
Nick. (With the beginning of a knowledge he cannot face) What are you two talking about?
George. I can kill him, Martha, if I want to.
Martha. HE IS OUR CHILD!
. . . .
George. AND I HAVE KILLED HIM! (VW, p. 235.)

Martha has broken the rules by talking about the son with outsiders. And so George has exercised his right to "kill" him. Nick (along with the audience) begins to understand that the son is a figment of Martha's (with George in collusion) imagination: "Jesus Christ, I think I understand this." With Honey as clerk, George finishes the party with a prayer: *Requiescat in pace. Amen.* The party is over.

It is clear that the games provide a comment on the masculine and feminine stereotypes outlined above and also on the relative values that American society places on them. Through antagonistic contact, the give-and-take of the game framework, Albee reverses the roles of the contenders. Nick, the virile, practical scientist, and Martha, Earth-goddess and mother, are cut down to size, and their masks destroyed. When Nick fails to give satisfaction in "Hump the Hostess," Martha declares that George is the only man who has ever done so and Nick is relegated to the role of houseboy, which was George's role in the first act: "Get over there and answer the door." (vw, p. 19.)

Martha. You can be houseboy around here for a while. You can start off being houseboy right now.
Nick. Look, lady, I'm no flunky to you.
Martha. (Cheerfully) Sure you are! You're ambitious, aren't you, boy? You didn't chase me around the kitchen and up the goddamn stairs out of mad, driven passion, did you now? You were thinking a little bit about your career, weren't you? Well, you can just houseboy your way up the ladder for a while. (vw, p. 194.)

The image of the sexually dominant and ambitious male loses stature when Nick is forced to accept this role. Martha alone is unscathed up to "Bringing Up Baby"; her image as the Earth-mother who teems with fertility and sex appeal is destroyed by that game. For all practical purposes her final status approximates Honey's; once George has destroyed the baby, Martha is infertile and childlike. The impractical and ineffectual George has established control over the threesome. These idols of American culture are shown to have clay feet.

The social satire that the playwright injects through the games is augmented by the use of ritual details. The subterranean seriousness of the play-world is underscored by a gradual progression from a house-party atmosphere into the atmosphere of ritual. The title of the second act "Walpurgisnacht" suggests a preternatural context that parallels the Witches' Sabbath in Goethe's *Faust*. In that play Mephistopheles describes the scene to his companion:

> Just look! You barely see the other end.
> A hundred fires in a row, my friend!
> They dance, they chat, they cook, they drink, they court.
> Now you tell me where there's better sport! [7]

As in the Witches' Sabbath, the couples drink, chat, and kiss; Martha and Nick dance as a prelude to the game of "Hump the Hostess." George remarks on the nature of the dance: "It's a familiar dance . . . It's a very old ritual . . . as old as they come." (vw, p. 131.) This New England house is also the mountaintop where the witches gather—those unholy souls who congregate to observe the May festival.[8]

The Faustian analogue includes another illuminating reference to the games. The celebrants of Walpurgisnacht participate in "half-childish games" and there is posed "many a riddle knottily tied." People crowd about the Devil, says Faust, "where many riddles must be solved," and the Devil, adds Mephistopheles, poses many new ones of his own.[9] The ritual riddle has a significance for the persons who must solve it; it is, in this context, a matter of life-and-death.

From one point of view all the games in *Virginia Woolf* are riddles, word-games in that they depend on the exercise of power in knowledge. The riddle is a means of expressing and concealing knowledge; in primitive cultures the secrets of the tribe are often concealed in a riddle. The man who could unknot it acquired the wisdom it contained, and with that wisdom, power.

The riddle is a sacred thing full of secret power, hence a dangerous thing. In its mythological or ritual context it is nearly always what German philologists know as the *Halsrätsel* or "capital riddle," which you either solve or forfeit. The player's life is at stake.[10]

Thus "Who's Afraid of Virginia Woolf?" can be read as a "capital riddle." It seems to require no answer at the outset but gathers significance in repetition. Unless it can be finally solved, the players are in danger of not finding an identity to replace the one they have lost in the games. Other riddling features of the games include the "bergin" narrative which gives the strangers the power of understanding George's past. Martha uses a riddle-form in framing her revelation about his past:

> Well, Georgie-boy had lots of big ambitions
> In spite of something funny in his past. . . .
> Which Georgie-boy turned into a novel
> His first attempt and also his last. . . .
> Hey! I rhymed! I rhymed! (vw, p. 133.)

Martha's insistence on the rhyme calls attention to the riddle-form—a capsulated mystery to be solved. George does not employ rhyme in his story of "Blondie and his frau," but the allegorical style, with its reference to "Childe Roland," achieves a similar effect. Both put their material into a formal pattern that at once reveals and conceals. The lives of the players do depend on the answers to these riddles in that, when the other players solve them, the individual loses identity and can no longer exercise the same kind of control over the situation. George, Nick and Honey are exposed, to some extent, in the first three games; Martha is exposed in "Bringing Up Baby," the climactic riddle-game which adds explicitly ritual actions.

The most notable ritual addition is George's use of the Roman Catholic funeral service as accompaniment to the news of "Baby's" passing. He has built up to this by bringing in snapdragons to the chant *"Flores par los muertos."* The mock solemnity of this chant, with its veiled threat, becomes explicitly antagonistic when George throws the flowers, spear-like, at Martha. But the antagonism goes underground and the ritual solemnity is focused when George begins to recite the requiem. He vouches for the objectivity of his message and the necessity of the death of the son by following the ritual. Though this "news" is part of the game, George is not joking. Baby is dead and cannot be resurrected by any effort on Martha's part. The ritual dimension guarantees the objectivity of this game and its far-reaching effect. What is destroyed here is not only a social stereotype but a conviction about procreation that reaches into the marrow of the human situation.

"Bringing Up Baby" raises a question about the nature of the union between husband and wife. Though all the games demonstrate that social conventions cannot be defenses against life-experience, the illusions attacked in the first three games are fostered by certain conventional American attitudes: that a man must be a success in his profession or trade, that marriage is a romantic adventure based on "true love," that adultery is "fun and games." "Bringing Up Baby" does not quite fit the pattern here. It attacks a convention less ephemeral than these: the notion that the child is (or can be) a real bond of union between husband and wife. While it can be argued that the child is imaginary and so hardly a fair test-case, the fact is that, in *Virginia Woolf,* even the couple that has a child is sterile. The child is laid to rest with the ritual solemnity of a funeral service, its relationship to each parent is argued at length, it has as much reality as the experiences that are related about

George's parents and Martha's father. Whether or not we like it, what the final game says is clear enough—the child functioned as an actual child of flesh and blood would function in marriage. George and Martha have stayed together "for the sake of the child." Albee is ultimately striking at a radical and accepted attitude toward marriage: the child as bond of union between the partners.

The episode of the "imaginary baby" has been the largest stumbling block for critics who have evaluated the play. They are in general agreement that introduction of the child is inept and incredible, and their judgment ranges from a gentle disagreement with this sequence to a bitter indictment of the entire play.[11] The issue is taken to be the credibility of the child. Certainly, if the play is seen as the tragedy of two incompatible neurotics, the imaginary baby should be thrown out with the bath-water. But the same difficulty regarding credibility can be leveled at the contents of the other games; histories narrated by George and Martha contain details that seem to contribute to an understanding of their present situation, but on reflection it is impossible to sort out fact from fiction. The "bergin" story seems to go far toward explaining George's lack of virility and passiveness in the marital situation. He hated his parents and destroyed them. But uncertainties proliferate as the factual contents of the stories are weighed in the balance. The conclusion of the murder tale that George tells Nick does not fit the facts. "He was put in an asylum. That was thirty years ago. . . . And I'm told for these thirty years he has . . . not . . . uttered . . . one . . . sound." (vw, p. 96.) On the other hand, Martha talks as if another detail were actually true: "You'd wish you'd died in that automobile, you bastard." (vw, p. 154.) Finally, there is no certainty at all about the actual events:

George. Once . . . once, when I was sailing past Majorca, drinking on deck with a correspondent who was talking about Roosevelt, the moon went down, thought about it for a little . . . considered it, you know what I mean: . . . and then, POP, came up again. Just like that.
Martha. That is not true! That is such a lie!
George. You must not call everything a lie, Martha. (To Nick) Must she?
Nick. Hell, I don't know when you people are lying, or what.

. . . .

Martha. You were never in the goddamn Mediterranean at all . . . ever. . . .

George. I certainly was! My Mommy and Daddy took me there as a college graduation present. (vw, pp. 199–200.)

It is not even clear how seriously we are to take Martha's story about the lawn boy, her first husband. When Nick brings him up again, she says: "I'd forgotten him. But when I think about him and me it's almost like being a voyeur." (vw, p. 190.) George sums up the situation in the prelude to the final game: "Truth and illusion. Who knows the difference, eh, toots?" (vw, p. 201.) The "truth" of the son's existence lies in the subjective reactions to it. The other games may involve illusions that are "true"; whether or not George actually killed his parents is not at issue. He may have created the experience for fictional purposes, but he treats it as real. Their son must "die" because he is—in some sense—real. Logically, then, it seems that what the critics are objecting to is not a breach of dramatic credibility, but rather the *significance* of the son's presence and demise. "Bringing Up Baby" makes an uncomfortable point; it is no wonder that the critics are restive under its impact.

We have seen, then, that the setting, character-types and the use of situations conspire to produce ironic contrasts between accepted social conventions, cultural stereotypes and the actual relationships between persons. The structure of the play reinforces these contrasts and makes a statement of its own about them.

Northrop Frye points out that "as structure, the central principle of ironic myth is best approached as a parody of romance: the application of romantic mythical forms to a more realistic content which fits them in unexpected ways." [12] The game-motif and what it reveals is the "realistic content" in *Virginia Woolf;* the structure is "romantic" in that it follows the comic pattern in outline and in detail. The movement of the plot, then, is the familiar one of temporary liaison followed by separation and alienation which heals into a new union at the conclusion of the play. Underneath the snarl and snap of the dialogue and the satiric twists given to the incidents, *Virginia Woolf* progresses to a wedding.

The phases of this comic structure are carefully defined in the action. It is important to notice that the incidents that define the structural movement occur outside the context of the games. At the outset, after the opening riddles, George and Martha make it clear that their marriage is not altogether satisfactory:

Martha. I swear . . . if you existed I'd divorce you. . . .
George. Well, just stay on your feet, that's all. . . . These people are your guests, you know, and. . . .
Martha. I can't even see you . . . I haven't been able to see you for years. . . .
George. . . . if you pass out, or throw up, or something. . . .
Martha. . . . I mean, you're a blank, a cipher. . . . (vw, p. 17.)

Their "communication" is a double monologue, each trying to hurt the other with invective and name-calling. There is vital contact, but this contact does nothing to reassure us about the future of their relationship.

The mutual violations of confidence that follow threaten this antagonistic mode of communication and, at the center of the drama, Martha announces that the order of their world has broken down. Outside of the game-context, she tells her husband:

You know what's happened, George? You want to know what's *really happened?* (Snaps her fingers) It's snapped, finally. Not me . . . *it.* The whole arrangement. You can go along . . . forever, and everything's manageable. You make all sorts of excuses to yourself . . . *you* know . . . this is life . . . the hell with it . . . maybe tomorrow he'll be dead . . . maybe tomorrow you'll be dead . . . all sorts of excuses. But then, one day, one night, something happens . . . and SNAP! It breaks. (vw, pp. 156–7.)

There is no further attempt to explain the "snap"; the pressure on the rapport, tenuous at best, is cumulative and the straw that breaks the camel's back snaps the bond. The point of complete separation is indicated clearly because, apparently, after the snap nothing has changed. The games go on; Martha continues to play, though "Hump the Hostess" is not just a word-game, and George plays by refusing to accept the stereotyped role of outraged husband. "I'll beat you at your own game." (vw, p. 158.) Thus the break, as described in the dialogue above, seems gratuitous. It functions rather to define the plot-pattern, to call attention to the divisions of structure.

The final movement of the structure, as we have come to expect, is the reconciliation of the principals, the "wedding" or conclusion of the pattern. We are prepared for this reconciliation by Martha's confession to Nick, again outside the games, that George is the man for her. She begins to face her own problems, but without much hope:

[To Nick] You're all flops. I am the Earth Mother, and you're all flops. (More or less to herself) I disgust me. I pass my life in crummy, totally pointless infidelities . . . (Laughs ruefully) *would*-be infidelities. Hump the Hostess? That's a laugh. A bunch of boozed-up . . . impotent lunk-heads. . . . That's how it is in civilized society. (To herself again) All the gorgeous lunk-heads. Poor babies. (To Nick, now: earnestly) There is only one man in my life who has ever made me happy. Do you know that? One! . . . George; my husband.

. . . .

George who is out somewhere there in the dark. . . . George who is good to me, and whom I revile; who understands me, and whom I push off; who can make me laugh, and I choke it back in my throat; who can hold me, at night, so that it's warm, and whom I will bite so there's blood; who keeps learning the games we play as quickly as I can change the rules; who can make me happy and I do not wish to be happy, and yes, I do wish to be happy. George and Martha: sad, sad, sad. (vw, pp. 189–91.)

Here Martha recognizes her problem—she wishes to be happy and she has no right to be happy. "They" are all flops and she is the Earth Mother, but she is not happy with her dominant role. George made the "hideous mistake" of loving her and "must be punished for it." (vw, p. 191.) Martha feels that she is not worth loving and she has punished herself for it. But there is no hope for her alone; "Bringing Up Baby" can save her, but only on George's initiative. The reconciliation occurs because George kills their son and, with him, the image of herself that holds Martha captive.

After the games are over and the ritual laid aside, George and Martha are reconciled. They find the answer to the "capital" riddle "Who's Afraid of Virginia Woolf?" in the destruction of Martha's fantasy. She is stripped of her role as Earth Mother, the fertile goddess, powerful and attractive, by George's refusal to "play." The sought-for communion becomes a possibility when Martha accepts their sterility, facing the truth rather than hiding in illusion; the communion which heretofore has been accessible only in the antagonism of the game-context is available in the cold, five-o'clock-in-the-morning world of a mutual need.

George. (Long silence) It will be better.
Martha. (Long silence) I don't . . . know.
George. It will be . . . maybe.

. . . .

Martha. Just . . . us?
George. Yes. (vw, pp. 240–1.)

Martha is now afraid of Virginia Woolf, of that private world of fantasy built into a public face according to what society expects and demands. Without masks, husband and wife can begin to create a new life, maybe, out of a mutual isolation and a mutual need.

The satiric tone of the play seems to have disappeared in this final scene—two exhausted people alone in the cold light of dawn seem to have little satiric potential left. Albee's use of the comic structure, however, continues to make its own comment. In the drawing-room comedy the "reconciliation" movement would have a bright uplift about it, "true" love triumphing in a sophisticated way. In a broader perspective, this "reconciliation" would involve a kômos, the "unmasking" of bride and bridegroom that reveals their true identity in a nuptial ceremony that celebrates fertility and the birth of a new society. The prototype here remains the wedding of the Earth-goddess and the Eniautos daimon; the resonances of fertility and new life that are explicit in that marriage endure in all the variations of it. In *Virginia Woolf* these resonances are established by the playwright to create an ironic contrast with the final situation of George and Martha.

The irony here is observable, first, in the identity of the reconciled parties. Martha, who claimed an Earth-goddess identity until unmasked by "Bringing Up Baby," is a tired and lonely child, dependent on George. George's "unmasking," however, does not involve so obvious a revelation. He never had a chance to disguise himself in an accepted stereotype; his pose as a detached intellectual is as much a weapon for attack as a mask for defense. Behind his egghead pose works the eiron who uses his detachment to destroy the alazontes, the intruders, that are in charge of society.[13] The function as eiron explains the quasi-heroic impression we have of George. His philosophic stance toward the situations he cannot change immediately liberates him for the attack when the time is ripe. Because of it, he is capable of seeing the complexities of data in experience. When he tries to warn Nick about the dangers of social-climbing by adultery, and Nick answers with an obscenity, "Up yours!" George replies:

You take the trouble to construct a civilization . . . to . . . build a society, based on principles of . . . of principle . . . you endeavor to make communicable sense out of natural order, morality out of the unnatural disorder of man's mind . . . you make government and art, and realize that they are, must be, both the same . . . you bring things to the saddest of all points . . . to the point where there *is* something to lose . . . then all at once, through all the music, through all the sensible sounds of men building, attempting, comes the *Dies Irae*. And what is it? What does the trumpet sound? Up yours. I suppose there's justice to it, after all the years. . . . Up yours. (vw, p. 117.)

George's warnings to Nick and to Martha are largely ignored so that he has to attack. This feature of his character reflects a specific eiron that has for its model a traditional figure from romance—the giant-killer.[14]

In the final phase, then, George's character appears "unmasked" as "giant-killing eiron." There has been considerable preparation for this revelation through the course of the play. After Martha's recitation of her one-punch knockout victory over George, he gives the company a turn by popping a parasol from a short-barreled shotgun. "POW! . . . You're dead! Pow! You're dead." He "might kill" the braying Earth-goddess someday. (vw, pp. 57, 60.) After "Get the Guests," Martha compliments George on his "pigmy-hunting." He replies: "Baby, if quarterback there is a pigmy, you've certainly changed your style. What are you after now . . . giants?" (vw, p. 151.) The "giant-killer" image continues into the last act when he throws the snapdragons at Martha. "Snap went the dragons!" (vw, p. 202.) This symbolic violence leads up to the slaying of the most significant dragon, the imaginary son. Like the over-matched Davids of the romance, he destroys those enemies of truth who are in charge of the society, the conventional images and attitudes, personified in Nick and Martha, that are obstacles to a communion in spirit and in truth.

Beside the unmaskings, the ironic conclusion of *Virginia Woolf* reverses the significance of other comic motifs: the celebration of fertility and the establishment of a new social order. Though

Albee uses some of the images that traditionally reinforce the fertility motif, he inverts their meaning. The snapdragons that George picks "in Daddy's greenhouse" by the light of the moon are "flowers for the dead." They do not come from the garden outside, but from the hothouse—force-fed and artificial. Martha sees them as a "wedding bouquet": "Pansies! Rosemary! Violence! My wedding bouquet!" (vw, p. 196.) The Ophelia overtones here connect the fertility images of flowers, water and the bridal with death. When George hurls the snapdragons at Martha, he echoes her "SNAP!" the breakdown of their tenuous relationship. The cumulative effect of this irony is added to the explicit development of the sterility motif in Honey's character. She is afraid of child-bearing and reverts to the child's role when she is threatened by it—lying in a foetal position "sucking her thumb" on the cool bathroom floor. When Martha's situation is finally equated with Honey's at the unmasking, the symbols of fecundity with which she is surrounded, ironically treated as they are, simply reinforce her sterile condition.

From this perspective the ritual killing of the child also reverses a traditional pattern. Instead of a wedding ceremony there is a funeral; the child, which could be seen as a new creation symbolic of rebirth, is shown to be an illusion, an obstacle to real communion. Martha does see the child as savior, a medium of reconciliation and redemption in a hostile universe.

And as he grew . . . and as he grew . . . oh! so wise! . . . he walked evenly between us . . . (She spreads her hands) . . . a hand out to each of us for what we could offer by way of support, affection, teaching, even love . . . and these hands, still, to hold us off a bit, for mutual protection, to protect us all from George's . . . weakness . . . and my . . . necessary greater strength . . . to protect himself and *us*. (vw, p. 222.)

In Martha's fantasy, this savior-child is "poor lamb" who broke his arm when a cow moo'd back at him—the two sacrificial symbols of Dionysus and Christ are morticed together here by an allusion to James Joyce.[15] (vw, p. 221.) He is also a child of the sun, Apollo, with his rubber-tipped bow and arrow under his bed, and a *lux oriens:* [16] "the one light in all this hopeless *dark*ness . . . OUR SON." (vw, p. 227.) George sees the baby not as Dionysus or Christ born to inaugurate a new age or to save his people, but as a demon to be exorcized, the product of a Walpurgisnacht orgy. While Martha eulogizes the savior, George asks in ritual Latin that they be allowed to rest in peace when the Lord comes to judge the world by fire. *"Dum veneris judicare saeculum per ignem."* (vw, p. 227.) The suitable rite is the funeral service and a judgment on the world. There is no savior, neither Dionysus nor Christ, available to the cosmos of New Carthage.

The "new social order" established by this conclusion is "just us," two people alone in their weakness and their need. Martha sends Nick and Honey home; they leave wordlessly, for there is nothing to be said. George shows his concern for Martha in this late, cold and tired world.

George. Do you want anything, Martha?
Martha. (Still looking away) No . . . nothing.
George. All right. (Pause) Time for bed.
Martha. Yes. (vw, p. 239.)

This mutual concern, for the truth as they see it and for each other with George exercising his role as protector and with Martha accepting him in it, is all the couple has to work with. Tomorrow is another day—"Sunday, all day"—and perhaps, with the evil giants dead and the riddle of *Virginia Woolf* solved, things will be better . . . perhaps.

We now perceive that the "convention" that is being attacked finally in *Virginia Woolf* is the notion that we can expect salvation from without. The standards of politeness that govern social intercourse serve to conceal a basic antagonism. Once the veneer has been peeled off, like the label on Honey's brandy bottle, and the essential problem of communication is revealed, Albee is able to strike at the radical "illusion," as he sees it, the hope of salvation from some agent outside the individual. History and religious cult do not hold out any such hope; George, quoting Spengler, demolishes progressive optimism: "And the west, encumbered by crippling alliances, and burdened with a morality too rigid to accommodate itself to the swing of events, must . . . eventually . . . fall." (vw, p. 174.) The only applicable rituals are the "capital-riddle," a witches' sabbath and the requiem Mass. Biology, as typified by Nick, offers only the tyranny of the super-man, a race of smooth,

blond men right at the middleweight limit "dedicated to and working for the greater glory of the super-civilization." (vw, p. 66.) The
forces of nature no longer offer ground for hope; entering into the
creation of new life does not afford a psychological basis for the
union of husband and wife. The creative urge has no magic in it
that can unify the procreators. It is simple biology, mechanistic and
impersonal. The tendency to deify this urge in the "divine child" is
one more convention that keeps man from realizing the truth of his
condition.

Whether or not *Virginia Woolf* is a fair test of this latter view can
be questioned. The critical dissatisfaction with the device of the
"imaginary child" seems ultimately to stem from a restiveness about
the validity of Albee's treatment. By introducing the ritual details,
Albee is trying to universalize a particular case, that is, he moves
from satire on *American* attitudes to an ironic comment on values
that permeate all Western culture. George and Martha's last name
may be "Washington"; we are not so willing to accept "Mankind."
We find it hard to believe that the birth of an actual child would
have made no difference at all in their relationship. The cultural
generalization is much too sweeping. Thus the dissatisfaction with
the denouement is more than an objection to the imaginary nature
of the baby. The unitive potential of procreation is still an accepted
value in our society; it is precisely this value that Albee calls into
question in *Virginia Woolf*.

Uneasiness over this issue of creative potential is increased by the
fact that *Virginia Woolf*, in the final scene, ceases to be satire. In
his one-act plays Albee often reaches into the vitals of American
attitudes to strike at what he thinks sham and superficiality. In *The
Zoo Story* he reveals the complacent businessman to be a vegetable
incapable of experiencing any kind of real feeling; in *The American
Dream* he presents our idealization of physical beauty and sexual
power in all its vacuity. The validity of the satire in these plays rests
on the exposure of the veneer that disguises fear, ruthlessness, sav-
agery and self-interest without any attempt to solve the problems.
There is always an implicit recognition of the depth of the problem.
It cannot be solved by any quick panacea. It is the mark of the
satirist that he avoids the simple solution: "It is precisely the complexity of data in experience which the satirist insists on and the
simple set of standards that he distrusts." [17] The conclusion of *Vir-*

ginia Woolf, however, advocates a simple standard: no salvation from without, a reliance on "truth" and the resources of the personality. Though Albee sounds the "maybe" of caution with regard to the final situation of George and Martha, he also holds out a "romantic" hope that "it will be better." But the ironist of the first two-and-a-half acts has left his imprint on the play. There seems no reason why the old cycle of games should not begin again.

Though George and Martha do find a new basis for union, their union is isolationist, sterile, dependent on a mutual need. They are left facing the Void. When all the props of manners and mores have been kicked away, there is only the wasteland into which no life-giving streams flow. The note of hope that rings in their mutual concern seems like whistling in the graveyard. In the last analysis being afraid of Virginia Woolf in the world of New Carthage is not much different than simply being afraid.

Conclusion:

The Vision of American Drama

From its inception, the theater of the Western world has been an expression of communal beliefs experienced in community. The worshippers of Dionysus cried out in choral ecstasy around the altar of the god in testimony of the power of their communal belief; the Athenian throngs that poured into the theatre of Dionysus witnessed an action that was at once a religious celebration and a dramatic representation. When drama was resuscitated in the cathedrals of Europe, mysteries and miracles presented a Christian world-view in dramatic form—the cycle of salvation from the Creation to the Last Judgment. In Elizabethan England, when the flag flew over the Globe, the gentry, craftsmen and apprentices of London came to an entertainment that presumed their Englishness, their mutual membership in an organic body-politic. For these societies, drama drew into an integral experience the individual's everyday situation and the community's beliefs.

American drama, as we have viewed it in these representative plays, does not celebrate such a community of belief. The polarities that exist within a given cultural attitude and the opposition that exists between actual experience and the cultural attitude (what *should be* and what *is*) are not reconciled in these plays. Thus, for example, the myth of the Law insists on the one hand that it is the strong bulwark for the protection of individual rights; on the other hand, neither the Law itself nor society contains a remedy for an unjust law and a fanatical judge. A baby is, in one view, a biological accident, a mechanical conjunction of egg and sperm; in another, it is a bond of love between the parents. The criminal is a menace to society and must be destroyed; the criminal is a human being who has made a pitiable mistake and must be forgiven. Success belongs to the elect but the failure is not to be excommunicated for his failure. The individual playgoer leaves a "serious" drama with these attitudinal polarities unresolved, without the sense that his experience and his beliefs have been integrated. Thus he is isolated with the problem; he has no satisfying sense of closure or community.

There is considerable evidence that the modern American audience retains something of the ritual expectation that a play should resolve polarities, that it should reconcile communal belief and individual experience so that the community feels the completeness of its identity in belief. Each new talent that appears with a meaningful dramatic expression of our cultural problems or aspirations is lionized by reviewer and public alike; he is elected Messiah of the moment. Perhaps this is the man who knows the secret, who will be able to draw together in a satisfying whole those oppositions that vex us. Miller, Williams and, lately, Edward Albee held out such hopes; we patiently waited for the masterpiece. *After the Fall, The Milk Train Doesn't Stop Here Any More, Tiny Alice* mitigated those expectations. A sense of disappointment lingers on. There is a faint, nagging suspicion that the playwright has betrayed his trust. Whatever attitude the pundit might take—optimistic anticipation of the newest talent or philosophical resignation to a fragmented approach, the traditional expectation of a communal fulfillment turns the public away from serious drama to the stereotyped offerings of television, the movies and, if a theatre is available, the latest sugar-coated musical.

Evidence for this ritual expectation is also noticeable in scholarly-critical circles. The theories of "Orphic" and prophetic literature found in writers like Yeats, Maud Bodkin, Robert Graves and Richard Chase insist that the writer be a myth-maker whose mission is to create belief.[1] As these critics see the artist generally in this role, men like John Gassner and Eric Bentley apply this theory to the playwright. Gassner believes—with an almost transcendent faith—that the great American playwright will appear and heralds each new talent with apostolic fervor. Bentley manifests considerable disillusion with the present crop and continues to see salvation in the dry intellectualism of Shaw and Chekhov (as he reads them). Francis Fergusson, the most thoughtful of contemporary critics, tries in the most heroic way to demonstrate why this ritual expectancy is doomed to disappointment by the contemporary *théâtre manqué*.

Behind the flight of the public to the reassuring sub-literary stereotypes and the disillusionment of the critic lies the assumption that
the playwright can create meaning where none is evident, that out of
the chaos of a fragmented culture he can bring an ordered cosmos.

The playwrights we have considered represent a peak of American
dramatic achievement. Their plays deal with those attitudes that are
basic to the American view of life: success, the law, crime and punishment, the democratic individual and society, the individual and
his God. They cut to the heart of American experience and try to
deal with the problems it contains. The analyses above are an attempt to demonstrate how the cultural attitudes work by supplying
the dramatist with structural principles and character-types. It
should be clear from these same analyses that the playwrights do
not transcend the culture, that they do not resolve the polarities
they present. They are not Messiahs and their plays do not contain
a gospel for Americans. What they show us are the forms and pressures of the times, but without fulfilling the ritual expectation that
would resolve those forms and pressures into an ordered vision.

How can we characterize the actual theatric experience for which
the American audience is looking? In the foregoing chapters we have
talked about "epiphany" in the concluding movements of the comic
and tragic structures. We also pointed out that this epiphany traditionally—in Greek and Elizabethan drama, for instance—involved
overtones of regeneration. In the tragic pattern the individual is
purged of his guilt and readmitted into society; in the comic pattern
harmony is restored to society and the cosmos. The polarities of
belief and experience are resolved in the ending. This resolution is
the dramatic "discovery" of the meaning of human action for the
audience-community. When the epiphany is regenerative in accordance with cultural beliefs, the ritual expectation of the audience is
satisfied. Whether or not this expectation issues from the nature of
the dramatic form is not the issue here; the fact is that we look for,
hope for, this kind of resolution. The impulse to blame the playwright when no regeneration occurs is a measure at once of our
optimism and our disappointment.

The conclusions of the dramas we have discussed above suggest
not regeneration, but isolation or despair. Because they are serious
treatments of basic cultural problems, the conflict (agon) and the
suffering in the action speak to the culture. But what is affirmed in

the epiphany is either a personal vision that disregards the polar opposition dramatized in the action or a confrontation with the Void. The Freudian motivation in *Mourning Becomes Electra* moves Orin and Lavinia to a fate consistent with psychological theory; both return to a "womb." O'Neill tries to make a myth that involves a regeneration of sorts, but in his myth "rebirth" is simply a synonym for oblivion and entombment. Eliot's gnostic comedy depends for its force on a tradition which the playwright selects for the cognoscenti; only careful explanation makes the play—and its point—communicable. Considered without its rhetoric, the resolution of *J.B.* is positive, but less than honest. MacLeish trades a Calvinist God of thunder for a soft and secret Nature-god who blindly turns the wheel of "life" and "love." Miller's Salesman cannot come to grips with his problem without destroying his own identity so that it is the same old Willy who goes to his death, hoping for love and success, at least in the eyes of his family. In *Streetcar* Blanche's final response to the challenge of the Kowalski present is complete withdrawal into the past through madness. John Proctor may vindicate his "name" before the community, but his sacrifice does not destroy the shadow of the fanatical judge and the unjust law. Wilder suggests that each day offers an opportunity for new life if only the individual recognizes his opportunity. But his world is generated by an ideal out of the past, and Emily's rebirth is from a grave to which she must return. Albee leaves his society sterile and isolated, with only a mutual need and a mutual fear on which to build.

These conclusions underscore the polar opposites that the cultural attitudes contain or the actual situations to which they have no answer. The playwright may cast about for an integrating epiphany, but he can only illustrate the dilemma. The audience looks for the moment of insight, the symbol of regeneration, that should bring the pattern to closure. When it does not appear, each member is left to cast about for his own solution. The dramatist has said *A* and should say *B*, but the cultural attitudes with which he is working do not provide for such consistency.

The absence of any acceptable regeneration symbol explains the frustration of audience-expectation; it also makes a statement about the nature of the hero as he appears in these plays. We have noticed that frequently the hero's personality splits in two; he is detective and husband or Salesman and family-man or citizen and adulterer.

The cultural attitude dictates the principles upon which the economic or social or political facet of the character acts and upon which he is to be judged, but it does not touch the private area of the psyche. McLeod can judge the criminal as long as the criminal is not himself; the Salesman knows how he must manipulate the buyers, but he has no stick by which to measure his own performance as husband and father. There is always a part of the personality that remains autonomous, beyond the realm of communal judgment.

The American credo says that, as long as a man does no palpable harm to his fellows, his interior life is his own business. No one can tell him what to think or how to act in the moral sphere. "Never argue about religion or politics" applies to the private area of personal conviction. Once the principle of autonomy is established, it is equally true that no one can help him in these areas. A sense of personal guilt belongs to his privacy; society cannot absolve him. If he cannot manage to absolve himself, then he must learn to live with his guilt. No Olympian god can cast a deciding vote that will lift the blood-guilt; there can be no recognition of "the Turk within" who can be slain with a dagger-stroke. McLeod cannot remove his brain and wash away under the faucet the dirty pictures his wife put there. The strategies that the culture provides for removing guilt only operate in the public eye, to redeem a man's good name. They do not free him from the interior burdens of guilt and isolation.

Neither can society bless his marriage-bed and put man and wife in communion with the fertile rhythms of nature. The only valid principle for a lasting communion is "true love," essentially a mystery. In the "gimmick" Broadway comedy or the stereotype television show "true love" triumphs to the wish-fulfilling satisfaction of the audience. It only does so because the polarity established by the imprecision of this attitude is carefully eliminated by the stereotype —"they lived happily ever after." J.B. is declared autonomous before he achieves union with his wife. Martha is stripped of her Earth-mother image in order to better her condition. Within the mystery of "true love" the destiny of lovers is confected. Like guilt, it is an individual experience that is self-determined.

This "romantic" view of the hero who is captain of his fate in splendid (or sordid) isolation seems to accept the situation as it is, making a virtue of necessity.[2] This figure, at his best admirable in his fortitude, has a counterpart, a *Doppelgänger,* in the ghost of the

Puritan whose fate is determined by decree so that neither sacrament nor society can help him toward it or rescue him from it.

The images of space and time in these plays moreover testify to our unwillingness to accept this isolated destiny, however noble. The recurring motifs of renewal through escape imply an uneasiness and constitute a search for regeneration strategies.

Idealization of, and nostalgia for, the past is a prominent feature of the plays. There is a search in the past for the happy or innocent person we once were. It is also, correlatively, an attempt to halt the inexorable forward progress of time, the destroyer. J.B.'s view of the god-like qualities of Nature gets its sanction from the agrarian society of the past, Blanche is obsessed by the values of plantation life now lost to her, the history of the Lomans has a frontier flavor, the climax of *Our Town* moves back into the horse-and-buggy days when life was simpler. The past is Edenic; we can only look longingly over our shoulders as we are carried forward. The fact that time can only be stopped momentarily by a backward glance is a manifestation of our desire to stop it and a proof that we cannot stop it at all.

Another symptom of the desire for regeneration is the spatial remove. The longing for "another time" is paralleled by the longing for "another country," and—in the dramas considered—is just as futile. In fact, despite the resources of modern stagecraft, there is a surprising, almost neo-classical adherence to unity of place. Travel is much talked of, sought after and hoped for, but seldom shown. O'Neill's characters, after turning this way and that, are finally trapped in the Mannon mansion. Eliot's heroine Celia meets her destiny on an ant-hill among savages, but the "ordinary people" whose fate lies in making the best of a bad lot live out their lives in a London drawing-room. The "old plantation" is separated spatially as well as temporally from the Kowalski flat. Willy Loman is "walled in" by the bricks of the apartment houses around him. Nick and Honey come out of the plain states, an ill-advised move to the decadent society of New Carthage. Only *Our Town* manages to break away from the confinement of space. The cemetery in Grover's Corners involves a journey that changes the condition of the people who make it. As time cannot be reversed and its burden of guilt and isolation removed, so the escape to a frontier that once offered new life has lost its magic.

The contemporary American feels himself at the mercy of linear time and delimited space; confinement to this dimension does not allow any room for release. The Greek drama had an Olympian dimension that allowed the gods to enter history and so to resolve the polarity of mother-murder and father-revenge by dissolving the blood code. This dimension operates (without the deus-ex-machina) in a play like *Oedipus* where suffering is a necessary step to the knowledge that man cannot exercise complete providential control over the cosmos. The three-tiered world of the Elizabethan included the fretted canopy of Heaven and the trapdoor to Hell. The ghost of the elder Hamlet walks abroad to see justice done, to point to the rottenness of the state of Denmark, to commission his son avenger. No gods from Olympus compose our dilemmas, no spirits from St. Patrick's Purgatory convict our world of sin and judgment. The transcendent sphere that can reconcile dichotomies is not available to the space-and-time-bound American dramatist.

The composite image of American drama—as we can assemble it from these plays—is the image of an individual moving through a series of experiences like points on a line stretched between two infinities. The unaccommodated hero comes out of the first infinity at birth; he travels through life, making what he can of each experience—trying to be a success, a friend, the head of a family, a servant of God. Each situation has its own set of values and a strategy for realizing the value of that experience, but these strategies are frequently unrelated and juxtaposing them uncovers polarities. Willy, for example, cannot understand how his philandering on the road constitutes a betrayal of his wife; the ethos of the traveling salesman has no relation to home conduct. In fact, the traveling salesman of the blue joke *has* no home and no family. All the determinants of heredity and environmental influences and the strategies recommended by cultural attitudes pressure the hero to react to the immediate situation, the present point on the line, without regard for a wider context.

Even should the polarities set up by differing strategies be resolved in a given case, the hero must confront the second infinity at the end of the line. "Death," oblivion, an imprecise eternity, swallows him up. We are not suggesting here that the burden of Greek or Elizabethan drama is an escape from death for the individual, or that their epiphanies convey to him a sense of personal immortality. Rather, the point is that this linear view of experience points inevitably to the "end of the line" for the individual, to a confrontation with the Void. Greek and Elizabethan plays do not operate in a time-space continuum that focuses on this inevitability. Orestes, Oedipus, Hamlet had a relationship with nature and with society that situates their problem in the larger context in the City or the kingdom, among the gods or flights of angels. Willy Loman, Blanche Dubois, John Proctor have no such solidarity with their cosmos; their time runs out.

The plays, then, dramatize the situation of the American individual within linear time and delimited space. The movement of dramatic action in this cosmos presses the individual to a confrontation with the Void, the jumping-off place that makes calamity of so long life, where the recipe for success, the even hand of justice, the consolations of human love recede into a limbo of meaninglessness.

Under the pressure of this confrontation, the American public tries to turn its collective head away. Its members, except for the intellectual in-group, do not favor the European insistence on this confrontation in the Theatre of the Absurd. The Absurd playwright takes the content of the final movement of the traditional pattern, the epiphany, which fails to reconcile opposites and he creates a dramatic form from this failure. The isolation of the individual in the face of oblivion makes all communication ultimately meaningless. There are no values on which all can agree; such agreement is pointless when the individual will be blotted out by an indifferent universe. Godot will never appear; the "Eternal Emperor" is just another empty chair and the "message" depends on a deaf-and-dumb orator. *Waiting for Godot* may enjoy a reputation at San Quentin, but it has not swept the nation.

This aversion is also indicated by the slick Broadway box-office success. This type of play avoids the boundary-situation and keeps well within the safe-zone of conformity to accepted dramatic and cultural convention. The Broadway comedy depends on clever dialogue, an in-group flavor and the traditional comic formula. *Take Her, She's Mine, A Thousand Clowns, The Owl and the Pussycat,* to pick three typical examples, each focus on a social situation that provides for humor. *Take Her, She's Mine* deals with a father's anxiety when his favorite daughter leaves home for a fashionable college in the East. The father suffers through the various "stages" of her adaptation to college life, proves himself unselfish and intelligent, and allows her to marry a properly matured graduate student.

No danger really lowers anywhere in the experience; the audience is reassured at every turn. *A Thousand Clowns* raises the issue of individuality and conformity while satirizing television and institutional supervision of the guardian-ward relationship by social workers. The psychological case worker, an attractive and unspoiled lady Ph.D., after the classic contre-temps of separation, returns to decorate the apartment of the individualistic unemployed television writer who accepts her tacit offer to allow him his eccentricities. In *The Owl and the Pussycat* two lonely and disturbed people, a prostitute who sees herself as "actress and model" and a book clerk who imagines himself a "writer" discover that their lives can be straightened out only if they confess to their fantasies and acknowledge their "real" identities. The audience is protected from the polarities in the situations by a firm adherence to the conventional structure: the daughter discovers a husband who resembles her overprotective father, "true love" insures the compatibility of the writer's individuality and the case-worker's conformity, a simple acknowledgement of identity breaks down the antipathy of the book clerk and the prostitute. This kind of formula play can satirize selected social attitudes as long as they simultaneously guarantee more universally held cultural values: the solidarity of the American family, worth of individuality, honesty in personal relationships as the best policy. The "gimmick" play is essentially wish-fulfillment that masquerades as "problem" drama by focusing on a segment of society. It is also a recognition of the enduring vitality of the traditional comic pattern.

The decline of serious drama as popular entertainment, then, is related to the vision of the life that it incorporates. No one likes to be reminded of his plight, especially if he is asked to pay for such a reminder. When the public goes to a Miller or a Williams or an Albee play, its values and attitudes suffer under the pressure of the dramatic experience. Resources for coping with this experience are meager. As Augustine remarks in the third book of his *Confessions,* why should a man suffer through a drama when he would not personally undertake such suffering in real life for all the world? The satisfaction that Western drama has traditionally afforded flows through the conflict and the suffering to an assurance that it is worthwhile. Drama that continually impresses on the spectator the image of his own hapless situation is not calculated to appeal to a wide popular audience.

Finally, these representative plays dramatize unreconciled polarities that can be summarized thus: the image of the self-sufficient hero in control of his own interior life versus the structural image of the dramatic pattern that expresses a desire to escape isolation and guilt through community. The traditional comic and tragic patterns that result in a rebirth epiphany, whatever other functions they perform aesthetically, resemble ritual in that they do cope with isolation and guilt. The comic pattern with its progress to a wedding, its fertility overtones, its empathic harmony with nature provides a schema that celebrates societal rebirth. What is dramatized in the pattern is the desire for insertion in a community. Whether the pattern is used to integrate polar oppositions in a culture or to pillory deviations from the norm by satirical inversions, the movement of the action reflects the ideal of "belonging." The tragic pattern moves the hero from guilt through suffering to a purgation that readmits him to the company of men. His guilt is purged either by trial according to the norms of the culture or by knowledge gained through suffering. The large outlines of these patterns, then, are themselves an image of the universal human aspiration for communion and purgation. When the patterns remain unfulfilled, the experience of the playgoer is a reaction to this unresolved tension between content and form, between the "statement" of the structural pattern and the image of the unaccommodated hero in the epiphany.

If we were to cast these observations as a judgment, the prognosis for American drama would be bleak indeed. It should be clear that the fault is not in our stars, the dramatists, but in ourselves, in the cultural situation. We have been trying to deal here with the facts of the case. The serious dramatists actually use these patterns out of their literary background and because of their exposure to popular models. The ritual expectancy of the audience results from the working out of these patterns in popular genres like the "gimmick" play and the television serial. Whether these traditional structures are the *only* possible patterns for contemporary drama is a question that requires another book. This much is true: it is hard to see how the stuff of drama could be other than an imitation of those actions that realize two of man's fundamental desires—communion and purgation. It is equally hard to imagine how an increasingly aware American public can continue to tolerate contradiction at the heart of its beliefs.

Notes

CHAPTER 1

1. Arthur Miller has called attention to this propensity in American criticism for dealing almost exclusively with character motivation: "Our critics will be inclined to see the hero of a play as a psychological figure, a special case always, and their interest flags beyond this point. . . . The European, however, while interested in the character's manifest surface, is equally intent upon discovering what generality he represents"—"The Playwright in the Atomic World," in *The Theatre in the Twentieth Century,* ed. R. W. Corrigan (New York, 1963), pp. 36–37.
2. See Francis Fergusson, *The Idea of a Theatre* (Princeton, 1949), pp. 14–15.
3. For us "guilt" has an exclusively moral connotation. In speaking of tragedy, we must be careful to broaden its meaning. "Guilt" here means more than a deliberately malicious act; it is a violation of a tabu, conscious or unconscious, that puts a man outside the society in which he has lived. Oedipus violates tabu by murdering his father and marrying his mother. Willy Loman violates tabu by failing as a salesman and as a father.
4. In his recent study Walter Kerr sees the essence of comedy as an insistence on man's limitations in his cosmos. He must always deal with the needs of his own clay and the persistent opacity of his situation; no matter what his aspirations, he must eat, drink, breed and belch. The fun lies in his having to cope with the immovable object—which he is trying to move. This view of comedy focuses on man's efforts rather than on the function of the pattern in the total context of the play. Comic action is not simply a picture of man's imprisonment in matter; it is more fundamentally a dynamic presentation of man's desire to harmonize with his environment and his difficulties as he makes the attempt. Compare Walter Kerr, *Tragedy and Comedy* (New York, 1967), pp. 146–49 with William F. Lynch, S.J., *Christ and Apollo* (New York, 1960), pp. 91–93 for two different views of the significance of comic limitation.

CHAPTER 2

1. Quoted in A. H. Quinn, *A History of American Drama* (New York, 1927), I, 44.
2. *Nine Plays by Eugene O'Neill,* ed. Joseph Wood Krutch (New York, 1932), p. xii (Introduction).
3. See, for example, Arthur and Barbara Gelb, *O'Neill* (New York, 1962).

4. Letter to A. H. Quinn, quoted in *A History of American Drama*, II, 199.

5. "Working Notes and Extracts from a Fragmentary Work Diary" in *European Theories of the Drama: with a Supplement on the American Drama*, ed. Barrett H. Clark (New York, 1947), p. 530. In a recent article in *American Literature* (XXXVIII [March, 1966], 85–100), Horst Frenz and Martin Mueller suggest that *Mourning Becomes Electra* contains more parallels with *Hamlet* than with the *Oresteia*. Their essential point is well taken: the total effect of *Mourning Becomes Electra* is quite different from the total effect of the *Oresteia*. The same can be said about the endings of *Hamlet* and *Mourning Becomes Electra*. Gilbert Murray, some years ago, pointed out the parallels between Orestes and Hamlet. The modifications which O'Neill makes to fit the New England milieu are more significant critically than the *Hamlet* analogues.

6. The plot structure of Greek tragedy reflects a pattern that has overtones of religious ritual. The movement of the plays from agon, through pathos, to epiphany, according to the findings of the Cambridge Anthropological school of critics, is derived from the Dionysiac rebirth ritual. Gilbert Murray has documented the persistence of this structural pattern in Greek tragedy. (See Murray, "Excursus on the Ritual Forms Preserved in Greek Tragedy," in Jane Ellen Harrison, *Themis* [Cambridge, 1912], pp. 342–43.) Not every scholar has accepted the historical conclusions of Murray's study; there are notable gaps in the historical evidence. For a dissenting view, see Gerald F. Else, *The Origins and Early Form of Greek Tragedy* (Cambridge, Mass., 1965), pp. 27–30. We are not concerned here with the *historical* controversy, but with the internal evidence in the plays themselves. Murray points to a pattern in the plays, the audiences saw these dramas in the context of the Dionysian festival; *culturally*, the evidence for a resurrectional ritual model is strong.

7. Norman T. Pratt, "Aeschylus and O'Neill," *Classical Journal*, LI (January, 1956), 163.

8. William Arrowsmith, "The Criticism of Greek Tragedy," *Tulane Drama Review*, III (1958–59), 45.

9. Harrison, *Themis*, p. 249.

10. Ibid., p. 232.

11. Gilbert Murray takes these structural divisions more literally: he says that "in the trilogy the full theophany is reserved for the last play and consequently the sequence in the individual plays is upset and confused." (Murray, "Excursus," *Themis*, p. 358.) Individual agones and pathoi can be picked out in the various episodes; the basis for them is reducible to the conflict between piety and revenge according to the code.

12. In his depiction of Electra O'Neill departs from Aeschylus. In the *Oresteia* Electra plays a subordinate role. She functions as surrogate to Agamemnon; as her visit to her father's tomb opens the *Choephori*, she is immediately identified with his cause. She also serves to introduce

Orestes by lamenting his absence and recognizing him on his appearance. Lavinia, on the other hand, appears in the first scene of *Homecoming*. She has previous knowledge of her mother's infidelity; she attempts to warn her father of his danger; she discovers evidence, immediately after Ezra's death, of Christine's treachery. Apropos of the title, Lavinia assumes the role of heroine in *Mourning*. O'Neill has a precedent for her centrality from Euripides' version of the legend. His notes indicate that he also made use of that play. But the main outlines of *Mourning* follow Aeschylus.

13. H. L. Mencken, *Book of Prefaces* (Garden City, N.Y., 1924), p. 205.
14. "We are living in a country governed by Puritans and it is useless to attempt to beat them in a frontal attack—at least, at present. . . . My whole life, once I get free from my present engagements, will be devoted to combating Puritanism." Letter to Theodore Dreiser, July 28, 1916; *Letters of H. L. Mencken,* ed. Guy J. Forgue (New York, 1961).
15. H. L. Mencken, *Prejudices, 4th Series* (New York, 1924), p. 165.
16. "The religion of America . . . began to lose its inward direction; it became less and less a scheme of personal salvation and more and more a scheme of pious derring-do. The revivals of the '70s had all the bounce and fervor of those of a half century before, but the mourner's bench began to lose its standing as their symbol and in its place appeared the collection basket. Instead of accusing himself, the convert volunteered to track down and bring in the other fellow. . . . These various Puritan enterprises had one character in common: they were all efforts to combat immorality with the weapons designed for crime. . . . Beneath them all then was the dubious principle . . . that it is competent for the community to limit and condition the private acts of its members." H. L. Mencken, *Books of Prefaces,* 236–37, 242.
17. Gelb, *O'Neill,* p. 399.
18. Ludwig Lewisohn, *Expression in America* (New York, 1932), p. 392.
19. Eugene O'Neill, *Mourning Becomes Electra* (New York, 1931), p. 17. All quotations taken from this edition. Hereafter abbreviated MBE.
20. Max Weber, *The Protestant Ethic and the Rise of Capitalism,* trans. Talcott Parsons (New York, 1930), pp. 108–109.
21. One of the few direct references to God in the play comes from Christine, the "pagan," and credits him with destroying the lives he touches.

> *Christine.* Why can't we all remain innocent and loving and trusting? God won't leave us alone. He twists and tortures our lives until—we poison each other to death. (MBE, p. 110)

Here God is described as the creator of time who moves his creatures through suffering toward the finality of death. Experience corrupts to no purpose. He is, then, a surrogate for necessary guilt, not a providential force for good.
22. Lewisohn, *Expression in America,* p. 282.
23. Mencken, *Prejudices, 4th Series,* p. 165.

24. Leslie Fiedler advances the thesis that literature of the American male shows him to be constantly in search of a "nobler companionship" than that of woman. Thus the threat of incest, the ultimate sexual degradation, is the "essential erotic theme of the novel." What he says of the homosexual implications of this thesis might be equally applied to the act of incest (in fact or desire): "The event of such love is only guilt and death and a retreat into a dark house." *Love and Death in the American Novel* (Cleveland, 1960), p. 396. This is exactly what happens to Orin and Lavinia after Orin makes his proposal: guilt, death, a retreat into a dark house.

25. W. David Sievers, *Freud on Broadway* (New York, 1955), pp. 122–23.

26. See Frederick J. Hoffman, *Freudianism and the Literary Mind* (Baton Rouge, La., 1945), pp. 58–69.

27. Ibid., p. 30.

28. Letter to Martha Carolyn Sparrow, October 13, 1929; quoted in Arthur H. Nethercot, "The Psychoanalyzing of Eugene O'Neill," *Modern Drama,* III (December, 1960), 248.

29. Gelb, *O'Neill*, p. 69.

30. Lewisohn, *Expression in America*, p. 219.

31. One important difference that sets off American interpretations of Freud from the European is the centrality of the mother. European familial structure emphasized the tyrannical father, but the case was otherwise in America. "In the late nineteenth century the typical case was that of the neurasthenic upper-class woman who convinced her family and herself of her chronic invalidism and used it to tyrannize the household. To some degree she is still a fixture on the American psychic landscape, disillusioned after an impossibly romantic courtship, using the psychoanalytic couch to give her life some importance. . . . There is the daughter or son who, within an overprotected milieu, has been torn away from many of the life experiences which once gave the young American a sense of identity. . . . There is the "silver cord" relations between an obsessive mother and a weak son which has blighted the lives of many young Americans." Max Lerner, *America as a Civilization* (New York, 1957), pp. 696–97.

32. Doris M. Alexander has pointed out striking parallels between the parent-child, husband-wife situations in *Mourning* and the analysis of these relationships in *What Is Wrong with Marriage*, a popularization of Freudian theory published in 1929 by Dr. G. V. Hamilton and Kenneth MacGowan. The Oedipus and Electra complexes which form part of the "family doom" are, according to Miss Alexander, described as O'Neill has them in the play. She also establishes the distinct possibility that O'Neill knew this book; he was a friend (and perhaps a patient) of Doctor Hamilton's and an associate of Kenneth MacGowan. Whether or not O'Neill consciously used this book (we have seen that he denies using a source), *What Is Wrong with Marriage* expresses popular conceptions to which he had easy access. See Doris M. Alexander, "Psy-

chological Fate in 'Mourning Becomes Electra,' " *PMLA*, LXVIII (December, 1953), 923–34.

33. Eugene O'Neill, "Working Notes," *Chief European Theories of Drama*, p. 535.

34. The Islands—real and ideal—embody an American folk-myth that the audience would recognize. In the American experience, the frontier held out the hope of an escape from the problems and difficulties of the settled community. A man could win a new identity and a fresh start by pulling up stakes and heading west. This vision of the frontier as an escape was compounded quite early with the vision of a vast and constantly growing agricultural society based on close ties with the fecund land. Cultivation by industrious settlers would turn the wilderness into a garden. (Henry Nash Smith, *Virgin Land* [Cambridge, Mass., 1950], pp. 138–39.) Escape to the frontier suggested, then, not only escape from the social, economic and personal problems of the old, settled life, but also an escape to regeneration in a paradisiacal environment. When the frontier closed at the end of the nineteenth century, this vision was retouched by the mythologizing spirit. Frederick Jackson Turner—"The West and American Ideals," *Washington Historical Quarterly*, V (October, 1914), 245—presented a view of American history that pivoted on the premise that the frontier shaped the American ideal of democracy. And, if we imagine that this vision is moribund today, we need only recall the slogan of the Kennedy administration.

35. The yearning to return to paradise, a common theme in Western literature, is often associated with sexual freedom, nudity, the feminine characteristics of the tropics. See Mircea Eliade, *Myth, Dreams and Mysteries*, trans. Philip Maigret (London, 1946), p. 42.

36. Doris Falk, *Eugene O'Neill and the Tragic Tension* (New Brunswick, N.J., 1958), pp. 6–7.

37. Eliade, *Myth, Dreams and Mysteries*, p. 235.

CHAPTER 3

1. T. S. Eliot, *The Sacred Wood* (London, 1920), p. 51.

2. T. S. Eliot, *The Use of Poetry and the Use of Criticism* (Cambridge, Mass., 1933), p. 5.

3. *Sacred Wood*, pp. 62–63.

4. T. S. Eliot, *Essays on Elizabethan Drama* (New York, 1932), p. 173.

5. *Poetry and Drama*, p. 26.

6. Northrop Frye, *Anatomy of Criticism* (Princeton, 1957), p. 163.

7. F. M. Cornford, *The Origins of Attic Comedy* (Cambridge, 1934), p. 17.

8. *Sacred Wood*, p. 67.

9. Ibid., p. 76.

10. "London Letter," *The Dial*, LXXI (October, 1921), 453.

11. Frye, *Anatomy of Criticism*, p. 163.

12. T. S. Eliot, *The Cocktail Party* (New York, 1950), p. 9. Hereafter all quotations from this edition, abbreviated CP.
13. Noel Coward, "Design for Living," *Play Parade* (Garden City, N.Y., 1933), pp. 91–92.
14. Murray, "Excursus," *Themis*, p. 354.
15. Gilbert Murray, *Euripides and His Age* (New York, 1913), p. 66.
16. Cornford, *Attic Comedy*, p. 246.
17. Carol H. Smith points out this resemblance: "Eliot even presents a triumphal marriage procession, like that at the end of the ritual drama when all the guests of the first party, except Celia, appear before the beginning of the second." *T. S. Eliot's Dramatic Theory and Practice* (Princeton, 1963), p. 181.
18. W. K. Wimsatt, "Eliot's Comedy," *Sewanee Review*, LVIII (Autumn, 1950), pp. 672–73.
19. Cornford, *Attic Comedy*, pp. 188–89.
20. Ibid., p. 174.
21. Carol Smith notes the ritual nature of the Doctor and Cook roles without, however, relating them to Cornford's analysis. See *Eliot's Dramatic Theory and Practice*, pp. 179–80.
22. *Attic Comedy*, pp. 188–89.
23. E. K. Chambers comments on the Doctor in the Mummers' Play: "One or more of the champions falls, and then appears upon the scene a Doctor, who brings the dead to life again. The Doctor is a comic character." (*The Medieval Stage* [Oxford, 1933], I, 213.) Cornford notes the relationship between the Mummers cast of characters and that of the Northern Greek Festival plays: "By this time, moreover, it must have occurred to the reader that they are fundamentally the same troupe as we have made out behind the Aristophanic play. . . . They are the set required for the fertility drama of the marriage of the Old Year transformed into the New, that marriage which is interrupted by the death and revival of the hero." (*Attic Comedy*, p. 188.)
24. *Attic Comedy*, p. 189.
25. A. B. Cook, *Zeus* (Cambridge, England, 1914), I, 675.
26. *Attic Comedy*, p. 165.
27. *Frag.*, 146, 14.
28. The surprise is concocted from eggs; Smith points out that these ingredients are a commentary on Edward's sterility. In Eliot's poetry the egg is a favorite symbol for fertility. *Eliot's Dramatic Theory and Practice*, p. 180.
29. *Alcestis*, trans. Dudley Fitts and Robert Fitzgerald (New York, 1936), p. 18.
30. This aspect of the drama has led Wimsatt to call *The Cocktail Party* "the best morality play in English since *Everyman* and the only comical morality." ("Eliot's Comedy," *Sewanee Review*, LVIII, 677.)
31. I am indebted to a student, Mr. Paul Devlin, for pointing out that wine mixed with water also accompanies the invocation of "Zeus

Savior." See Harrison, *Prolegomena to the Study of Greek Religion* (New York, 1955), p. 448.

32. Eliot, *Poetry and Drama*, p. 32.

33. Robert Colby, in his article "Orpheus in the Counting House" (*PMLA*, LXXII [September, 1957], 794), calls attention, in passing, to this relationship.

34. T. S. Eliot, *Idea of a Christian Society* (New York, 1940), p. 33.

35. Ibid., p. 34.

36. Ibid., p. 61.

37. Sandra Wood, "Weston Revisited," *Accent*, X (Autumn, 1950), 211.

38. William Arrowsmith, "The Cocktail Party," *Hudson Review*, III (Autumn, 1950), 413, 414.

39. Walter Stein, "After the Cocktails," *Essays in Criticism*, III (January, 1953), 90, 94.

40. *Idea of a Christian Society*, p. 33.

41. Arrowsmith, "The Cocktail Party," *Hudson Review*, III, 428.

42. See R. B. Heilman, "Alcestis and the Cocktail Party," *Comparative Literature*, V (1953), 114–15.

43. William Lynch, S.J., "Confusion in Our Theatre," *Thought*, XXVI (September, 1951), 351.

44. Mircea Eliade, *The Myth of the Eternal Return*, trans. W. R. Trask (New York, 1954), p. 34.

45. Ernst Cassirer, *The Philosophy of Symbolic Forms*, trans. R. Manheim (New Haven, 1955), I, 2.

46. Lynch, "Confusion in Our Theatre," *Thought*, XXVI, 351.

CHAPTER 4

1. Archibald MacLeish, "Trespass on a Monument," New York *Times* (December 7, 1958), Section 2, p. 1.

2. *Actfive and Other Poems* (New York, 1948), p. 33.

3. MacLeish, "Trespass," New York *Times* (December 7, 1958), Section 2, p. 1.

4. *Paradise Regained*, I, 149. William Blake, who came to grips with the evils of a later age, uses the Book of Job to thrash Milton's "rationalism." According to Blake, Milton's Messiah is the governing reason, and "in the Book of Job Milton's Messiah is called Satan." (*The Complete Writings of William Blake*, ed. Geoffrey Keynes [London, 1966], p. 150.)

5. Max Weber, *The Protestant Ethic*, p. 164.

6. See Louis B. Wright, "Franklin's Legacy to the Gilded Age," *Virginia Quarterly Review*, XXII (1946), 268–79.

7. H. M. Kallen, *The Book of Job as Greek Tragedy* (New York, 1918).

8. R. B. Sewall, *The Vision of Tragedy* (New Haven, 1959), p. 24.

9. Ibid., p. 13.

10. Herbert Weiner, "Job on Broadway," *Commentary*, XXVII (February, 1959), 154.

11. Carl Jung, *Answer to Job*, trans. R. F. C. Hull (London, 1954), p. xiv.

12. Archibald MacLeish, "Book of Job," *Christian Century*, LXXVI (April 8, 1959), 419.

13. Archibald MacLeish, "The Man Behind J.B.," *Theatre Arts*, XLIII (April, 1959), p. 61.

14. "Staging of a Play: Notebooks and Letters Behind Elia Kazan's staging of Archibald MacLeish's 'J.B.'," *Esquire*, LI (May, 1959), 146.

15. "J.B.," *Theatre Arts*, XLIV (February, 1960), 33. Hereafter this version will be cited as "TA, XLIV."

16. The meaning of this symbolism is clear from some of MacLeish's early poetry. In "The End of the World," the poet describes a circus performance; in the middle of the show

> Quite unexpectedly the top blew off:
> And there, there overhead, there, there hung over
> Those thousands of white faces, those dazed eyes
> There in the starless dark, the poise, the hover,
> There with vast wings across the cancelled skies,
> There in the sudden blackness, the black pall
> Of nothing, nothing, nothing—nothing at all.

(*Streets in the Moon* [Cambridge, Mass., 1926], p. 101.) The setting in *J.B.* is not so explicit about the "nothing at all," but the black backdrop dwarfs the personae on stage. They work in a circle of light surrounded by blackness. The visual impact approximates the last lines of the poem. See S. L. Falk, *Archibald MacLeish* (New York, 1965), pp. 139–40.

17. Perhaps MacLeish's inspiration for this device can be traced to Jung's book. He remarks on the "stage-managing of this imaginary duel between God and Job-Satan." (Jung, *Answer to Job*, pp. 29–30.)

18. Their ambiguity has disturbed some of the commentators. Joseph Wood Krutch, who admired the play generally, felt uneasy about this device: "To me they seem the least satisfactory personages and the least satisfactory device in the play, partly because they are the most conventionally unconventional figures, rather obviously reminiscent of Pirandello and conceived in a fashion that suggests the sinister, half-witted clowns of Beckett and other contemporary surrealists." ("The Universe at Stage Center," *Theatre Arts*, XLII [August, 1958], 10–11.)

19. This Kantian antinomy is glossed in *Answer to Job*. "God in His omniscience would never make a mistake if only he consulted with it. He has equipped his human creatures with a modicum of consciousness and a corresponding degree of free will, but he must also know that by doing so he leads them into the temptation of falling into a dangerous independence. That would be too great a risk if man had to do with a creator who was only kind and good." (Jung, *Answer to Job*, p. 87.)

20. The Nickles character underwent an evolution through various versions of the play. In the published version he was a cynical old man, disillusioned with the world. Kazan suggested that his attitudes reflected a youthful rebelliousness. MacLeish modified the character along these lines for the Broadway production.

21. In the published version (Boston, 1958), MacLeish makes this point more explicitly:

> *Sarah.* Let me say it! Let me say it!
>
> . . . .
>
> Nobody knows of it but me.
> You never let them know: not anyone—
> Even your children. They don't know. (*J.B.*, p. 39.)

The revelation about "it" is never made; J. B. cuts her off. The mystery presumably refers to anonymous kindnesses, secret philanthropies.

22. In the book version Sarah comments on J.B.'s habit of reveling in Nature.

> He lies there watching
> Long before I see the light—
> Can't bear to miss a minute of it:
> Sun at morning, moon at night,
> The last red apple, the first peas. (*J.B.*, p. 32.)

23. In her article, "MacLeish and the Fortunate Fall" (*American Literature*, XXXV [May, 1963], 207–208), Eleanor Sickles relates this song and the tree imagery in it to the poet's use of the tree in *Songs for Eve*. In this collection the "green" tree is the tree of experience and consciousness. "Apple eaten of that tree,/Animal I ceased to be." (Archibald MacLeish, *Songs for Eve* [Boston, 1954], p. 29.)

24. In Hebrew theology, God is known and addressed primarily in terms that relate him to society and history. He is the Lord, King, Judge, shepherd, father, husband. Nature imagery, when it appears in the Bible, is usually derived from a pagan milieu and accommodated to Yahweh. In the Book of Job this personal and societal relationship is taken for granted. Yahweh is Job's personal God; Job is Yahweh's servant. See George Ernest Wright, *The God Who Acts* (Naperville, Ill., 1952), p. 49.

25. As President Eisenhower once put it in his own inimitable syntax, "our form of government has no sense unless it is founded in a deeply felt religious faith, and I don't care what it is." (Quoted in Max Lerner, *America as a Civilization*, p. 715.)

26. This idea is made explicit in the book version. In this scene Zuss too is dissatisfied because J.B. has acted as though his suffering were justified "not by the Will of God but Job's Acceptance of the Will of God." (*J.B.*, p. 139.)

27. "Staging of a Play," *Esquire*, LI, 157.

28. Jung, *Answer to Job*, p. 63.

29. Eliade, *Myths, Dreams and Mysteries*, pp. 138–39.

30. *Answer to Job,* p. 133.

31. In the published version the emphasis was completely on the comic aspect of the conclusion. Sarah is in control; she delivers the crucial speech to the silent J.B.:

> *Sarah.* Even the forsythia beside the
> Stair could stop me.
> *J.B.* It's too dark to see.
> *Sarah.* Then blow on the coal of the heart, my darling.
>
> . . . .
>
> The candles in churches are out.
> The lights have gone out of the sky.
> Blow on the coal of the heart
> And we'll see by and by . . . (The light increases, plain white
> daylight from the door as they work.)   (*J.B.,* pp. 152–53.)

The play, in this version, ends here on a note of optimism, and it is the woman who announces the message of love and hope.

32. The modification of the ending in the action version was suggested by Kazan's objections to the earlier conclusion. In a letter dated August 15, 1958, he writes to MacLeish:

> "The end does not seem satisfying to me. Possible reasons . . . 1. It seems small. The problem J.B. has been confronting has nothing to do with love, so we cannot solve it satisfactorily through love. J.B.'s been up against the biggest and most modern of all problems: i.e., Man's sudden inheritance of the earth and of 'Everything.' Man's resultant isolation. Man's sudden awareness of meaninglessness. The problem has been put two ways, one by Nickles, one by Zuss. . . . Shall he reject the human condition as n.g. [no good] and cut his throat? Or should he accept the condition of meaninglessness because it is God's will. My point is that the solution has to be through repeat *through* a confrontation of this issue on this level. . . . It's irrelevant why Sarah came back. I'm caught up in J.B.'s problem. . . . 3. J.B.'s return to Sarah is too easy. . . . 4. I sort of resent having Sarah say the last lines. It's been J.B. I've been going with. And I want to come to a climax through and with him. . . . 5. J.B. at the end is not tough enough. He's not the man who's been able to come through all he's come through." ("Staging of a Play," *Esquire,* LI, 149.)

Thus the rhetorical emphasis on J.B.'s sufferings and isolation and the consequent reduction of Sarah's role are the result of Kazan's concern about the focus of the play. What he does not see, and perhaps could not see, is that the problem lies with the comic structure that is established early, runs through the play and provides for a positive conclusion. It is essential to MacLeish's concept.

33. Archibald MacLeish, "Humanism and the Belief in Man," *Atlantic Monthly,* CLXXIV (November, 1949), 76.

34. MacLeish summarized his message in lectures and articles in widely

scattered publications. For example, see "The Men Behind J.B.," *Theatre Arts,* XLIII, 61–62; "Book of Job," *Christian Century,* LXXXVI, 61–62. Many of the comments of the reviewers were directed at correcting MacLeish's exegesis. For a negative appraisal, see Weiner, "Job on Broadway," *Commentary,* XXVII, 153–58; supporting Mac-Leish's adaptation, see Henry Van Dusen, "Third Thoughts on *J.B.,*" *Christian Century,* LXXVI (January 28, 1959), 106–107.

CHAPTER 5

1. Eliade, *Myth, Dreams and Mysteries,* p. 36.
2. William O. Aydelotte, "The Detective Story as Historical Source," *Yale Review* XXXIX (n.s.) (September, 1949), 92.
3. John P. Sisk, "Crime and Criticism," *Commonweal,* LXIV (April 20, 1959), 72, 74.
4. W. H. Auden, "The Guilty Vicarage," in *The Critical Performance,* ed. Stanley Edgar Hyman (New York, 1956), p. 313. This essay first appeared in *Harper's Magazine* for May, 1948.
5. Auden, "The Guilty Vicarage," *The Critical Performance,* p. 302.
6. J. Patterson, "A Cosmic View of the Private Eye," *Saturday Review,* XXXVI (August 22, 1953), 8.
7. Philip Durham, *Down These Mean Streets a Man Must Go* (Chapel Hill, 1963), pp. 80–81.
8. *Raymond Chandler Speaking,* eds. Dorothy Gardiner and Katherine Sorley Walker (Boston, 1962), p. 219.
9. Patterson, "Cosmic View," *Saturday Review,* XXXVI, 31.
10. "The Play that was Born in a Speech," New York *Times* (March 20, 1949), Section 2, pp. 1, 3.
11. John Gassner, *Best American Plays, 3rd Series* (New York, 1952), p. 318.
12. Harold Clurman, "Good Show," *New Republic,* CXX (April 11, 1949), 25.
13. W. H. Wright [S. S. Van Dine], *The Great Detective Stories* (New York, 1942), p. 6 (Introduction).
14. Auden, "The Guilty Vicarage," *The Critical Performance,* p. 306.
15. Sidney Kingsley, *Detective Story* (New York, 1949), p. 18. Hereafter cited as DS.
16. Marshall McLuhan, "Footsteps in the Sands of Crime," *Sewanee Review,* LIV (October, 1946), 629.
17. Norbert Muhlen, "The Thinker and the Tough Guy," *Commonweal,* LI (November 25, 1949), 217.
18. "The Play that was Born in a Speech," New York *Times* (March 20, 1949), Section 2, p. 3.
19. John Mason Brown, "Seeing Things: Constabulary Duty," *Saturday Review of Literature,* XXXII (April 16, 1949), 51.
20. Luke Parsons, "On the Novels of Raymond Chandler," *Fortnightly Review,* CLXXXI [CLXXV n.s.] (May, 1954), 350.

21. Even in an author as realistic as Kingsley, something can be made of the names of the personae. "Kurt Schneider," as noted above, is a (somewhat gross) description of the abortionist's occupation. Mary is "Mary Immaculate." Giacoppetti may be translated "Little Jim."

22. "The Theatre," *Time*, LIII (April 4, 1949), 75.

23. Fergusson, *The Idea of a Theatre*, p. 28.

24. Leo Gurko, *Heroes, Highbrows and the Popular Mind* (Indianapolis, 1953), p. 168.

CHAPTER 6

1. Ivor Brown, "As London Sees Willy Loman," New York *Times* (August 28, 1949), Book Section, p. 59.

2. "Death of a Salesman," New York *Times* (February 11, 1949), p. 27.

3. See Sewall, *The Vision of Tragedy*, pp. 130, 167; H. J. Mueller, *The Spirit of Tragedy* (New York, 1956), pp. 316–17; T. R. Henn, *The Harvest of Tragedy* (London, 1956), p. 268.

4. Henry Popkin, "The Strange Encounter," *Sewanee Review*, LXVIII (Winter, 1960), 53.

5. The enormous success of this tract and its perennial appeal are attested by its frequent republication. In 1826 Simon Ide republished the essay along with Franklin's "Advice to Young Tradesmen." Much later, in 1921, Roger Babson's *Making Good in Business* reiterated the major points of Franklin's essay as part of Babson's advice to the success-seeker.

6. Ralph Waldo Emerson, *The Conduct of Life* (Boston, 1904), p. 95.

7. *Acres of Diamonds* (New York, 1915), p. 18.

8. Kenneth S. Lynn, *The Dream of Success* (Boston, 1955), pp. 6–7.

9. Irwin G. Wyllie, *The Self-Made Man in America* (New Brunswick, N.J., 1954), p. 27.

10. Orison Marsden, *Entering Business* (New York, 1903), p. 27.

11. Arthur Miller, *Death of a Salesman* (New York, 1949), p. 11. Subsequent references to this edition are marked SALESMAN.

12. Arthur Miller, "The Family in Modern Drama," *Atlantic Monthly*, CXCVII (April, 1956), 37.

13. See John Gassner, *Form and Idea in Modern Theatre* (New York, 1956), p. 13.

14. There have been attempts to give Willy a specific ethnic heritage. After seeing Thomas Mitchell do Willy, Miller himself commented that he did not realize he had written a play about an Irish family. (Popkin, "Strange Encounter," *Sewanee Review*, LXVIII, 35.) George Ross reviewed a Yiddish production, pointing out underlying Jewish elements in the play. He felt that Miller had "censored out" the specifically Jewish in favor of an anonymous Americanism. (*"Death of a Salesman* in the Original," *Commentary*, XI [1951], 184–86.) This controversy

underscores the point—relating the Lomans to any ethnic background destroys Miller's perspective.

15. Roger Babson, *Making Good in Business* (New York, 1921), pp. 98–9.
16. Wyllie, *Self-Made Man in America,* p. 107.
17. W. J. Ong, *Frontiers in American Catholicism* (New York, 1957), p. 31.
18. Henn, *Harvest of Tragedy,* p. 29.
19. "Pathetic" is used here, not in the sentimental, nice-doggy sense, but in the root meaning. Willy is acted upon by outside forces; he suffers the incursion of societal pressures. As he is shaped by these forces, he is "pathetic."
20. "Shadows of the Gods," *Harper's Magazine,* CCXVII (August, 1958), 36.
21. Willy has an unhappy penchant for falling into their hands. He owns and operates a Hastings refrigerator and a Studebaker car.
22. Miller, "The Family in Modern Drama," *Atlantic Monthly,* CXCVII, 39–40.
23. *Making Good in Business,* p. 73.
24. Miller emphasizes this view. He is convinced that drama can instruct, that its power to move an audience can be reformatory: "There lies in the dramatic form the ultimate possibility of raising the truth-consciousness of mankind to a level of intensity as to transform those who observe it." ("The Family in Modern Drama, *Atlantic Monthly,* CXCVII, 41.)
25. Popkin, "Strange Encounter," *Sewanee Review,* LXIII, 55.

CHAPTER 7

1. For a symbolic interpretation of Williams' Southern heritage, see Esther M. Jackson, *The Broken World of Tennessee Williams* (Madison, 1965), p. 46.
2. Williams, *Facts About Me,* quoted in Benjamin Nelson, *Tennessee Williams* (New York, 1961), p. 6.
3. Malcolm Cowley, "Going with the Wind," *New Republic,* LXXXVIII (September 16, 1936), 161.
4. W. J. Cash, *The Mind of the South* (New York, 1941), pp. 430–31.
5. James Dickey, "Notes on the Decline of Outrage" in *South,* eds. Louis D. Rubin and Robert D. Jacobs (Garden City, N.Y., 1961), pp. 87–88.
6. Alfred Kazin, *On Native Ground* (New York, 1942), p. 460.
7. See Cash, *Mind of the South,* pp. 44–51.
8. Ibid., p. 60.
9. Francis P. Gaines, *The Southern Plantation* (New York, 1925), p. 174.
10. Ibid., p. 175.
11. William R. Taylor, *Cavalier and Yankee* (New York, 1961), p. 161.
12. Kazin, *On Native Ground,* p. 465.

13. Williams, *A Streetcar Named Desire* (New York, 1947), p. 9. All subsequent references to this edition are marked STREETCAR.
14. Mary Boykin Chesnut, *Diary from Dixie,* ed. Ben Ames Williams (Cambridge, Mass., 1961), p. 157.
15. There is an interesting story in Mary Chesnut's diary that serves as comment on this scene and testifies to the division in the Southern attitude toward womanhood.

   "March 11th.—A freshman came quite eager to try his hand at a flirtation. 'Dance with her,' he was told, 'and talk with her; walk with her and flatter her; dance until she is warm and tired; then propose to walk in a cool shady piazza. It must be a somewhat dark piazza. Begin your promenade slowly; warm up to your work; draw her arm closer and closer; then, break her wing' . . . The aspirant for fame as a flirt followed these lucid directions literally, but when he seized the poor girl and kissed her, she uplifted her voice in terror and screamed as if the house was on fire. . . . The girl's brother challenged him. There was no mortal combat, however, for the gay young fellow who had led the freshman's ignorance astray stepped forward and put things straight. An explanation and an apology at every turn hushed it all up." (*Diary from Dixie,* pp. 196–97.)

   While the company at the Charleston lady's party laughed heartily at this "foolish story," the possible consequences are something to consider.
16. *Sights and Spectacles, 1937–1956* (New York, 1956), p. 132.
17. Cornford, *Attic Comedy,* p. 137.
18. Ibid., p. 149.
19. Nelson, *Tennessee Williams,* p. 25.
20. The similarity between the Reconstruction era in the South and the emancipation of the serfs in Russia inspired Josh Logan to adapt *The Cherry Orchard* to a Southern setting. His *Wisteria Trees* (1950) dramatizes correspondences that Williams had come upon earlier.
21. Toby Cole and Helen Krich Chinoy, *Directing the Play* (Indianapolis, 1953), p. 307.
22. *"Modernism" in Modern Drama* (Ithaca, N.Y., 1953), p. 128.
23. S. L. Falk, *Tennessee Williams* (New York, 1961), p. 81.
24. Nancy Tischler, *Tennessee Williams: Rebellious Puritan* (New York, 1961), p. 144.
25. Popkin, "Plays of Tennessee Williams," *Tulane Drama Review,* IV (March, 1960), 54.
26. Tischler, *Tennessee Williams,* p. 144.

CHAPTER 8

1. Ralph Henry Gabriel, *The Course of American Democratic Thought* (New York, 1940), p. 16.

2. Thurman W. Arnold, *The Symbols of Government* (New Haven, 1935), p. 127.

3. Henry Steele Commager, *The American Mind* (New Haven, 1950), p. 363.

4. Arnold, *Symbols of Government,* p. 134.

5. Ibid., pp. 136–37.

6. Ibid., pp. 143–44.

7. Arthur Miller, *Collected Plays* (New York, 1957), pp. 24–25 (Introduction). In view of this remark, Miller's choice of lawyer as hero in his autobiographical play *After the Fall* is not surprising.

8. Ibid., p. 39.

9. Ibid., p. 11.

10. Ibid., p. 47.

11. Arnold, *Symbols of Government,* p. 141.

12. *Collected Plays,* p. 41. It speaks well of the judges of the Salem trials that Miller was able to draw on official records in constructing his play. The preservation of these documents indicates that the judges felt fully justified in their course of action. For them, the letter of the law was clear and they applied it with what they considered a rigorous fairness. Had the witches been stabbed in the dark and the record either not taken or destroyed, no redress would have been possible. The material is so complete that Miller could not only reconstruct the event and include accurate historical detail, but he was also able to supply credible motivations from hints in the testimony.

13. Ibid., p. 47.

14. The modified realism of the setting used in the 1953 production—rough wooden beams and period set-pieces—was changed to black draperies in the more successful 1958 revival. This change underscored the modern dimension by giving the *mise en scene* more universality.

15. *The Crucible* in *Collected Plays,* p. 239. Quotations from the play are from this version, hereafter referred to as CRUCIBLE.

16. "So critics have taken exception, for instance, to the unrelieved badness of the prosecution in my play. I understand how this is possible and I plead no mitigation, but I was up against historical facts which were immutable. I do not think that either the record itself or the numerous commentaries upon it reveal any mitigation of the unrelieved, straightforward, and absolute dedication to evil displayed by the judges of these trials and the prosecutors." (Miller, *Collected Plays,* p. 43.)

17. The "secularization" of American society is a point at issue here. For Justice Holmes, a leading American jurist, the American system of morality is "a body of imperfect social generalizations expressed in terms of emotion." The Law can dispense with emotion and evolve toward a better understanding of the deepest instincts of man. Through this understanding men can connect the Law with "the universe and catch an echo of the infinite, a glimpse of its unfathomable process, a hint of the universal law." Practically, then, without prejudice to a higher order, the Law can become an ever more effective instrument for

justice here and now. (Oliver Wendell Holmes, *Collected Legal Papers* [New York, 1952], pp. 306, 202.)

CHAPTER 9

1. "The Play," New York *Times* (February 5, 1938), p. 18.
2. The term "displacement" is Northrop Frye's, who seems to be echoing Freud. Frye points out that both the mythic and the realistic approaches use the same structural principles and that realism fits these principles into a context of plausibility. "The presence of mythical structure in realistic fiction . . . poses certain technical problems for making it plausible, and the devices used in solving these problems may be given the general name of 'displacement.' " (Frye, *Anatomy of Criticism*, p. 136.)
3. *The Beginnings of Critical Realism in America: 1860–1920* (New York, 1930), p. 374.
4. Thornton Wilder, *Our Town* (New York, 1938), p. 10. All subsequent quotations and references from this edition, abbreviated OUR TOWN.
5. Henry Bamford Parkes, *The American Experience* (New York, 1957), p. 353.
6. Wilder, "A Preface to 'Our Town,' " New York *Times* (February 13, 1938), Section 10, p. 1.
7. In *The Intent of the Artist*, ed. August Centeno (Princeton, 1941), p. 90.
8. Frye, *Anatomy of Criticism*, p. 136.
9. *Intent of the Artist*, p. 96.
10. Wilder, *Three Plays* (New York, 1957), p. xii.
11. Rex Burbank, *Thornton Wilder* (New York, 1961), pp. 23–24.
12. *Intent of the Artist*, p. 97.
13. Eliade, *Myth of the Eternal Return*, p. 34.
14. Critics do not hesitate to use this expression of *Our Town*. Alan Thompson, for example, says: "The play required a strong illusion of reality, and on the whole I think that the illusion was as strong as it would have been if aided by all the elaborate realism of conventional productions." (*The Anatomy of Drama* [Berkeley, California, 1946], p. 103.)
15. Roy C. Flickinger, *The Greek Theatre and Its Drama* (Chicago, 1918), p. 16.
16. H. D. F. Kitto, *Greek Tragedy* (London, 1950), p. 83.
17. Theodor H. Gaster, *Thespis* (New York, 1950), p. 71.
18. Eliade, *Myth of the Eternal Return*, pp. 85–86.
19. Ibid., p. 10.
20. Ibid., p. 12.
21. See Frye, *Anatomy of Criticism*, pp. 158–237.
22. Ibid., pp. 203–204.
23. In Gertrude Stein, *Four in America* (New Haven, 1947), pp. xviii–xix.

24. Frye, *Anatomy of Criticism*, p. 145.
25. Amos N. Wilder, *The Spiritual Aspects of the New Poetry* (New York, 1940), p. 220.
26. Gaster, *Thespis*, p. 4.
27. Campbell, *Hero with a Thousand Faces*, pp. 245–56.
28. Compare Francis Fergusson, *The Human Image in Dramatic Literature* (Garden City, N.Y., 1957), pp. 50–60 and Burbank, *Wilder*, pp. 94–97.
29. As a pragmatic test of this assertion, the reader should recall the movie. Though the director tried to reproduce many of the devices in the play, the realistic settings and the lack of audience participation wiped out much of the play's impact. When Frank Craven was off-screen, it looked like another nostalgic salute to the "good old days."

CHAPTER 10

1. Martin Esslin, *The Theatre of the Absurd* (Garden City, N.Y., 1961), p. 292.
2. *Anatomy of Criticism*, p. 223.
3. There is a striking parallel to the *Virginia Woolf* situation and an illustration of the "polite" level of concealment in a poem from another era, George Meredith's sonnet sequence "Modern Love." Meredith treats the theme of alienation and infidelity in marriage. Sonnet 17 in the sequence describes a dinner party with husband and wife presiding:

> At dinner she is hostess, I am host.
> Went the feast ever cheerfuller? She keeps
> The Topic over intellectual deeps
> In buoyancy afloat. They see no ghost.
> With sparkling surface-eyes we ply the ball:
> It is in truth a most contagious game:
> HIDING THE SKELETON, shall be its name.
> Such a play as this the devils might appall!

4. Edward Albee, *Who's Afraid of Virginia Woolf?* (New York, 1965), p. 85. Subsequent citations in the text, abbreviated vw, refer to this edition.
5. See J. Huizinga, *Homo Ludens* (London, 1949), pp. 7–15.
6. Ibid., pp. 74–75.
7. *Faust,* trans. Walter Kaufmann (Garden City, N.Y., 1961), 11. 4056–9.
8. The Faustian allusion tempts the reader to allegorize. Identifying Faust and Mephistopheles with Nick and George respectively (or vice versa) is a fascinating intellectual exercise, but the parallels do not work out. For instance, when Mephistopheles leads Faust from a larger celebration to a small conclave of minor pleasures, Mephistopheles announces that he will be matchmaker and Faust suitor. Faust dances with a young witch, Mephistopheles dances with the "old" witch. (*Faust*, 11. 4123–27.) The reference to *Faust* is rather a matter of atmosphere. The trip

to Brocken is phantasmagoric, a transition to the world of the grotesque. "The Walpurgisnacht is a dream sequence mirroring an inner state of moral and emotional confusion . . . Spring rites in which the humanist might discern survivals of ancient fertility worship are viewed . . . as a cult of obscenity and bestiality, so that pregnancy and birth—the theme is traditional in the lore of witchcraft, but the emphasis given it would indicate that Faust has at least considered the possibility of Margarete's being with child—represent only ugliness and evil." See Stuart Atkins, *Goethe's Faust* (Cambridge, Mass., 1958), pp. 90–93.

9. *Faust*, ll. 4039–41.

10. Huizinga, *Homo Ludens*, p. 108.

11. The favorable critical extreme is represented by John Gassner ("Broadway in Review," *Educational Theatre Journal*, XV [March, 1963], 77–80) who compares Albee with O'Neill, then states: "Does not the play move to a veritable anticlimax, moreover, when cause and effect are so disproportionate; when we learn at the end that they never had a son to whom something terrible had happened? They have been tearing at each other's vitals for a deprivation that does not prevent some human beings from behaving with decency and consideration toward each other." At the other extreme, Richard Schnechner ("Who's Afraid of Edward Albee?" *Tulane Drama Review*, VII [Spring, 1963], 7–10) writes: "There is no real, hard bed-rock of suffering in *Virginia Woolf*—it is all illusory, depending on a "child" who never was born: a gimmick, a trick, a trap. And there is no solid creative suffering in the writer who meanders through a scene stopping here and there for the sake of a joke or an easy allusion that almost fits." Neither critic considers the satiric nature of the play; *Virginia Woolf* is not a tragedy or a near-tragedy.

12. *The Anatomy of Criticism*, p. 223.

13. "The *eiron* is the man who deprecates himself, as opposed to the *alazon*. Such a man makes himself invulnerable, and though Aristotle disapproved of him, there is no question that he is a predestined artist, just as the alazon is one of his predestined victims." See Northrop Frye, *Anatomy of Criticism*, p. 40.

14. Ibid., pp. 227–28.

15. "once upon a time and a very good time it was there was a moocow coming down along the road and this moocow that was coming down along the road met a nicens little boy named baby tuckoo. . . ." This "moocow" image is later transmogrified into the image of the "crowned bull, *bous stephanoforos*, that is identified with the hero Stephen Daedalus. (*A Portrait of the Artist* [New York, 1964], p. 7.) The *bous stephanoforos* leads the procession in a late spring festival of Dionysus. (See *Themis*, pp. 153–4.) This connection is strengthened by the earlier reference to Martha's paganism: "Martha is the only true pagan on the eastern seaboard." (vw, p. 73.) It is confirmed by Martha's claim to the title of "Earth Mother." Dionysus, Zeus-Young Man, is the son of Semele, the Thracian Earth Mother. (See Jane Ellen Harrison,

Mythology [Boston, 1924], p. 134.) This Dionysian reference is bracketed by Christ imagery. George quotes the sequence of the funeral Mass: *"Et gratia tua illis succurrente, merantur evadere judicium ultionis*—And with the help of your grace, may they be able to escape the vengeful judgment." The boy breaks his arm—"poor lamb." Both Christ and Dionysus were "sons of God," suffered, died and were resurrected. It suffices to say that, in *Virginia Woolf,* the savior-image is firmly attached by these resonances to the child.

16. In his first appearances in Greek literature, the bow-and-arrow is the equipment of Apollo. In the Homeric hymn he draws near with his shining bended bow. In the first Book of the Iliad he appears as "Far-darting Apollo, and "fierce is the clang of the silver bow." Later he appears as his own counterpart, that is, the Destroyer is also Healer. He is also equated, in Orphic literature, with the sun. "Helios = supreme god = Dionysus = Apollo." (See W. K. C. Guthrie, *Orpheus and Greek Religion* [London, 1952], p. 43.) To this resonance is added that of "fleece": "in the sun his hair . . . became . . . fleece." (vw, p. 220.) The boy, relates Martha, scooped out a banana to make a boat with green-grape oarsmen and orange-slice shields—a miniature *Argos* in the light of the above reference. The story of the golden fleece combines the motif of sacrifice with that of sterility. A famine in Alus is to be adverted by sacrifice of the King's children who escape on the ram with the golden fleece. (J. G. Fraser, *The New Golden Bough,* ed. Theodor H. Gaster [New York, 1964], pp. 296–7.) Martha's vision of her child makes him savior and hero; he *will* die for his parents, but ironically, according to George's formula.

17. Frye, *Anatomy of Criticism,* p. 232.

CHAPTER 11

1. This view of art emphasizes the sacramental-symbolical nature of the literary work. It accepts on faith that, by an act of the will, the artist can create a myth that will substitute for religious experience, or that he can reverse the historical process so that, out of something that was not religion, religion may come again.

2. The romantic hero has a mythos of his own. Joseph Campbell testifies to his aspirations for community while insisting that he must achieve it alone:

> "The modern hero, the modern individual who are to heed the call and seek the mansion of that presence [the multifarious divine presence within that is the life of all] with whom it is our destiny to be atoned [at-oned] cannot, indeed must not, wait for his community to cast off its slough of pride, fear, rationalized avarice and sanctified misunderstanding. . . . It is not society that is to guide and save the creative hero, but precisely the reverse. And so everyone of us shares the supreme ordeal—carries the cross of the

Notes to p. 252

redeemer—not in the bright moments of his tribe's great victories, but in the silences of his personal despair." (*The Hero with a Thousand Faces*, p. 391.)

For a less triumphant view of this isolation, see William Lynch, *Christ and Apollo*, pp. 79–81.

Selected Bibliography

BOOKS

Aeschylus. *Orestia*. Trans. Richmond Lattimore. Chicago, 1953.

Arnold, Thurman W. *The Symbols of Government*. New Haven, 1935.

Burbank, Rex. *Thornton Wilder*. New York, 1961.

Campbell, Joseph. *The Hero with a Thousand Faces*. New York, 1949.

Cash, W. J. *The Mind of the South*. New York, 1941.

Centeno, August, ed. *The Intent of the Artist*. Princeton, 1941.

Clark, Barrett H., ed. *European Theories of the Drama: with a Supplement on the American Drama*. New York, 1947.

Conwell, Russell H. *Acres of Diamonds*. New York, 1915.

Cornford, F. M. *The Origins of Attic Comedy*. Cambridge, 1934.

Eliade, Mircea. *Myth, Dreams and Mysteries*. Trans. Philip Maigret. London, 1946.

——, *The Myth of the Eternal Return*. Trans. W. R. Trask, New York, 1954.

Eliot, T. S. *The Cocktail Party*. New York, 1950.

——, *Essays on Elizabethan Drama*. New York, 1932.

——, *The Idea of a Christian Society*. New York, 1940.

——, *Poetry and Drama*. London, 1950.

——, *The Sacred Wood*. London, 1920.

——, *The Use of Poetry and the Use of Criticism*. Cambridge, Mass., 1933.

Euripides. *Alcestis*. Trans. Dudley Fitts and Robert Fitzgerald. New York, 1936.

Falk, Doris. *Eugene O'Neill and the Tragic Tension*. New Brunswick, N.J., 1958.

Falk, Signi L. *Tennessee Williams*. New York, 1961.

Fergusson, Francis. *The Human Image in Dramatic Literature*. Garden City, N.Y., 1957.

——, *The Idea of a Theatre*. Princeton, 1949.

Frye, Northrop. *Anatomy of Criticism*. Princeton, 1957.

Gassner, John. *Form and Idea in Modern Theatre*. New York, 1956.

——, ed. *Best American Plays, 3rd Series*, New York, 1952.

Gelb, Arthur and Barbara. *O'Neill*. New York, 1962.

Gurko, Leo. *Heroes, Highbrows and the Popular Mind*. Indianapolis, 1953.

Harrison, Jane Ellen. *Themis*. Cambridge, 1912.

Hoffman, Frederick J. *Freudianism and the Literary Mind*. Baton Rouge, La., 1945.

Hyman, Stanley Edgar, ed. *The Critical Performance*. New York, 1956.

Jung, Carl. *Answer to Job*. Trans. R. F. C. Hull. London, 1954.

Kallen, H. M. *The Book of Job as Greek Tragedy*. New York, 1918.

Kerr, Walter. *Tragedy and Comedy*. New York, 1967.

Kingsley, Sidney. *Detective Story*. New York, 1949.

Kitto, H. D. F. *Greek Tragedy*. London, 1950.

Lerner, Max. *America as a Civilization*. New York, 1957.

Lynn, Kenneth S. *The Dream of Success*. Boston, 1955.

MacLeish, Archibald. *Actfive and Other Poems*. New York, 1948.

——, *J.B.*, Boston, 1958.

——, *Songs for Eve*. Boston, 1954.

——, *Streets in the Moon*. Cambridge, Mass., 1926.

Mencken, H. L. *A Book of Prefaces*. Garden City, N.Y., 1924.

——, *Prejudices, 4th Series*. New York, 1924.

Miller, Arthur. *Collected Plays*. New York, 1957.

——, *Death of a Salesman*. New York, 1949.

Nelson, Benjamin. *Tennessee Williams*. New York, 1961.

O'Neill, Eugene. *Mourning Becomes Electra*. New York, 1931.

Ong, S. J., Walter J. *The Barbarian Within*. New York, 1962.

——, *Frontiers in American Catholicism*. New York, 1957.

Quinn, Arthur Hobson. *A History of American Drama*. 2 Vols. New York, 1927.

Rubin, Louis D., and Robert D. Jacobs, eds. *South: Modern Southern Literature in Its Cultural Setting*. Garden City, N.Y., 1961.

Sewall, R. B. *The Vision of Tragedy*. New Haven, 1959.

Sievers, W. David. *Freud on Broadway*. New York, 1955.

Smith, Henry Nash. *Virgin Land*. Cambridge, Mass., 1950.

Thompson, G. D. *Aeschylus and Athens*. London, 1941.

Tischler, Nancy M. *Tennessee Williams: Rebellious Puritan*. New York, 1961.

Weber, Max. *The Protestant Ethic and the Rise of Capitalism*. Trans. Talcott Parsons. New York, 1930.

Wilder, Amos N. *The Spiritual Aspects of the New Poetry*. New York, 1940.

Wilder, Thornton. *Three Plays*. New York, 1957.

Williams, Tennessee. *A Streetcar Named Desire*. New York, 1947.

Wright, George Ernest. *The God Who Acts*. Naperville, Ill., 1952.

Selected Bibliography

PERIODICALS

Alexander, Doris M. "Psychological Fate in 'Mourning Becomes Electra,'" *PMLA,* LXVIII (December, 1953), 923–34.

Atkinson, Brooks. "The Play" [*Our Town*], New York *Times* (February 5, 1938), p. 18.

Arrowsmith, William. "The Cocktail Party," *Hudson Review,* III (Autumn, 1950), 411–30.

——, "The Criticism of Greek Tragedy," *Tulane Drama Review,* III (1958–1959), 31–57.

Aydelotte, William O. "The Detective Story as Historical Source," *Yale Review,* (n.s.) XXXIX (September, 1949), 76–95.

Brown, Ivor. "As London Sees Willy Loman," New York *Times* (August 28, 1949), Book Section, pp. 11, 59.

Brown, John Mason. "Seeing Things: Constabulary Duty." *Saturday Review of Literature.* XXXII (April 16, 1949), 50–2.

Clurman, Harold. "Good Show," *New Republic,* CXX (April 11, 1949), 25–6.

Eliot, T. S. "London Letter," *The Dial,* LXXI (October, 1921), 453.

Heilman, R. B. "Alcestis and the Cocktail Party," *Comparative Literature,* V (1953), 105–16.

Kazin, Alfred. "Psychoanalysis and Literary Criticism Today," *Partisan Review,* XXVI (Winter, 1959), 45–54.

Krutch, Joseph Wood. "The Universe at Stage Center," *Theatre Arts,* XLII (August, 1958), 9–11.

Lynch, S. J., William F. "Confusion in Our Theatre," *Thought,* XXVI (Autumn, 1951), 342–60.

[MacLeish, Archibald, and Elia Kazan.] "The Staging of a Play: Notebooks and Letters behind Elia Kazan's Staging of Archibald MacLeish's 'J.B.'" *Esquire,* LI (May, 1959), 144–58.

MacLeish, Archibald. "Book of Job," *Christian Century,* LXXVI (April 8, 1959), 61–2.

——, "Humanism and the Belief in Man," *Atlantic Monthly,* CLXXIV (November, 1949), 72–8.

——, "J.B.," *Theatre Arts,* XLIV (February, 1960), 33–64.

——, "The Men behind J.B.," *Theatre Arts,* XLIII (April, 1959), 61–3.

——, "Trespass on a Monument," New York *Times* (December 7, 1958), Section 2, pp. 1, 7.

McLuhan, Herbert Marshall. "Footsteps in the Sands of Crime," *Sewanee Review,* LIV (October, 1946), 617–34.

Miller, Arthur. "The Family in Modern Drama," *Atlantic Monthly,* CXCVII (April, 1956), 35–41.

——, "Shadows of the Gods," *Harper's Magazine,* CCXVII (August, 1958), 35–43.

Muhlen, Norbert. "The Thinker and the Tough Guy," *Commonweal,* LI (November 25, 1949), 216–7.

Nethercot, Arthur H. "The Psychoanalyzing of Eugene O'Neill," *Modern Drama,* III (December, 1960), 242–56.

Paterson, J. "A Cosmic View of the Private Eye," *Saturday Review of Literature,* XXVI (August 22, 1953), 31–2.

"The Play that was Born in a Speech," New York *Times* (March 20, 1949), Section 2, pp. 1, 3.

Popkin, Henry. "The Plays of Tennessee Williams," *Tulane Drama Review,* IV (March, 1960), 45–64.

——, "The Strange Encounter," *Sewanee Review,* LXVIII (Winter, 1960), 34–60.

Pratt, Norman T. "Aeschylus and O'Neill," *Classical Journal,* LI (January, 1956), 163–7.

Rahv, Philip. "Myth and the Powerhouse," *Partisan Review,* XX (Fall, 1953), 641–5.

Ross, George. *"Death of a Salesman* in the Original," *Commentary,* XI (1951), 184–6.

Sickles, Eleanor. "MacLeish and the Fortunate Fall," *American Literature,* XXXV (May, 1963), 205–17.

Sisk, John P. "Crime and Criticism," *Commonweal,* LXIV (April 20, 1959), 72–4.

Stein, Walter. "After the Cocktails," *Essays in Criticism,* III (January, 1953), 85–104.

"The Theatre," [*Detective Story*], anon. rev., *Time,* LIII (April 4, 1949), 75–6.

Van Dusen, Henry. "Third Thoughts on *J.B.,*" *Christian Century,* LXXVI (January 28, 1959), 106–107.

Weiner, Herbert. "Job on Broadway," *Commentary,* XXVII (February, 1959), 153–8.

Wilder, Thornton. "A Preface to 'Our Town,'" New York *Times* (February 13, 1938), Section 10, pp. 1, 3.

Wimsatt, W. K. "Eliot's Comedy," *Sewanee Review,* LVIII (Autumn, 1950), 666–78.

Wood, Sandra. "Weston Revisited," *Accent,* X (Autumn, 1950), 207–12.

Wright, Louis B. "Franklin's Legacy to the Gilded Age," *Virginia Quarterly Review,* XXII (1946), 268–79.

Index

Index

Index

Thomas E. Porter, S. J. received his Ph.D. in English from the University of North Carolina in 1965. He was Dean of Colombiere College of the University of Detroit from 1965–1967 and is currently Associate Professor of English at the University of Detroit.

The manuscript was edited by Sandra Shapiro. The book was designed by Sylvia Winter. The type face for the book is linotype Old Style No. 7; and the display face is Garamond.

The book is printed on S. D. Warren's Olde Style Antique paper and bound in Bancroft's Oxford cloth over binders board. Manufactured in the United States of America.